Women Playwrights
The Best Plays
of 1992

Smith and Kraus *Books For Actors*

THE MONOLOGUE SERIES

The Best Men's Stage Monologues of 1992
The Best Men's Stage Monologues of 1991
The Best Men's Stage Monologues of 1990
The Best Women's Stage Monologues of 1992
The Best Women's Stage Monologues of 1991
The Best Women's Stage Monologues of 1990
One Hundred Men's Stage Monologues from the 1980's
One Hundred Women's Stage Monologues from the 1980's
Street Talk: Character Monologues for Actors
Uptown: Character Monologues for Actors
Monologues from Contemporary Literature: Volume I
Monologues from Classic Plays
Kiss and Tell: The Art of the Restoration Monologue

FESTIVAL MONOLOGUE SERIES

The Great Monologues from the Humana Festival
The Great Monologues from the EST Marathon
The Great Monologues from the Women's Project
The Great Monologues from the Mark Taper Forum

YOUNG ACTORS SERIES

Great Scenes and Monologues for Children
New Plays from A.C.T.'s Young Conservatory
Great Scenes for Young Actors from the Stage
Great Monologues for Young Actors

SCENE STUDY SERIES

The Best Stage Scenes for Women from the 1980's
The Best Stage Scenes for Men from the 1980's
The Best Stage Scenes of 1992

PLAYS FOR ACTORS SERIES

Seventeen Short Plays by Romulus Linney
Lanford Wilson: 21 Short Plays
William Mastrosimone: Collected Plays
Eric Overmeyer: Collected Plays
Terrence McNally: Collected Plays

GREAT TRANSLATION FOR ACTORS SERIES

The Wood Demon by Anton Chekhov

OTHER BOOKS IN OUR COLLECTION

The Actor's Chekhov
Humana Festival '93: The Collected Plays
Break A Leg! Daily Inspiration for the Actor

If you require pre-publication information about upcoming Smith and Kraus monologues collections, scene collections, play anthologies, advanced acting books, and books for young actors, you may receive our semi-annual catalogue, free of charge, by sending your name and address to **Smith and Kraus Catalogue, P.O. Box 10, Newbury, VT 05051.**

Women Playwrights
The Best Plays
of 1992

Edited by Robyn Goodman
and Marisa Smith

Correction to Back Cover

C. West
T. Rebeck   P. Scanlon   C. Butterfield
S. Pearson
P. Vogel

SK
A Smith and Kraus Book

A Smith and Kraus Book
Published by Smith and Kraus, Inc.

First Edition: March 1993
10 9 8 7 6 5 4 3 2 1
Publisher's Cataloging in Publication (Prepared by Quality Books Inc.)
Women playwrights: the best plays of 1992 / Robyn Goodman, Marisa Smith.
    p. cm. - (Women playwrights annual series)
    ISSN: 1067-327X
1. American drama - Women authors. 2. American Drama - 20th century. I. Goodman, Robyn. II. Smith, Marisa. III. Series.
PS628.W6W6 1993   812'.954'0809287
                    QBI93-498

Table of Contents

Foreword *by Robyn Goodman*

Introduction *by Marsha Mason*

Foreword

When Smith and Kraus approached me to edit this volume I was delighted. I have always felt that there was a wealth of dramtic literature written by women that deserved special attention. Playwrights who happen to be women are grappling with some of the most potent issues of our culture. Under-represented on Broadway, their voices can be heard loud and clear in theaters all across this country.

I saw *Baltimore Waltz*, *Jar the Floor* and *Joined at the Head* onstage in exhilarating productions. *Spike Heels* was the last play I produced with Carole Rothman at Second Stage. *Unfinished Stories* captivated me when I read it. Patricia Scanlon is an offbeat artist whose work I've admired for some time. It gives me great pleasure to bring these six plays together in one collection based on their merit rather than on the sex of their authors. I invite you to savor their diversity.

Robyn Goodman
Winter, 1992

Introduction

When I was asked to write the introduction to this book of plays by women I surprised myself and eagerly said yes. I realized I was hungry to know what other women were feeling and thinking these days. Especially women who wanted to write for the theater.

Well! Hold on! Are we in luck! These women are thinking and writing about everything from relationship between mothers, daughters, sons, husbands, fathers, lovers friends, to issues as diverse as AIDS, sexual harassment, cancer, sexism, classism, euthanasia, fear, personal truth, and the existential crisis called living!

Plays are like doors to me. They can be as massive and ornate as cathedrals or as small and intimate as keyholes. They can be as real as the kitchen sink or as ephemeral as dreams. When we read them in the quiet or sit in a darkened theatre space and listen we step over the threshold of the door that the playwright has opened for us. We walk into their secret garden or jungle and hopefully we are taken on an adventurous odyssey.

Something in each play in this collection surprised me, grabbed at my heart, nudged my mind, arrested my thinking, and moved my emotional balance. Each playwright has passionately revealed their work with flaming energy and creative wit. Each focuses her light of uncompromising honesty on a diversity of form, style, subject, place and relationship.

In "Spike Heels", the character Georgie pounds on a door and then bursts onto the stage, taking us, pell mell, through the war zone of male / female relationships. Her vehemence and fearsomeness propels the action as sexual harassment and classism are laid bare in an intricate pattern between friends and lovers. Theresa Rebeck's characters are bright and intelligent and verbal. They hold nothing back. She pounds, picks and chisels away at that mountain of sexism and class with Georgie's spike heels. Theatre means dialogue to me and in Ms. Rebeck's play the dialogue is brittle, fast, intelligent and funny. Language flys and leaps and smacks in this urban environment. Hearts are heard and minds are bent as Edward, Andrew, Lydia and Georgie negotiate their way through the landscape of American relationships.

In Cheryl L. West's "Jar The Floor" we enter the rich, sensual, quirky world of four generations of contemporary black women on the occasion of their great grandmother's ninetieth birthday. In this Illinois home we find out that no matter how hard we work at being distant and different from our mothers we are all inextricably joined at the hip. Ms. West helps us experience and understand that we are joined, not so much by blood, as we are by our inner and outer scars. We are all entertwined with our mothers by our desire to belong. Our experience of exile and our need to go home.

Paula Vogel has done something remarkable in "The Baltimore Waltz." She has found a charming and witty metaphor for a disease that could never be described in a charming or witty way. Ms. Vogel opens a dreamy door in a hospital room with humor, and sensitivity and introduces us to a sister and a brother and their relationship to his illness, AIDS. She draws us in effectively conveying their love for each other and their history in this funny and touching play. Together Anna and Carl take us on a trip much longed for trip to Europe and experience and express all that comes with mortality.

In Sybille Pearson's "Unfinished Stories" we enter another world of family. This one is peopled with three generations of men and one woman. The men Ms. Pearson creates are as unique and quirky as Ms. West's women. In Gaby's upper west side apartment in New York City she is queen, caretaker, ex-wife, mother, activist, ex-daughter-in-law and Wise Woman. She is the quiet center of this politically active family and it is her relationship with her father-in-law and his understanding of her that propels the play as each character confronts death in this unsentimental view of euthanasia. And it is Gaby's sorrow, anger and pain that reverberates of the walls of her world and pierces ours.

The litany of personal and philosophical fears that Trash and Dirty Diggin Man recite in scene seven of "What Is This Everything?" is the stuff that dreams are made of. Patricia Scanlon's one act play takes place on the landscape found inside a dream - a piece of time out of time. Trash is a child / woman who is twelve years old one minute and thirty the next. The feelings and thoughts she poignantly shares in this dream play remind me of me at twelve and every year in between. But she is sharing them all simultaneously. She and Dirty Diggin Man, (a philosopher poet,) communicate their existential crises in a surrealistic setting overshadowed by a Father/Waiter character. They are all, to me, aspects of a single personality grappling with the existential fairy tale called life.

In "Joined At The Head" Catherine Butterfield relates the story ofMaggie, a successful novelist, who goes to Boston on a book signing trip and is contacted by Jim, her high school love. She goes to dinner at his home and meets his wife, "Maggy." This warm, funny play focuses in on how stories are told: what's truthfully real and what's really true. Although there are 3 characters on stage the play has a palpable fourth character; the audience. Ms. Butterfield's characters suddenly, unexpectedly draw us into the story as each of them takes turnes addressing us the audience. This device isn't arbitrary. I've often read or heard writers explain that their characters take on a life of their own that is expressed with a voice so strong , so clear that they draw out the writer's best intentions. It is the characters that keep the writer honest after all.

So, there you have it. I have come full circle and a very full circle it is. I'm back from an adventurous odyssey; a trip taken with six wildly diverse women and all their glorious characters and return enriched, expanded and inspired. Now it's you turn to step over the threshold and into your adventure. You won't be disappointed.

Marsha Mason
Los Angeles, California
January, 1993

Women Playwrights
The Best Plays
of 1992

SPIKE HEELS
by Theresa Rebeck

Playwright's Biography

NY Stage: *Does This Woman Have a Name?* (Double Image, Alice's Fourth Floor) *Sex With Censor* (Naked Angels Censorship Project) *The Bar Plays* (Westbank Cafe) and readings and workshops at MTC, EST, the Women's Project and New York Stage and Film. Television: *American Dreamer, Brooklyn Bridge*, and the HBO comedy *Dream On*.

Playwright's Note

In the spring of 1992, I was discussing "Spike Heels" with a group of graduate students from the NYU theatre program, and one of them asked me why the play's central character swore so much. She was bothered by this, because, she told me, "Where I come from, girls who say the f-word also do the f-word." To which I could only reply, where I come from, women generally say and do both, so I feel compelled to grant my characters the same liberties.

Her comment was remarkable to me mostly because it wasn't; more than any other question about my work, I am asked why my women say fuck. Frankly, I don't know many women - of all ages, levels of education, backgrounds, professions - who don't say it, with greater or lesser degrees of abandon, at one time or another. (My mother is one noteworthy exception.) But apparently, no matter what we do or say in real life, when we are represented on the stage, we still are half-expected to act like ladies; we're still not supposed to swear, or sleep around, or have abortions, or get angry at men. Women on stage are seen through a frame of cultural assumptions, and the simple facts of our lives - the drama of our lives, the things that happen to us - are, too often, cultural taboos.

Not surprisingly, I am less interested in those cultural taboos than I am in women's voices and our points of view. I am interested in framing incidents the way the culture tends to frame them - oh, look, two men fighting over a beautiful woman - and then hearing what the woman's perspective on that cultural stereotype might be. That is how "Spike Heels" began.

The incident of sexual harassment at the center of this play is part of a continuum; the battle of desire which the men wage over Georgie, and which she wages with them, has many colors and incidents. Even as she objects to what they do and say to her, she participates: She gets angry, she makes jokes, she colludes, she feels self-loathing. Like many women, she needs the job, so she does not merely walk away. What Edward had done is harassment nonetheless. The fact that all the participants in this comedy eventually can see beyond that moment toward affectionate equality in the battle of the sexes is, I hope, redemptive rather than foolhardy.

Theresa Rebeck
November 10, 1992

CHARACTERS

ANDREW, 35, quiet, friendly, idealistic, earnest.
GEORGIE, a volatile and intelligent young woman, mid/late 20s.
EDWARD, 35, sophisticated and pragmatic, dangerously charming.
LYDIA, early 30s, elegant and direct.

ORIGINAL CAST

Spike Heels was produced in workshop by New York Stage and Film Company in association with the Powerhouse Theatre at Vassar, July, 1990.

Spike Heels was originally produced in New York by the Second Stage Theatre on June 4, 1992. It was directed by Michael Greif and had the following cast:

ANDREW..Tony Goldwyn
GEORGIE...Saundra Santiago
EDWARD..Kevin Bacon
LYDIA...Julie White

SETTING Boston

TIME The present

Spike Heels

Scene 1

Loud classical music, Vivaldi or Mozart, on the radio. There is a long moment of pounding at the door. Lights come up on the main room of Andrew's apartment, the orderly environment of a scholar.

GEORGIE: *(Offstage.)* Andrew! Are you in there? Dammit, Goddammit, are you home, goddam you – Andrew!

ANDREW: *(Overlapping, offstage.)* Wait a minute – I'm coming –

GEORGIE: *(Overlapping, offstage.)* Open up the goddam door – are you home or WHAT – Jesus CHRIST I am going to KILL myself I swear to God I will DAMMIT, ANDREW! *(Andrew crosses the stage quickly, wiping his hands on a towel, snaps off the radio and opens the door.)*

ANDREW: What, what, what – *(Georgie bursts into the room, crosses center and tears off her shoes.)*

GEORGIE: I have been on the stupid goddam subway for twelve hours, so help me God, squished between four of the smelliest fat men on earth, all of them with their armpits in my goddam fucking FACE, in high heels - Oh. *(Suddenly polite)* Am I interrupting?

ANDREW: *(Surprised)* No, I was just making dinner. Lydia's coming over in about an hour, but -

GEORGIE: I'm interrupting -

ANDREW: You're not interrupting! You know I'm always glad to see you. I something wrong?

GEORGIE: *(Mad again)* Goddammit, I hate heels. I have ruined my arches for the rest of my life just so a bunch of stupid men can have a good time looking at my fucking LEGS.

ANDREW: Nice to see you too.

GEORGIE: If I had a fucking car I wouldn't have to take the fucking T. Do you know how long I have been in transit? An hour and a half. An HOUR and a HALF.

ANDREW: You said twelve a second ago.

GEORGIE: It felt like twelve. I swear to God, the mass transportation system in this entire country is just a mess, and do you know why? Because rich people do not take the subway. Rich people own cars. This is the richest goddam country in the world; there is no reason that we couldn't have decent subway systems in our stupid major cities. It's totally a class issue.

ANDREW: It's only six o'clock now; you've only been in transit for an hour.

GEORGIE: An hour and a HALF. Do you think I don't know the difference between an hour, and an hour and a half? Excuse me? I left work at 4:30, it is now 6:00, and I have been on the goddam subway for an hour and a HALF.

ANDREW: Edward let you off at 4:30? That's out of character. What, did he have a nervous breakdown or something?

GEORGIE: I hope so. I hope he totally loses his mind. I hope he has a vision of how useless his whole stupid life has been, and I hope he jumps out his spectacular little office window and into the fucking Charles River, that is what I hope.

ANDREW: Come on, he's not that bad.

GEORGIE: I wish I still smoked. Why the hell did I have to quit smoking? I loved smoking. Do you have any cigarettes? How the hell are we supposed to survive in this stupid country without cigarettes? I mean, they invent this terrific little antidote to everything, *cigarettes,* and then after they get you hooked on it they tell you that it's going to kill you. And you know, the thing is, I think I'd rather be killed by cancer than by life in general. I really think that. *(She circles the room gingerly, trying to get some feeling back in her feet.)*

ANDREW: Are you going to tell me what happened?

GEORGIE: I threw a pencil at Edward, okay? He was getting on my nerves, so I said, fuck you, Edward, and threw a pencil at him. *(She starts to laugh.)*

ANDREW: Oh, Jesus.

GEORGIE: Oh, fuck that shit. I mean, just fuck it, you know? Look. Look. There's this other secretary at work who wears blouses that have bows at the collar, and she has these little tiny initials on the corner of her glasses. You know, little tiny gold letters with sticky crap on the back; she puts these damn things on the corner of her glasses. People do that out in the so-called real world, Andrew. You didn't tell me about this shit.

ANDREW: Georgie –

GEORGIE: So this secretary, her life is like this open book, not that anyone really gives a shit. She comes in every morning with some new thing, you know this – I don't know, this thing that she's got to talk about. So she comes in, and throws things around her desk so that everybody knows she's upset, and the next thing you know, every secretary in the office is listening to this endless fucking story about her stupid landlady who is just being a bitch. I mean, who cares? If your landlady is a bitch, you just say: My landlady is a bitch. I know what that means.

ANDREW: What does this have to do with Edward?

GEORGIE: Nothing. This has nothing to do with Edward.

ANDREW: Georgie – you just said you threw a pencil at him. Before you started ranting about this other person, this –

GEORGIE: Mary Louise. Can you believe that name? *Mary Louise.*

ANDREW: Whatever. Why are you telling me about this woman? I mean, what is your point?

GEORGIE: My point is – I don't know what my point is. My point is, there's something wrong with that whole place. All these people talking about their binky little landladies, or the nuances of the new tax law – like these things matter, like they're even real – *(Pause).* My point is, I can't do it, Andrew. I know you thought I could, but I can't. I mean, I can do the work, but – I'm scared all the time down there. They're different from me. You know?

ANDREW: No –

GEORGIE: Yeah. They are. And I don't like it. It just doesn't make any sense, and everyone – they're all kind of mean. Polite and mean, and I don't – I get wigged, you know? There's something wrong with the whole thing. Doesn't the whole thing scare you?

ANDREW: Oh, sweetheart. Here, give me your foot.

GEORGIE: Excuse me? I say doesn't that scare you and you say give me your foot? What is that supposed to mean? Are we having a conversation here, or is this like some sort of art film or what? *(He crosses to the couch, throws her shoes aside and begins to massage her foot.)*

ANDREW: No wonder you're in a bad mood. These shoes look like some sort of medieval torture device.

GEORGIE: Don't just throw those around, those cost a fortune. What are you – Andrew, excuse me, but what are you doing?

ANDREW: I'm massaging your foot. It's supposed to be soothing. Isn't it soothing?

GEORGIE: Yes, it's very – I don't know if soothing is what I would call this.

ANDREW: Supposedly the muscles in the foot are connected to almost every other part of your body. So it's important that your feet are always relaxed. That's why you're in a bad mood; you've been abusing your feet.

GEORGIE: That's not why I'm in a bad mood.

ANDREW: *(Pause)* How's that?

GEORGIE: It's nice. It's very nice. *(Pause. Andrew looks up at her for a moment, and becomes suddenly awkward. He quickly sets her foot down and moves to the kitchen.)*

ANDREW: I better get to work on dinner. *(Georgie watches him exit, then sits in silence for a moment.)*

GEORGIE: So how's Lydia?

ANDREW: *(Off.)* She's fine. Fine. She's good –

GEORGIE: Good. How's the wedding?

ANDREW: *(Pause.)* Fine. It's still a ways off, so nobody's too hysterical yet.

GEORGIE: That's good.

ANDREW: She wants to meet you.

GEORGIE: She does?

ANDREW: Yeah. She's coming over for dinner later on. You should stick around. It really is ridiculous that you two haven't met yet.

GEORGIE: Yeah, that's ridiculous, all right. *(Andrew reenters, carrying a cutting board and vegetables.)*

ANDREW: So, can you stay?

GEORGIE: Right. She's gonna come over for some romantic little vegetable thing and find me. I'm sure. *(She starts to leave.)*

ANDREW: She said we should all go out sometime –

GEORGIE: Fine, we'll do that sometime.

ANDREW: Georgie –

GEORGIE: What? I'm all sweaty and gross. My shirt is sticking to everything and I stink. I can't meet Lydia smelling like a sewer. She'll faint or gag or something.

ANDREW: Don't start.

GEORGIE: I'm sorry. I'm just not up to it, okay?

ANDREW: So don't stay for dinner. She won't be here for another hour. Just stick around for a while.

GEORGIE: Look – these clothes are killing me. I need to go upstairs. I can come back tomorrow.

ANDREW: Go put on one of my t-shirts; they're in the top drawer of the dresser. Come on. You still haven't told me the details of your assault on Edward.

GEORGIE: Andrew –

ANDREW: There's some shorts in there, too.

GEORGIE: Oh, fuck. *(She heads off, peeling her jacket as she goes. Andrew cleans his books, etc.)*

ANDREW: *(Calling.)* You'll be fine. It's just going to take a little while to get used to it all. You know, actually, you're doing great. I talked to Edward last week, and he said you're the best secretary he's ever had. So you should just chill out and be nice to him. He's not that bad, and he likes you a lot. As a matter of fact, I think he has a crush on you. Oh, goddammit – *(He sees something on the coffee table, picks up a book and slams it down. He takes the book to a small garbage can by his desk and knocks the dead bug off.)* These goddam bugs are invading my living room now. Did you ever get a hold of Renzella? I thought he was sending somebody over. *(Pause.)* Georgie?

GEORGIE: *(Off.)* You got a regular boudoir in here. Lydia's been lending you some of her clothes, huh?

ANDREW: Hey, leave that stuff alone. *(Pause.)* Georgie?

GEORGIE: *(Off.)* I don't want to wear one of your t-shirts. I want to wear this. *(She appears in the doorway, wearing an elegant patterned silk dress. She slinks into the room.)*

ANDREW: I asked you not to start.

GEORGIE: Thank you. I picked it up at Saks. Usually I don't appreciate his line, but when I found this I was just devastated –

ANDREW: Take off the dress. Take it off now.

GEORGIE: I particularly like the bow.

ANDREW: I don't find this funny.

GEORGIE: I just thought I could pick up some fashion tips. So I look presentable when we all go out to dinner.

ANDREW: *This is not funny. (Pause.)*

GEORGIE: Okay. It's not funny. Fine. *(Pause.)* I didn't mean anything. I just meant – this is a nice dress. Silk, huh? Lydia's kind of loaded, huh? *(Pause.)* You think this looks good on me? I mean, I got some money coming in now, maybe I should try to dress better.

ANDREW: I think you should take it off.

GEORGIE: Yeah. I guess I look pretty stupid. *(She crosses back to the bedroom.)*

ANDREW: I'm sorry. That's her favorite dress. I just – you don't even know her. She's nothing like that. *(Georgie exits.) (Calling.)* We'll set up a date this week and actually do it: we'll go out to dinner. The three of us. You two can spend the evening trashing Edward. It'll be fun. You'll be thick as thieves by dawn.

GEORGIE: *(Off.)* She doesn't like him either, huh?

ANDREW: Both of you, you're both heartbreakers. *(Georgie reenters and stands in the doorway, without her shirt on, wearing a slip and a bra. She carries the t-shirt in her hands.)*

GEORGIE: What is that supposed to mean?

ANDREW: Nothing. I told you; I think he has a crush on you. I talked to him last week, and –

GEORGIE: You talked to him? You talked to him. What did he say?

ANDREW: Georgie.

GEORGIE: What?

ANDREW: Put your shirt on. *(She puts the t-shirt on. It is long and loose, with sleeves and neck cut out.)*

GEORGIE: You talked to him?

ANDREW: I talk to him all the time. You know that.

GEORGIE: So what did he say?

ANDREW: He said he liked you.

GEORGIE: Great. That's just – and what did you say?

ANDREW: I said I liked you, too.

GEORGIE: That's what you said? You said, "I like her, too." That's all you said? *(Pause.)*

ANDREW: *(Perplexed.)* Yes. That's all I said. *(Pause.)*

GEORGIE: Great. Well, you know, as far as I'm concerned, Edward can just go fuck himself. I mean, your little friend is just a prince, isn't he? He's just a delight. *(She goes back into the bedroom.)*

ANDREW: *(Calling.)* Look – he hired you. You didn't have any references, you didn't have any legal experience, you didn't have a college degree. And he didn't ask any questions. You might think about that. *(She reenters, carrying a pair of gym shorts. While she speaks, she takes off her slip and pantyhose.)*

GEORGIE: Oh, I might, might I? All right. I'm thinking about that. Nothing is coming to me, Andrew. What is your point here?

ANDREW: My point is, he gave you a job. I'm not saying the man is a saint. But he gave you a job.

GEORGIE: Yeah, right, he "gave" me the damn job. I fucking work my ass off for that jerk; he doesn't give me shit. I earn it, you know? He "gave" me the job. I just love that. What does that mean, that I should be working at McDonald's or something, that's what I really deserve or something?

ANDREW: You wouldn't last two hours at McDonald's. Some customer would complain about their french fries and you'd tell him to fuck off and die, and that would be the end of that.

GEORGIE: Bullshit. Fuck you, that is such fucking bullshit. You think I don't know how to behave in public or something?

ANDREW: Georgie – could you put your clothes on – Georgie –

GEORGIE: *(Ignoring him, overlapping.)* Jesus, I was a goddam waitress for seven years, the customers fucking loved me. You think I talk like this in front of strangers; you think I don't have a brain in my head or something? That is so fucking condescending. Anytime I lose my temper, I'm crazy, is that it? You don't know why I threw that pencil, you just assume. You just make these assumptions.

Well, fuck you, Andrew. I mean it. Fuck you. *(She takes her clothes in her hands and heads for the door.)*
ANDREW: You can't go out in the hall like that –
GEORGIE: I mean, I just love that. You don't even know. You've never seen me in that office. You think I'm like, incapable of acting like somebody I'm not? For four months I've been scared to death but I do it, you know, I take messages, I call the court, I write his damn letters. I watch my mouth, I dress like this – whatever this is; these are the ugliest clothes I have ever seen – I am gracious, I am bright, I am promising. I am being this other person for them because I do want this job but there is a point beyond which I will not be fucked with! So you finally push me beyond that point, and I throw the pencil and now you're going to tell me that that is *my* problem? What, do you guys think you hold all the cards or something? You think you have the last word on reality? You do, you think that anything you do to me is okay as long as it's phrased properly, and anything I do is fucked because I'm not using the right words. I'm, like, throwing pencils and saying fuck you, I'm speaking another language, that's my problem. And the thing is – I am America. You know? You guys are not America. You think you are; Jesus Christ, you guys think you own the world. It's like, you guys think you can say anything you want if you phrase it right and look good while you say it! I mean, who made up that rule, Andrew? And do you actually think we're buying it? *(Pause.)*
ANDREW: Maybe you should sit down and tell me what's going on.
GEORGIE: Yeah, and maybe you should go fuck yourself. *(Pause.)* I'm sorry, okay?
ANDREW: Are you okay?
GEORGIE: Yes! No. Christ. I'm sorry. I'm sorry. *(Pause. They stand for a moment in silence. Andrew crosses and puts his arm around her. She leans against him.)*
ANDREW: What happened at the office?
GEORGIE: I don't know. You got anything to drink around here? I mean, could I have a drink?
ANDREW: Do you want some tea?
GEORGIE: Tea? Are you kidding? I mean, is that supposed to soothe me or something? I hate to break the news to you, but I really think that that is like, just a myth, Andrew. I think that in reality vodka is far more soothing than tea.
ANDREW: I don't have any vodka.
GEORGIE: Bourbon works too.
ANDREW: I have half a bottle of white zinfandel.
GEORGIE: Oh, Jesus. Make me tea. *(He exits to the kitchen. Georgie crosses, picks up the gym shorts and puts them on. Andrew reenters and sits her on the couch.)*
ANDREW: All right. Now tell me what happened.
GEORGIE: Nothing happened. I mean, it's stupid.
ANDREW: *(Pause.)* That's it. It's stupid? You can talk for hours about absolutely nothing, and now all you have to say about something that is clearly upsetting you is, it's stupid?
GEORGIE: I feel stupid.

ANDREW: What are you talking about, you feel stupid? You just walked in here and insulted me for ten minutes.

GEORGIE: That was different. I was mad.

ANDREW: You have to be mad to talk?

GEORGIE: No, come on – I don't know –

ANDREW: I could make you mad.

GEORGIE: No, you couldn't. You're too nice.

ANDREW: Fuck you.

GEORGIE: – Andrew –

ANDREW: Fuck you. Come on, fuck you.

GEORGIE: *(Calm.)* Yeah, fuck you too.

ANDREW: Fuck you.

GEORGIE: Fuck you.

ANDREW: Fuck you.

GEORGIE: You look really stupid saying fuck you –

ANDREW: Fuck you. Fuck you! Fuck you.

GEORGIE: *(Laughing, overlap.)* Andrew, stop it. Cut it out. It sounds weird when you say it. You shouldn't talk like that.

ANDREW: You talk like that all the time!

GEORGIE: I'm different. I mean, I know how to swear. You don't. It's like, fuck you. Fuck you. Or, you know, fuck you. It's just – you know. You got to know how to say it.

ANDREW: Fuck you.

GEORGIE: Forget it. You look really stupid. You look the way I look when I try to talk like you.

ANDREW: You've tried it:? Really? I must have missed that day.

GEORGIE: Oh, fuck you. You know I can do it; I can be as snotty and polite as anybody and it just makes me look stupid.

ANDREW: Georgie, it doesn't. You just – look. The English language is one of the most elegant and sophisticated languages on earth, and it will let you be whatever you want. If you use it carefully, and with respect, it can teach you things, it will allow you to uncover thoughts and ideas you never knew you were capable of; it will give you access to wisdom. Sophistication. Knowledge. Language is a gift that humanity has given itself to describe the world within, and without, with grace and wonder, and you can do that. Or you can use it badly and just be a, a fucking--cunt, if that's all you ever--

GEORGIE: UGGH. I can't believe you used that word. Oh, my God. You should see these words coming out of your mouth. It's so fucking weird. I'm not kidding, Andrew. I wouldn't swear if I was you.

ANDREW: Forget it. You want that fucking tea?

GEORGIE: No. I don't want the fucking tea.

ANDREW: You want to tell me what happened?

GEORGIE: Oh, God. It really is stupid. I mean, what do you think happened? He wants to screw me is what happened. *(Pause.)*

ANDREW: Could you elaborate on that?

GEORGIE: What, you don't know what that means?

ANDREW: He propositioned you or he tried to rape you or what? You have to be more specific; "screw" covers a lot of ground.

GEORGIE: Well, in his own weird little way he tried both, okay?

ANDREW: *(Pause.)* Georgie, don't kid around with me now –

GEORGIE: Just sit down, Andrew. He didn't lay a hand on me, he just – Look. Last week he tells me we have to talk about my future with the firm so we go out to dinner and he tells me how amazing I am and I could be a paralegal if I keep this up. I spilled my soup, I got so excited. So then he takes me home and asks if he can come up, and I say sorry, but I would like to keep our relationship professional. See, I do know how to talk like you assholes when I want to, so you can just stop acting like I'm a fucking idiot with words.

ANDREW: So he propositioned you.

GEORGIE: Last week, that was last week. Yesterday, he has me stay late, right? He says, Georgie, could you stay late and type up some interrogatories? And I say, sure. Then after everybody's gone he invites me into his office and asks me if I knew his couch folds out into a bed. So I say I have to get to work, Edward. But he wants to have a debate about the pros and cons of whether or not I should screw him. It was amazing, it went on for 20 minutes, I am not kidding. So I finally said, Edward, I don't have to debate this with you. I don't have to be polite, you know? I'm not going to fuck you. So he says, he doesn't have to be polite either and he could just rape me if he wanted because everybody else is gone and the security guard isn't due until ten. And I stared at him – and, you know, I could see it in his little lawyer's face; he could've done it. *(Pause.)* I mean, on the one hand, it was no big deal; I just walked out of the office and took the stairs, 'cause I wasn't going to wait for any elevator. I mean, I was scared, but I didn't think he was going to do anything because it was pretty clear that in his own sick little mind, just saying it was as good as doing it. What a weirdo.

ANDREW: You went to work today? You went to work after that?

GEORGIE: That job means a lot to me! *(Pause.)* What was I supposed to do, just quit and go back to – fuck, I don't know – I mean – I don't want to go back and be a waitress! What was I supposed to do? Quit, because Edward is an asshole? I didn't care, I didn't think he'd try it again! I didn't; I thought that was it!

ANDREW: Wasn't it?

GEORGIE: Today, he comes out of his office at about 4:30 and asks me to stay late to type a pleading. And he kind of looks at me, you know? So I said, fuck you, Edward, and threw my pencil at him.

ANDREW: *(Pause.)* Why didn't you tell me? Dammit. Why didn't you tell me last night?

GEORGIE: It was something, it was something he said.

ANDREW: He said something *worse?*

GEORGIE: No. No. It was just talk. You know? It was just talk. I just – I didn't want to make a big deal about it.

ANDREW: It *is* a big deal. It's indecent. It's a big deal. *(He paces angrily.)*

GEORGIE: Andrew. You're mad. I've never seen you mad.

ANDREW: Yes, I'm mad! I'm mad! We'll sue him for harassment. We'll take him to court.

GEORGIE: What, are you kidding? He'll kill us. He's a really good lawyer.
ANDREW: I don't care. Dammit. Goddammit!
GEORGIE: You want some tea?
ANDREW: NO, I – *(Pause.)* I'm sorry. I shouldn't be yelling at you.
GEORGIE: It's okay. I mean, he didn't do anything. It was just talk. Okay? Let me make you some tea. *(She goes into the kitchen. Andrew prowls the room angrily for a moment, then picks up the phone and dials. Georgie reenters with the tea.)*
GEORGIE: Andrew, what are you doing? You're not calling him, are you? Don't call him, okay? Andrew. I mean it.
ANDREW: *(Into phone.)* Hello, Jennine? It's Andrew. Is Edward around? Yeah, could you?
GEORGIE: *(Overlap.)* Andrew, I'm not kidding. Could you put the – would you put the fucking receiver down? Oh, FUCK. *(She crosses and pulls the cord out of the wall. They stare at each other for a moment, startled.)* What, did you think I was kidding? Did you not understand that I was saying I do not want you calling that asshole? Do you not understand English? *(Andrew picks up the ends of the phone cord, angry.)*
ANDREW: Have you lost your mind?
GEORGIE: No, I have not lost my mind! What the fuck kind of question is that? I asked you nicely to put the phone down. It was your little macho choice to keep on dialing, so don't go acting like I'm insane. I just don't want you talking to him right now! I don't need you doing some sort of protective male thing here! Just for a minute, okay? *(Pause.)*
ANDREW: Okay.
GEORGIE: I'm sorry about your phone.
ANDREW: It's okay.
GEORGIE: I'll get you another one.
ANDREW: It's okay.
GEORGIE: God, I should just go home before I make everything worse –
ANDREW: No. It's okay. I'm sorry, okay? *(He takes her face in his hands for a moment; she pulls away nervously.)*
GEORGIE: Okay. Let's talk about something else. Here's your tea. Chop those vegetables. Let's talk about – books. That'll cheer you up.
ANDREW: Georgie –
GEORGIE: No, come on, you're always beating me over the head to talk about books. I finished that one you gave me. *(She pulls a book out of her purse. They talk nervously.)*
ANDREW: Already?
GEORGIE: It was good; it was a good read, you know? Reminded me of, like, Sydney Sheldon. A lot happened.
ANDREW: *The Iliad* reminds you of Sydney Sheldon. Great.
GEORGIE: Yeah, it would make a great mini series, you know? We should try the idea out on my sister; she's like this expert on junk TV. No shit, she lies around this apartment in the Bronx all day and – come on, Andrew, help me out here. I'm sorry, okay?

ANDREW: It's okay.
GEORGIE: What else you got? *(She picks up a book from the table. He takes it from her.)*
ANDREW: No, you can't have that. I'm using that.
GEORGIE: Oh. Right. Right! How's your book coming?
ANDREW: It's fine.
GEORGIE: You should let me help you with that. I mean, I'm out of work now. I could come down and plug it into your computer for you. No kidding, I'm fast. I'll type it up for you; you'll be done in a week.
ANDREW: Right.
GEORGIE: I could, I could help! I mean, as long as you're going to do this Pygmalion thing, you might as well get something out of it.
ANDREW: Do what?
GEORGIE: Isn't that what it's called? Pig something? I heard Edward – uh - you know, I heard That Guy we both can't stand right now tell one of the partners you were playing this pig game. So I asked Donna about it. Some guy wrote a whole book; I bought it.
ANDREW: George Bernard Shaw.
GEORGIE: Yeah. I mean, it didn't exactly hit me as being the same thing here –
ANDREW: It's not the same thing. It's not the same thing at all. Edward doesn't know shit, okay? *(He takes the vegetables into the kitchen.)*
GEORGIE: *(Calling.)* Well – okay, he doesn't know shit, but I thought there were similarities. And, you know, the whole point of the book is she teaches him things, too, so I just thought – *(He reenters with washcloth and begins wiping off the coffee table.)*
ANDREW: It's not the same thing.
GEORGIE: Then what is it? *(Pause.)* I mean it. What is this?
ANDREW: What is what?
GEORGIE: This. This. All the dinners and the books and the lessons and the job. What is this, anyway? We been doing this for like, six months or something, you know? I mean – what's going on here, Andrew?
ANDREW: Georgie. We can take him to court.
GEORGIE: NO. I'm not talking about him. I'm talking about this. What is this?
ANDREW: It's – friendship.
GEORGIE: Friendship.
ANDREW: Yes.
GEORGIE: You're sure about that.
ANDREW: Yes.
GEORGIE: You get that mad whenever anybody fucks around with your friends, huh?
ANDREW: Yes. *(She looks at him. Suddenly, she crosses and sits very close.)* What are you doing?
GEORGIE: Nothing.
ANDREW: Georgie –
GEORGIE: I'm not doing anything. I'm just sitting next to my friend here with hardly any clothes on.

ANDREW: Come on. Don't do this. Please?

GEORGIE: Just once, Andrew. Don't you want to try it just once? Really. Don't you, kind of?

ANDREW: I don't think a one night stand is what you're looking for.

GEORGIE: Fine. We'll do it twice. She'll never know.

ANDREW: She's not the one I'm worried about. Georgie – oh, boy. Look, you're upset about what happened with Edward –

GEORGIE: Do I look upset?

ANDREW: But this isn't going to fix that –

GEORGIE: I don't need to be fixed. Come on, Andrew, let's just do it today. I had a bad day. I'm not upset – but I had a bad day.

ANDREW: Georgie – no – If I – I would be just as bad as him if I – I'm not going to take advantage of you like that.

GEORGIE: Fuck, yes, take advantage of me. Please. Don't be noble, Andrew. For once, don't be noble.

ANDREW: Georgie, sweetheart –

GEORGIE: She's going to be here in half an hour. We don't have a lot of time to talk about this. *(She slides her arms up around his neck. Protesting, he tries to pull her away. She resists and they wrestle for a moment; Andrew finally gets her turned around and holds her in front of him with her arms crossed under his.)*

GEORGIE: Okay, okay, if you don't want to, just say so –

ANDREW: It's not that I don't want to! *(Pause.)* I want to, all right?

GEORGIE: You do?

ANDREW: Yes. Oh, yes. *(He buries his face in her hair for a moment. She waits, uncertain.)*

GEORGIE: Okay. *(Pause.)* Are we waiting for something?

ANDREW: It's not that simple.

GEORGIE: Trust me on this one. It is that simple. *(She pulls away; he holds her.)*

ANDREW: Not fifteen minutes ago, you were on a rampage; you were ready to murder me and every other man you've ever met. Now you want to make love?

GEORGIE: Sex is kind of spontaneous that way.

ANDREW: It's not what you want.

GEORGIE: I'm pretty sure it is.

ANDREW: Please. Listen to me. Will you please listen? *(She nods. He releases her. Pause.)* All right. Nietzche talks about the myth of eternal return.

GEORGIE: Oh, come on. Don't do this to me –

ANDREW: Thomas Hardy, historical repetition.

GEORGIE: Don't do this to me, Andrew – we don't have much time here!

ANDREW: *(Overlap.)* What history teaches you is that people have never learned anything from history. Hegel. History is a nightmare from which I am trying to escape. James Joyce.

GEORGIE: *(Overlap.)* This is your fucking book. I don't want to hear about your stupid book now!

ANDREW: You better want to hear about it, because I'm not talking about my stupid book, I'm talking about your life. Historical repetition. One man treats you bad so you fall in bed with another. God. The system eats up people like you and spits them out like chicken bones; it always has. You end up in deadend jobs, crummy apartments, bad neighborhoods, too many drugs, too much alcohol, meaningless relationships. They don't give you anything to live for, so you live for nothing! The complexities of what happens to the underclasses are so byzantine no one can make head or tail out of them anymore, we never could. We spin our theories, one after another, and it never amounts to anything; century after century we lose half the human race, more than half, to what? And why? I just didn't want to see you become a statistic.

GEORGIE: What does this have to do with whether or not we go to bed?

ANDREW: I will not become just another one of your lovers. We're both worth more than that.

GEORGIE: I didn't mean –

ANDREW: Relationships *mean* something. People *mean*. You don't sleep with every person you're attracted to; that's not the way it works. And aside from the crucial fact that I'm not about to betray Lydia, who I love, I'm not going to betray you. You want to know what this is? I am not your friend, okay? I am your teacher. And you don't sleep with your teacher; it screws up everything. You don't do it.

GEORGIE: I had a geometry teacher who came onto me in the tenth grade.

ANDREW: Did you ever learn anything from him? *(Pause.)*

GEORGIE: Fine. Okay, fine. I mean, I just wanted to sleep with you. I didn't mean to threaten world history, you know?

ANDREW: Georgie. It's not that I don't want to.

GEORGIE: No, it's fine, I don't care, I shouldn't have – I'm no better than Edward, am I?

ANDREW: No. You are.

GEORGIE: What's Lydia like? Is she like you? I mean, is she gentle, like you?

ANDREW: I guess so.

GEORGIE: Edward is so full of shit. You know, he told me – He told me the reason he came onto me was because you told him to.

ANDREW: What?

GEORGIE: Yeah. I mean, I didn't believe him. Because it was so creepy, and you're not – I mean, you're so Not That, but it just made me sick to hear it, you know?

ANDREW: *(Pause.)* What did he say?

GEORGIE: I don't know. He said you told him I was on the make or something and he should – you know? Then today when I got here, you said you talked to him, so I thought – I mean, I didn't want to think it, but – I'm sorry. I just – I got freaked out. I'm sorry.

ANDREW: It's okay.

GEORGIE: What a creep.

ANDREW: Yeah. *(Long pause.)* It's getting late. We should – get going on this dinner. *(He picks up the dishrag and crosses slowly to the kitchen. She watches him for an awful moment.)*

GEORGIE: *(Quiet.)* Andrew?

ANDREW: What?
GEORGIE: What did you say to him?
ANDREW: What?
GEORGIE: *(Pause.)* Oh, no. When I got here you said you talked to him. What did you say?
ANDREW: I said – I liked you. That was all I said.
GEORGIE: That was all?
ANDREW: Yes! I mean, no, I – of course, we talked about other things, but it wasn't anything – it wasn't –
GEORGIE: Why are you getting so nervous?
ANDREW: I'm not nervous! I'm trying to remember the conversation. He said – he wanted to ask you out, and I said I thought that would be okay. I told him you might be – I told him I thought you might need someone in your life, you seemed – Look. I thought you were getting a kind of crush on me, so it might be good for you –
GEORGIE: You gave me to him?
ANDREW: No. That's not what I did.
GEORGIE: What the fuck would you call it? Why was he asking your permission to go out with me in the first place? Am I like your property or something and he has to get your permission –
ANDREW: Georgie, no; it was a misunderstanding. He thought there was something going on between us and he just wanted to know –
GEORGIE: Something going on. Some *thing,* huh? Christ, Andrew. I am in love with you.
ANDREW: *(Pause.)* I'm sorry. I didn't know.
GEORGIE: You didn't know? How could you not know?
ANDREW: Please, believe me, if I had known, I never would have said –
GEORGIE: You never would have said what? You never would have said, Go ahead, take her? You never would have said that, huh? I can't believe you. You – you're just the same as the rest of them, aren't you? *(She picks up her bag and goes to the door quickly, furious.)*
ANDREW: No! That's not – Georgie, you're upset, you're not being fair, you're not thinking –
GEORGIE: Don't talk to me about fair, just don't even start!
ANDREW: Don't walk out. We have to talk about this. Georgie – *(He grabs her elbow. She slaps him hard. They stare at each other.)*
GEORGIE: Fuck that, Andrew. You don't like my language, and I don't like yours. I'm sick of talking, you know? You know what I mean? You guys – for all you know, you don't know shit. *(She exits. Blackout.)*

Scene 2

> Again, loud classical music on the radio; this time something more sinister – Stravinsky, Rachmaninoff. A bottle of scotch with a significant dent in it stands on the coffee table. After a moment, Andrew crosses into the room.

ANDREW: Yeah, yeah, I'm coming – *(He opens the door; Edward enters. Andrew stares at him, aghast.)*
EDWARD: Hi. How's it going?
ANDREW: Edward.
EDWARD: Nice. Nice welcome. Listen, your security's great here; your front door is wide open.
ANDREW: Edward, what are you doing here?
EDWARD: I'm returning your calls. Sorry I didn't get back to you; I was in court all day. Anyway, I'm supposed to have dinner with Georgie, so I thought I'd kill two birds with one stone. I won't stay.
ANDREW: *(Quietly astonished.)* What? You what?
EDWARD: Christ, what a day I've had. Can I use your phone? *(He dials.)*
ANDREW: She's having dinner with you?
EDWARD: Yeah. Can you turn that down? *(Andrew crosses to the music and snaps it off. Edwards speaks into the receiver.)* Georgie. It's Edward. *(Pause.)* No, no, I'm in the building. I'm at Andrew's. So, can you just meet me down here? *(Pause.)* Hello? *(Pause.)* No, I just – Andrew wanted to talk to me about something, so I – No, I just got here. *(Pause.)* It's okay – okay, take your time. *(Pause.)* Okay, great. Bye. *(He stares at the receiver, perplexed, and hangs up.)* Christ. You have anything to drink around here?
ANDREW: You're not staying. *(Edward finds the bottle of scotch.)*
EDWARD: Is this *scotch?* Andrew, congratulations. You learned how to drink scotch. *(He exits to the kitchen, delivers part of his speech there, reenters pouring scotch and sits.)*
ANDREW: Edward –
EDWARD: *(Calling.)* You would not believe the day I've had. I spent the entire afternoon in front of McGilla Gorilla trying to convince her that three Jamaican dope peddlers with a collective list of priors as long as the Old Testament had been denied their rights. Some of these judges – I mean, I didn't write the fucking constitution. It wasn't my idea to give everybody rights. That was our founding fathers, remember? If she doesn't like it, she can complain to the goddamn supreme court. The stupid cop violated their rights. He pulls them over – get this, the cop pulls them over because they ran a red light – and they all get into an argument, so he pulls a search and seizure and finds six pounds of marijuana in the trunk. Marijuana, okay, we're not even talking cocaine. And can you show me probable cause in an argument about whether the light was yellow or red? Can you do that for me, please? Four hours I'm arguing this shit. I mean, I got assigned this case; someone give me a fucking break! I hate this pro bono shit. If I'm going to defend criminals, I really prefer that they have lots and lots of money. *(Andrew crosses and takes the glass from him politely.)*
ANDREW: *(Quiet.)* Don't make yourself at home; you're not staying. I've been calling you all day to let you know that I want you to stay away from her. If you ever go near her again, I'll have you charged with assault. No. Forget that. If you go near her, I'll cut your throat out. Do you understand? now get out. *(Pause.)*
EDWARD: Well. That was aggressive. You want to tell me what this is about?
ANDREW: You know what this is about.

EDWARD: Well, no, really, I don't, but I can make some wild guesses. You talked to Georgie?

ANDREW: Yes. I talked to Georgie.

EDWARD: She told you about the fight we had, huh?

ANDREW: Actually, what she told me was that you threatened to rape her.

EDWARD: What? Oh, that is not –

ANDREW: Don't. Just don't even try to talk your way out of this one. You know, frankly, I never thought even you could sink this low. Christ, we've been friends for what, fifteen years, and I've seen you go through a lot of women and I'm not always crazy about the way you treat them, but this – if anyone had asked me, I would've said, no, he's bad but he's not that bad –

EDWARD: *(Overlap.)* Andrew. ANDREW. I didn't threaten her. I did not threaten her. Okay?

ANDREW: Spare me –

EDWARD: To the best of my recollection, in this country the accused is innocent until proven guilty, so can you give me a second here to tell you what happened?

ANDREW: Fine. Fine. Go right ahead.

EDWARD: Can I have my drink back, please? *(Andrew looks at him, hands him the drink.)* I'm glad to see you're bringing an open mind to this. Okay. You want to know what happened? I came onto her. I admit it. That's not a crime; she's an attractive woman. And as you'll recall, I told you about this ahead of time; I got clearance from you, pal.

ANDREW: Don't throw that at me –

EDWARD: *(Overlap.)* I asked you –

ANDREW: *(Overlap.)* – You said you wanted to start seeing her!

EDWARD: Did you think that meant I was going to take her on a picnic?

ANDREW: I certainly didn't think it meant rape.

EDWARD: Oh, for – Nothing happened! I came onto her and she wasn't interested and I got mad. That's it. I got mad.

ANDREW: What did you say to her?

EDWARD: Please. Who remembers? It turned into a huge fight. The woman is screaming at me. I know very little.

ANDREW: What did you say?

EDWARD: Andrew – this woman makes Godzilla look like a Barbie doll.

ANDREW: What did you say?

EDWARD: I don't remember the specifics of the fight.

ANDREW: You did it, didn't you. You said it.

EDWARD: I did not threaten her, okay? I mean, we were having an argument, a discussion in my office, and I said some things that perhaps I should not have said, but I did not threaten her –

ANDREW: *(Overlapping.)* Oh, what, "some things that I should not have said," like I could just rape you –

EDWARD: All right, yes, perhaps I said that, that is not the same thing –

ANDREW: That's it. Get out. *(He grabs at the drink. Edward resists and the drink goes flying, covering both of them with scotch.)*

EDWARD: Do you think we can discuss this like rational adults?

ANDREW: No, as a matter of fact, I don't think we can.

EDWARD: When I walked in, you said you wanted to slit my throat. That doesn't mean you'd actually do it, does it?

ANDREW: Oh, it might.

EDWARD: I was having a fight with my secretary, Andrew. We both said things we shouldn't have said. *(Edward turns away and goes to the kitchen. He returns a moment later with a towel. He dries himself off and throws it at Andrew.)*

ANDREW: It wasn't a fight. It was sexual harassment.

EDWARD: *(Overlap.)* As a term, "sexual harassment" is so overdefined it's almost meaningless. MacKinnon notwithstanding, at no point did I actually threaten her; and at no point did I suggest that her job security would be endangered by a failure to participate in a sexual act --

ANDREW: *(Overlap.)* Shut up. WOULD YOU PLEASE SHUT UP? *(Pause.)*

EDWARD: I'm sorry. I spend too much time in front of judges. *(Pause.)* Come on. Let's be reasonable about this. If I had threatened to rape her, would she be having dinner with me?

ANDREW: I don't know anything about any dinner.

EDWARD: You just heard me on the phone with her. I admit, we had a nasty fight, but she came back to the office today, we talked it out, and she went back to work. Now I'm taking her to dinner to smooth things over.

ANDREW: A dinner is supposed to smooth over rape?

EDWARD: I did not in fact rape her! Can we at least agree on that?

ANDREW: Fine.

EDWARD: Thank you. Now. May I take it that you object to this dinner?

ANDREW: Yes. I object to the dinner.

EDWARD: Why?

ANDREW: Edward –

EDWARD: Are you interested in her?

ANDREW: You know – she is not some thing we can pass around between us, Jesus –

EDWARD: You're objecting to a simple dinner. I'm trying to find out why. If there's something going on between you –

ANDREW: No, nothing is going on between us!

EDWARD: You don't want her, but you'd prefer that no one else had her?

ANDREW: I don't know what it is about you, but everything sounds so sleazy coming out of your mouth.

EDWARD: Yeah, they teach us how to do that in law school. I'm just trying to get a grip on this, man. I mean, it sounds to me like you want to fuck her.

ANDREW: Everything is not sex, you know?

EDWARD: I know. Do you want to fuck her or not?

ANDREW: Look, I'm engaged to another woman, I'm not about to – why am I even answering you? I'm not the one on trial here!

EDWARD: Oh, no. Not Lydia. I have told you, I absolutely refuse to believe that you are going to marry that woman –

ANDREW: We are not getting into this again –

EDWARD: Sleeping with Lydia is one thing, Andrew, but marrying her –

ANDREW: We are not discussing this –

EDWARD: Come on, the woman looks like a corpse! I mean, what happens when you dust her off and put her out in the sunlight?

ANDREW: You didn't object to her looks while you were going out with her! As I recall, before she dumped you, you thought she was "exquisite."

EDWARD: Oooo. Nice shot. That's a three pointer. *(He exits to the kitchen and returns a moment later with a can of peanuts which he eats happily.)*

ANDREW: *(Pause.)* I don't know why I even talk to you anymore.

EDWARD: *(Calling.)* I keep you sharp.

ANDREW: *(Calling.)* You give me a headache.

EDWARD: *(Reentering.)* I love fighting with you. You're so earnest.

ANDREW: Oh, for – yes, I'm earnest. Jesus CHRIST, I'm earnest! This is not a game –

EDWARD: ANDREW. CALM DOWN. I know it's not a game. I'm just being a jerk, okay?

ANDREW: Well, cut it out. I mean, some things are not just food for another argument. We're talking about a woman's soul here –

EDWARD: A woman's soul? Andrew, come back. We're not talking about anybody's *soul;* we're talking about whether or not I said something sleazy to my secretary. I'm not trying to be difficult; I'm just being realistic. I mean, I just, I don't want to have a little conversation about how we all should behave better so the world will be a better place. I'm not going to make the world a better place. The human race does not do that. We make it worse, we always have; if we're not killing each other, we're killing whales or buffalo or bald eagles, what have you, and if we're not doing that, we just pollute everything so nothing can survive here anyway. That is what the human race does; it's what we've always done. We have our moments. We have Shakespeare, the Declaration of Independence. The Taj Mahal. Smokey Robinson. We are capable of wisdom and compassion and genius, but most of the time we just throw it away. We yearn for meaning and then we squander our lives on drugs and television. We're corrupt. We are not good. I accept that. And this is why you're holed up in this nice little university teaching political philosophy, and I'm making $143,000 a year defending drug dealers. Because I like reality. And what is the moral of this story? The moral is: Georgie is real. She is *real*. And, frankly, your impulse to keep her at a distance, physically, at least, strikes me as a little academic.

ANDREW: Don't give me that. What are you saying, I'm stupid or insipid because I want to preserve some integrity in my private life, because I believe it's possible to – to – to care about her without screwing her? I believe in human dignity so I'm not an idiot, is that it? Well, fuck you, Edward. I mean it. That's a crock of shit. Next thing, you'll be telling me Ted Bundy is a national hero!

EDWARD: Don't twist my words. My position is offensive enough as it stands. Chill out. Have some scotch. *(He pours him a drink.)* Come on. We can talk about this. We've been through worse.

ANDREW: I don't know. I don't know. Sometimes, talking to you is like talking to a swamp.

EDWARD: It's a gift.

ANDREW: I have to admit, it is. *(They drink.)*
EDWARD: This is good scotch. When did you start drinking scotch?
ANDREW: Last night.
EDWARD: Oh?
ANDREW: Yeah. We had a fight of our own. She blames me for the whole thing. As far as she's concerned, I gave you permission to threaten rape.
EDWARD: Well – in a way –
ANDREW: Edward –
EDWARD: Sorry. I'm sorry. It's like a knee jerk reaction. I'm sorry.
ANDREW: Look. I admit this is largely my fault. I never should have sent her to you in the first place. I wasn't thinking. I thought you'd treat her differently because she came from me.
EDWARD: Andrew.
ANDREW: I know. That was pretty stupid, wasn't it? I am a stupid man.
EDWARD: Andrew – I'm sorry. I am sorry. I just don't know what I can do about it now. You want me to promise to behave myself? I can promise that.
ANDREW: Please don't take this wrong, but I would have to be crazy to trust your promises at this point. God only knows what the word "behave" means to you.
EDWARD: It has a series of definitions.
ANDREW: Exactly. I'll get her another job.
EDWARD: What?
ANDREW: Don't give me a hard time about this! If she goes back to work for you, it's like she's saying fine, treat me like dirt, I don't mind. Well, she's better than that, all right?
EDWARD: It's not like she's Joan of Arc, for God's sake.
ANDREW: I'm not going to argue about this anymore.
EDWARD: It just seems to me that complete relocation is a drastic solution to an essentially simple misunderstanding. I don't think it's necessary, okay?
ANDREW: Well, I think it is. *(Pause.)*
EDWARD: Well, what you think isn't entirely relevant anymore, is it?
ANDREW: *(Pause.)* Excuse me?
EDWARD: *(Dangerous.)* Look. I spent the last four months training that girl and she is now a damn good secretary. I'm not going to let you just walk off with her.
ANDREW: Oh, now everything's business all of a sudden –
EDWARD: What else would it be?
ANDREW: Was it business when you threatened to rape her? And this dinner, that's business too, huh? *(Pause.)*
EDWARD: You know, you're getting to be a real prick in your old age.
ANDREW: That's funny, coming from you. *(Pause.)*
EDWARD: So what are you going to do? You going to tell her that she can't work for me anymore? You're going to tell her that, huh?
ANDREW: I'm just going to talk to her. She'll quit.
EDWARD: She isn't going to quit! She doesn't give a fuck about your moral codes, Andrew! She needs the damn job.
ANDREW: I'm just going to talk to her.

EDWARD: Tell her what? We'll both talk to her. When she gets down here, we'll just ask her. The two of us. We'll just ask her if she wants to quit.

ANDREW: I would prefer to talk to her alone.

EDWARD: Uh huh. I just bet you would.

ANDREW: Listen –

EDWARD: No, I understand. You two need a little privacy to work out the details of this decent little friendship you've got.

ANDREW: It's not – *(Georgie knocks on the door.)*

EDWARD: How much time do you need?

ANDREW: I don't –

EDWARD: It took me five minutes to get her to come back. How much time do you need to get her to quit again?

GEORGIE: *(Knocking.)* Hey, are you guys in there?

EDWARD: Ten minutes? Will that do?

ANDREW: You know – Lydia really is right about you.

EDWARD: I'll give you fifteen. That's ten more than I had. And I'll bet you, you still can't do it. How about it, Andrew?

ANDREW: I'm not going to bet you –

GEORGIE: *(Pounding.)* You guys –

EDWARD: You're on. Come up with some excuse, okay? Hello, my darling. *(Edward opens the door. Georgie enters; she is dressed to the nines in a provocative outfit. In her hands, she carries a pair of gold spike heels.)*

GEORGIE: Hi, Eddie. Have a little trouble with the door there? *(She crosses in and puts on her shoes.)*

EDWARD: You're late.

GEORGIE: So fire me. The subway went insane yet again. It took me forever to get home. Hi, Andrew.

EDWARD: You should have said something. I could have given you a lift.

GEORGIE: No, it's okay, I love the subway. *(She puts on the second shoe and stands up a little too quickly. She staggers; Edward reaches out and steadies her.)*

EDWARD: Steady –

GEORGIE: Sorry, I haven't worn these things for a while and you have to get used to them, you know? It's kind of like walking on stilts.

EDWARD: They're fabulous. You really look stunning, Georgie.

GEORGIE: I'm not overdressed, am I?

EDWARD: No, no. I mean, you don't have to be. *(Pause.)* That's not what I mean. I mean, we can go someplace elegant. If – we go out, I mean.

GEORGIE: What do you mean, if?

EDWARD: Nothing.

GEORGIE: Great. Let's go. *(She turns for the door.)*

EDWARD: Andrew?

GEORGIE: Andrew. Well, what a fun idea. Andrew. Why don't you come along?

ANDREW: I don't think –

GEORGIE: If you're not hungry, you can always watch us eat. *(Pause.)*

ANDREW: No. Thank you.

GEORGIE: Suit yourself. *(To Edward.)* Andrew's in a snit, huh? He doesn't like it when I wear these shoes. He thinks they're bad for me. But you like them, don't you?

EDWARD: I have to admit, I do. Sorry, Andrew.

GEORGIE: I like them, too. I like the way they make my legs look kind of dangerous, you know? And I like being tall. *(She laughs.)* I like being able to look you both in the eye. It's the only chance I get, when I'm wearing these things. *(She crosses to Edward and stands close, looking him in the eye.)* See what I mean?

EDWARD: It's perfectly delightful.

GEORGIE: Thank you. *(She crosses back to Andrew, looks him in the eye.)* What do you think, Andrew?

ANDREW: I think they look sad and ridiculous.

GEORGIE: Then I guess it's a good thing you're not going out to dinner with us, huh? Come on, Edward. Let's hit the road.

ANDREW: What's your rush? *(Pause.)*

GEORGIE: Excuse me?

ANDREW: You don't have to rush off, do you? Why don't you guys stay and have a drink first?

GEORGIE: I think we're in kind of a hurry.

ANDREW: One drink.

GEORGIE: Aren't we in a hurry?

ANDREW: Are you? Edward?

EDWARD: I don't think so.

ANDREW: Maybe you could run downstairs and get a bottle of wine.

EDWARD: Well, there's an idea. I'll be right back.

GEORGIE: No, Edward – I mean, I don't like wine. Look, Andrew has this scotch here. So Andrew, you've taken up scotch, huh? Forget the wine. Let's have scotch.

ANDREW: I'd really like some wine.

GEORGIE: What are you talking about? You're drinking scotch.

ANDREW: I'd rather have wine.

GEORGIE: Well, fine, then you go get it.

EDWARD: No, that's okay, I'll get it. What would you like?

ANDREW: I don't – Champagne.

GEORGIE: What?

ANDREW: We'll have champagne. It'll be fun.

GEORGIE: Fun?

EDWARD: I'll be right back.

GEORGIE: No, come on – I mean – okay, I'll go get it.

ANDREW AND EDWARD: *(Overlapping.)* No, no, no – *(Georgie stares at them.)*

EDWARD: I mean – it'll just take a second. You two – can chat.

GEORGIE: I don't want to chat.

EDWARD: Chat. *(He exits. Georgie turns and stares at Andrew for a second, then crosses and pours herself a glass of scotch.)*

GEORGIE: Okay. What is going on?
ANDREW: I might ask you the same question.
GEORGIE: Hey, I'm not the one acting like the three stooges, okay?
ANDREW: What do you think you're doing?
GEORGIE: What do I think I'm doing? I think I'm giving Edward a hard-on.
What do you think I'm doing?
ANDREW: I don't know. *(Pause.)* Are you trying to make me jealous?
GEORGIE: Is it working?
ANDREW: Yeah. Sure.
GEORGIE: Good.
ANDREW: I can't believe you. You went back to work for him. After what he
did, you went back to work – you're going out to *dinner* –
GEORGIE: You're suggesting we all have champagne together. So get off my
fucking back, okay? It looks like we're two of a kind when it comes to Edward.
ANDREW: I was trying to get rid of him so I could talk to you for a few minutes!
GEORGIE: Really? Andrew, you're so sly.
ANDREW: Okay, fine. You're mad at me, you want to have a fight, fine –
GEORGIE: Gee, thanks for the permission, Teach –
ANDREW: But don't go back to work for him! Don't have dinner with him!
GEORGIE: Why not?
ANDREW: He threatened to rape you!
GEORGIE: He apologized!
ANDREW: I would like to think that some things go beyond apology.
GEORGIE: Like what? Like betrayal, maybe? Listen – I know he's still slime,
but you want to know what happened? I did go back to work, yeah. I went back in
to get my stuff – I had all this shit in my desk, you know? So I go in at about ten
to pick it all up, and it was amazing. Every secretary in the building has her own
little story to tell me about how she almost did the same thing but never had the
guts. I'm like this fucking hero, you know? So right in the middle of this big
scene, there's like fifteen people crowding around my desk, right, Edward comes
out and says he wants to talk to me. In his office. And he just stands there, and it's
like this dare, you now, it's like this fucking dare, and everyone goes real quiet,
just waiting to see what I'm gonna do. The whole fucking office is watching me.
And I don't know, when you get a dare like that – I mean, it was so out there. So
we go in his office, and he says: I want to apologize. And then he goes into it. He
apologizes for about five minutes. Swore he'd never do it again. Then he offers
me a two thousand dollar raise. Well – the whole thing just started to seem kind of
funny. Two thousand bucks? He never even touched me! I didn't even have to
kiss him. I just thought – hey, you know, two thousand bucks. Jesus. So – I didn't
quit. *(Pause.)* I didn't quit.
ANDREW: Do you believe him?
GEORGIE: Yeah. I believe he's going to give me a raise. He won't even feel it.
Two thousand is like what he pays to have his car waxed.
ANDREW: That's not what I mean.
GEORGIE: I know. *(Pause.)*
ANDREW: I can get you another job. Last night I called some people in the

department and I found some leads –
GEORGIE: I don't need a job. I got a job.
ANDREW: You don't have to put up with it. He'll try it again, you know he will –
GEORGIE: I can take care of myself; I been doing it for years. I don't need you to like, worry about me.
ANDREW: I beg to differ.
GEORGIE: Yeah, well, tough shit for you.
ANDREW: *(Pause.)* This isn't about the job.
GEORGIE: I'm getting out of here; you make me crazy – *(She goes for the door.)*
ANDREW: Last night you said you were in love with me.
GEORGIE: Yeah. I remember. *(Pause.)*
ANDREW: Come here. Please? I can't talk to you if you keep trying to leave. Come on, sit down – *(He crosses to her at the door. Instinctively, her arms fly up, defensive.)*
GEORGIE: Andrew, don't – *(Pause.)* I just – could you not get too close to me? *(Wounded, Andrew backs off. She stands at the door and looks at him.)*
ANDREW: I'm sorry about what happened. I didn't mean to betray you, and I certainly never meant to hurt you, and if that's why you're doing this –
GEORGIE: What exactly am I doing? *(Pause.)* You don't know, do you? You don't know if I'm just trying to make you jealous, or if this is just what is, you know, reality, why not sleep with him? Maybe this is me. Okay? I mean, I understand this. Hormones I get. Every man I've ever had to deal with – I fucking know how to deal with that. I know what to do, and when to do it, and how to get what I want. You know – I live in a whole different world from you. I'm in the receiver's position. I do what you guys tell me to; whether it's reading books or fucking, I do it. I make all this noise, you know; I scream and yell bloody fucking murder, but I always manage to do what you say. That's the way we survive. I'm just being realistic, okay? And yeah, maybe I am trying to make you jealous. Maybe I want to teach you something for a change, you could learn from me, but– fuck. Jesus. Forget it. *(She crosses away from him and sits.)*
ANDREW: You're not that. You're not.
GEORGIE: Yeah, well then you tell me what I am because I don't know anymore. Oh, fuck. Look – I'm sorry I'm being so awful, I don't – I'm just confused, okay? I don't want to talk about this. Fuck. I don't know what I'm doing, Andrew, I just don't know what else to –
ANDREW: It's okay. It's okay. *(Andrew crosses to her, tentative.)* Let me take those off. Please? Let me take your shoes off. *(She looks at him, amazed, as he kneels and takes her shoes off, setting them aside. He holds her feet between his hands for a moment.)*
GEORGIE: Andrew, don't. Come on. Don't. It's killing me, okay? I know it's nothing to you, but I can't take it. *(He looks at her.)*
ANDREW: It's not nothing. *(He holds her by the elbow and slowly leans in to kiss her. The kiss begins to become passionate and physical when he suddenly pulls away. Confused, she clings to him for a moment; he gently releases himself.)*

ANDREW: *(Pause.)* Oh, God. You scare me to death.

GEORGIE: What?

ANDREW: You – no. No.

GEORGIE: Wait a minute. Come on. Let's go back to this tender moment thing – *(She reaches for him; he pulls away.)*

ANDREW: Look at that dress.

GEORGIE: What?

ANDREW: You look ridiculous.

GEORGIE: You just said – could you not fuck with my brain here? I get enough of that at the office –

ANDREW: Why are you wearing those shoes?

GEORGIE: Because they make my legs look good! Why are you yelling at me?

ANDREW: Because you're making a spectacle of yourself.

GEORGIE: Listen, the popular opinion is that I clean up pretty good, so don't get started on me here –

ANDREW: You don't care, do you? You're just going to go ahead and squander yourself. This is enough for you? The shoes, the dress, the fancy dinner. That's what you want, is that it?

GEORGIE: No. No, I don't want him, I don't want to do this, if you don't want me to, I won't do it, I – Why are you yelling at me? A minute ago you were kissing me, and you meant it. What the FUCK is going on here?

ANDREW: It wouldn't work. We are too different. There is an abyss between us; not a crevice, not a difference of opinion. An abyss. The void. It would be a nightmare to negotiate, and you're not exactly the calmest person I've ever met, you know what I mean? Who do you think you'd take it out on?

GEORGIE: I wouldn't.

ANDREW: Who are you kidding? It's inevitable with you; there's no peace in you. The only reason we've lasted as long as we have is because we don't sleep together. I listen to you, and I feel battered. I wouldn't survive. I'm telling you, if it got to be any more than this, I would not survive. Sometimes – sometimes I think you understand that life is not just a rage, it's better than that, but other times – I just don't know. *(Pause.)* It doesn't have to be like this. That's what I wanted to teach you. Life doesn't have to be just this long scream of rage, Georgie. You're better than this. I made you better than this. *(Pause.)*

GEORGIE: What?

ANDREW: I'm sorry. I didn't mean that.

GEORGIE: What did you say? You made me better? Did you actually say that?

ANDREW: Please don't go off again, I cannot take any more of this – *(She picks up the shoes.)*

GEORGIE: Well, I won't be better. I won't be better anymore. I'll be as bad as I want. Why didn't you just let me be whatever I was? At least I was happy. *(She starts to put on the shoes again.)*

ANDREW: You weren't happy.

GEORGIE: Fuck you. I'm not happy now.

ANDREW: You were not happy. You were so bored with your life you were killing yourself. You came home drunk after every shift; you were sleeping with

every guy who looked at you –
GEORGIE: That's what this is all about, isn't it? Fuck the abyss, this isn't about any abyss, this is about sex! All the guys. That's what bothers you, really. Isn't it?
ANDREW: Oh, for God's sake, I'm not judging you. Your apartment's right above mine. I couldn't help – the whole building knew about it. Christ.
GEORGIE: Why don't you just cut my heart out and get it over with? Compared to you, Edward really is a prince. Tell him I went upstairs to wait.
ANDREW: Georgie –
GEORGIE: TELL HIM I'M WAITING FOR HIM UPSTAIRS.
ANDREW: It won't prove anything.
GEORGIE: Oh, yeah. It will. Think about it, Andrew. Think about it tonight, while you're listening to your little ceiling here. Think about it. (She exits. Andrew stands for a moment, then viciously shoves a pile of books off the bookcase. Blackout.)

END ACT ONE

ACT II

Scene 1

Loud music is heard on the boombox, Elvis Costello singing "Romeo was restless, he was ready to kill..." The lights come up on Georgie's apartment, layout identical to Andrew's apartment, but all particulars – knickknacks, books, pillows, etc., different. This apartment is a comfortable mess. Georgie actually has more books than Andrew; they sprawl everywhere, as do her tapes.

Edward and Georgie are discovered entwined in a serious clinch on the couch. Georgie's legs are wrapped around Edward's body, the spike heels clearly visible. After a moment, Edward suddenly pulls away. He looks down at Georgie for a moment, stands, crosses to the music and snaps it off. Georgie watches him, astonished. He remains standing by the silent boombox for a moment before she speaks.

GEORGIE: Is something wrong?
EDWARD: The music. It seemed a little loud to me.
GEORGIE: Oh. *(Pause.)* Well, then, why don't you turn it off?
EDWARD: Thanks, I think I will. *(Pause. He stands there, thinking. She looks at him.)*
GEORGIE: Edward –
EDWARD: Could I have something to drink?
GEORGIE: Excuse me?
EDWARD: You invited me up for a drink. I'd like a drink.
GEORGIE: I'm sorry. I'm a little confused. I thought we got *past* the drink.
EDWARD: I'm kind of thirsty. *(Pause.)*
GEORGIE: Okay. What would you like to drink?
EDWARD: I don't know, I – tea? Could I have a cup of tea?
GEORGIE: Excuse me?
EDWARD: I think I'd like some tea.
GEORGIE: Why?
EDWARD: Don't you have any tea?
GEORGIE: I don't know, you know, I kind of doubt it –
EDWARD: I'll look.
GEORGIE: Edward – *(He exits to the kitchen. Noise. Georgie looks after him, annoyed, then sits and stares at the coffee table for a moment. She suddenly picks up a pile of books and drops them on the floor, crosses to the table, pours herself a drink.) (Calling loudly.)* I think you're going to have to settle for scotch, Edward. Personally, I have always thought scotch was much more to the point than almost anything else available in most situations.
EDWARD: *(Calling.)* I'd like to keep my wits about me, if you don't mind.
GEORGIE: *(Drinking.)* Oh, you plan on needing your wits? What for?
EDWARD: *(Reentering.)* One never knows. You know, your kitchen is a disaster

area. And how old is this stuff? *(He carries a mashed box of tea.)*
GEORGIE: I have no idea.
EDWARD: That milk in there, you know, that stuff is really frightening. *(He goes back into the kitchen.)*
GEORGIE: *(Calling.)* Edward –
EDWARD: *(Calling, sound of dishes.)* Don't you ever wash your dishes? Andrew's always complaining about the bugs in this building; I don't see how you can just leave dirty plates lying around like this. It's like an invitation –
GEORGIE: Edward – EDWARD. You are not doing my dishes. YOU ARE NOT – *(She stands and crosses quickly. Edward meets her in the doorway.)*
EDWARD: SHHH. Could – would you be quiet, please? You are one of the noisiest people I've ever met. It's the middle of the night, people are trying to sleep.
GEORGIE: Not everyone. Some of them, I'm sure, are doing other things. People do all sorts of things in the middle of the night. Didn't you know that?
EDWARD: Yes. I know that.
GEORGIE: I thought maybe you did. So – what's the problem here, Edward? All of a sudden you're acting like – I mean, what, is this your first time?
EDWARD: No.
GEORGIE: You a little nervous? You want me to be gentle? I can be gentle. *(She starts to close in.)*
EDWARD: That's not necessary.
GEORGIE: I didn't think it was. So what's the problem?
EDWARD: I'm just trying to get a grip on this. I mean, not two days ago, you did tell me, and I quote, "Even if you were the last fucking asshole on the planet, Edward –"
GEORGIE: Yeah, yeah, yeah. What can I say? I came to my senses.
EDWARD: Yes, well –
GEORGIE: You can be very persuasive.
EDWARD: I'm aware of that; still –
GEORGIE: You changing your mind about this?
EDWARD: No, that's not exactly –
GEORGIE: So what's the problem? *(She's getting close.)*
EDWARD: There's no problem. I just – I want that tea. *(He goes back to the kitchen. Georgie looks after him, seriously annoyed.)*
GEORGIE: I swear, sex was never this complicated in high school. *(She looks at the floor.) (To floor.)* You getting all this? *(She glances back at the kitchen for a moment, then stomps on the floor several times. Edward enters with a mug of tea and watches her.)*
EDWARD: Is something wrong?
GEORGIE: *(Starts.)* Oh. You know. Bugs. *(She takes off her shoe, crosses to the trash can and scrapes the bug off, puts the shoe back on.)* Got your tea there? Mmm, that looks delicious.
EDWARD: Could you turn down the sarcasm for just a few minutes, please? I mean, I would just like a minute, a tiny oasis of time that is not smothered in attitude. Just a moment of normal conversation. If you don't mind. I would like to

talk.

GEORGIE: We talked at dinner.

EDWARD: No, we chatted at dinner. We had three hours of chat, and I'm feeling a little disoriented, and I would like to talk.

GEORGIE: Why?

EDWARD: What's the matter, don't you know *how* to talk?

GEORGIE: Of *course* I know how to talk. I talk constantly! I just don't want to talk now! Christ, you're as bad as Andrew!

EDWARD: Oh? How so?

GEORGIE: *(Pause.)* I don't want to talk about Andrew.

EDWARD: Why not?

GEORGIE: Edward –

EDWARD: What?

GEORGIE: You are driving me crazy.

EDWARD: Why are you getting so defensive?

GEORGIE: I'm not – I hate this.

EDWARD: I just asked a simple question –

GEORGIE: You did not, you –

EDWARD: Yes, I did –

GEORGIE: You're right, this talking is really fun. I'm so glad we're *talking*. *(Pause.)* Okay. So fine. So what was the question?

EDWARD: Actually, there was no question. The subject of Andrew came up and you got all tense.

GEORGIE: I did not get tense.

EDWARD: Yes, you're very tense.

GEORGIE: I am not tense.

EDWARD: Yes, you are.

GEORGIE: Why don't you pick a subject. You want to have a discussion here? Then pick a subject and let's get on with it, all right?

EDWARD: All right. *(Pause.)* What do you and Andrew talk about?

GEORGIE: *(Pause.)* We talk about many things. Books and shit. America. You name it, we talk about it. Andrew and I have a very conversational relationship.

EDWARD: Does that bother you?

GEORGIE: *(Pause.)* What is that supposed to mean?

EDWARD: Nothing. He told me you had a crush on him, so I just thought –

GEORGIE: Well, he was wrong.

EDWARD: How did you two meet, anyway?

GEORGIE: Edward, what is it, am I on trial here –

EDWARD: You have something to hide?

GEORGIE: No, I – Fuck. We met on the elevator. We live in the same building, it's not unusual –

EDWARD: What, did he try to pick you up?

GEORGIE: I hardly think so.

EDWARD: You tried to pick him up.

GEORGIE: Is there a point to this? Cause I got to tell you, you're kind of wrecking the mood here; you're like doing a demolition job on my hormones.

EDWARD: I just want to know how you two met! He never told me.
GEORGIE: He gave me a book. We were in the elevator, and he handed me this book and said, here, I think you'll like this.That was it. He gave me this book.
EDWARD: He gave you a book?
GEORGIE: Yes.
EDWARD: You didn't think that was a pickup?
GEORGIE: No, I thought he was a Jehovah's Witness.
EDWARD: What?
GEORGIE: I thought he was a Jehovah's Witness! I have this ongoing relationship with those guys; I'm like, a sucker for the Jehovah's Witnesses. So when this guy on the elevator gave me a book I thought it was gonna be about the end of the world or what God really thinks or something. I mean, I got like the collected edition of those things –
EDWARD: You actually buy those?
GEORGIE: *(A little self-conscious.)* Yeah – well, yeah, I – I got a whole shelf of them, I got like twenty of them – *(She indicates. He goes over to look at her books. He picks one up and pages through it, amazed.)* What? They just get to me, okay? I mean, those fucking moonies, or the dianetics people, you can see it in their eyes, their brains are fried; they'd just as soon kill you as anything. But the Jehovah's Witnesses are always so nerdy I believe them. What? It's not like I go to their meetings or anything. I just talk to them. I like what they say. Resurrection. Life everlasting. It just sounds nice. I mean, I don't believe this shit at all, but I just – I end up listening because it's so – I don't know. They're always so kind. *(Pause.)* You can borrow that if you want. It's okay. You might like it. Some of it's very hopeful. *(He looks at her and smiles.)*
EDWARD: Thank you.
GEORGIE: So that's why I talked to Andrew in the elevator. I thought he was a Jehovah's Witness. *(Pause.)* So. You want to do it or not? *(Edward looks at her, startled and suddenly uncomfortable. The mood is seriously broken.)*
EDWARD: Excuse me?
GEORGIE: Oh, come on, Edward. We both know why you're here.
EDWARD: *(Recovering.)* Yes, we do, I just – I was momentarily stunned by your subtlety. I mean – never mind. Never mind. I think I will have that drink after all. This tea is not actually doing the trick. *(He picks the scotch bottle off the bookshelf, crosses to the kitchen and finds some ice and glasses.)*
GEORGIE: Oh, for God's sake. We're drinking now? Now we're drinking? Why are we drinking?
EDWARD: We're drinking because I want to drink!
GEORGIE: Are we going to have more conversation, too?
EDWARD: We will if I want to!
GEORGIE: Yeah, well, as long as we're taking a poll here, I gotta say, I'm not particularly interested in more conversation, Edward! I mean it. If you think this is going to go on all night or something, maybe you should just leave.
EDWARD: You're not throwing me out. *(He reenters, pours scotch into her glass and hands it to her.)*
GEORGIE: You say one more word, and I am.

EDWARD: No, you're not.
GEORGIE: Yes, I am.
EDWARD: Drink your scotch.
GEORGIE: Fuck you.
EDWARD: Yeah, fuck you too. *(He bumps her glass in a forced toast. They both drink.)*
GEORGIE: Now what? Should we have another? Maybe we should go out to dinner again. No, I know. How about a game of cards?
EDWARD: You know, I have to say, you really – your technique just leaves me breathless. Really.
GEORGIE: I gave you technique all night, Edward, and it didn't get either of us anywhere. But the gig is up. I don't know what's buggin' you but it's time to get over it. You want to do it or not? This is your last shot.
EDWARD: *(Pause.)* My last shot?
GEORGIE: Yeah. This is it. This is the offer. So what's it going to be?
EDWARD: Well. Since you put it that way. *(He sets his drink down and looks at her. He does not move. After a moment, she crosses slowly, eases into him and almost kisses him. He speaks.)*
EDWARD: Thank you very much, but since you put it that way, I'm afraid I'm going to have to decline your generous offer.
GEORGIE: *(Pause.)* Suit yourself. *(She crosses away from him, furious, and picks up her drink.)*
EDWARD: Please don't take this wrong. I just don't like being used.
GEORGIE: Oh, cut me a break. You want it; I'm saying here it is. Who cares about being used at a time like this?
EDWARD: I do.
GEORGIE: Yeah, I guess you can dish it out but you can't take it. Well, fine. That's fine. But trust me on this one: You just passed up the most interesting fuck of your life.
EDWARD: That may be. But it also may be that I prefer sleeping with one person at a time. Maybe I simply want to preserve as one of the ground rules of the increasingly neurotic relationship we seem to have established between us that if I ever do take you to bed, it will be on the condition that Andrew does not come along! *(He puts on his jacket and starts to leave.)*
GEORGIE: Andrew – fuck Andrew, I am tired of talking about Andrew!
EDWARD: What happened, he broke your heart so now you're bitter? You poor thing.
GEORGIE: Oh, shut up –
EDWARD: And now you're going to seduce his best friend to get back at him, is that it? That's the oldest trick in the book!
GEORGIE: Yeah, it's so old you almost fell for it.
EDWARD: What do you think you're doing? You think this is going to prove something? All it proves is what I suspected from the start: You are nothing but bad news.
GEORGIE: Look who's talking.
EDWARD: I am. And I know you. I know exactly who you are.

GEORGIE: You don't know the first thing about me.

EDWARD: I know everything about you. I see you every fucking day down at the courthouse, hanging all over your junkie boyfriend, screaming at your pimp -

GEORGIE: I don't know what you're talking about.

EDWARD: *(Overlap.)* I know where you grew up. I know your family. I know how your mother can't hold down a job –

GEORGIE: This doesn't have anything to do with anything –

EDWARD: I know how she drinks! I know how she leeches money out of you! I know about the arrests –

GEORGIE: STOP IT. *(Pause.)* So what? So you listen in on my phone calls, so what is that supposed to prove?

EDWARD: I don't listen to your phone calls. I don't have to. You're a dime a dozen, Georgie; you are as common as dirt.

GEORGIE: Yeah, I'm so common you've been trying to screw me for four months.

EDWARD: You think that makes you something? That doesn't make you anything. This is all – this is a fucking game to guys like me; you're a piece of furniture, for God's sake! I could go through three of you in a week.

GEORGIE: *(Overlap.)* Shut up. SHUT UP.

EDWARD: Come to think of it, I will take you up on that offer. Why the hell not?

GEORGIE: SHUT UP. You SHUT UP – *(She takes a swing at him. Edward grabs her arms; they struggle for a second.)*

EDWARD: Georgie –

GEORGIE: Oh, shit, I can't see anything. Edward –

EDWARD: What? Here, put your head down – you're okay – *(He sets her on the couch and tries to put her head down.)*

GEORGIE: No, I need air – *(Scared.)* I can't see, Edward –

EDWARD: *(Starting to panic.)* You're okay. You're fine. Just shut your eyes for a second. Take a breath. Georgie?

GEORGIE: I can't see. *(She leans back on the couch. He puts his arm around her.)*

EDWARD: You're okay. You're okay. Are you okay? Come on. Sweetheart. Are you okay? *(She suddenly shoves him away.)*

GEORGIE: Don't you touch me. *(He backs away, startled. Pause.)* Just stay away from me, okay?

EDWARD: Yeah. Yeah. I'm sorry. I'm sorry, okay? I'm sorry. Christ. What am I doing? *(He sits. Pause. She watches him. He finally looks at her.)* Are you okay?

GEORGIE: Yeah.

EDWARD: I'm sorry. I don't know why I did that.

GEORGIE: Me neither.

EDWARD: Can you see me?

GEORGIE: Yeah. I can see you. It just went funny, you know? When you just see stars? It went funny. I couldn't see anything. It scared me.

EDWARD: Me too. *(She sits up. He starts for her, then stops.)* Come on. Just lie there for a second, would you?

Theresa Rebeck 33

GEORGIE: I'm okay.

EDWARD: You're not okay. You're drunk.

GEORGIE: No, I'm not. I didn't drink hardly anything. I just – I got so mad at you. That never happened to me before. I mean, I'm like, mad all the time, but that never happened before.

EDWARD: You just never had me around to provoke you. And that was nothing. Stick with me, baby. I'll *really* piss you off.

GEORGIE: It's not funny.

EDWARD: I know.

GEORGIE: You were being a big jerk.

EDWARD: I know. I'm sorry.

GEORGIE: Why did you do that? *(He starts to cross again, and stops himself uncertainly.)*

EDWARD: Don't think about it for a minute.

GEORGIE: Man. I have to stop getting so mad all the time.

EDWARD: You scared me half to death. Do you want a glass of water?

GEORGIE: What is this thing you have with liquids? Andrew's the same way; something goes wrong and he just dives for the liquids. I don't know, they teach you this in college? Is this a class thing?

EDWARD: I'll get you a glass of water. *(He goes into the kitchen. Georgie curls up on the couch. He returns a moment later with a glass of water and a washcloth. He approaches her carefully, then feeds her the water as if she were a child. She resists for a moment.)* Come on, sweetheart. Just drink it. It's good for you.

GEORGIE: It's just water, Edward.

EDWARD: Water is very good for you – there you go. Here. Come on. *(She drinks. He takes the cloth and wipes her face.)* Is that better?

GEORGIE: Yeah.

EDWARD: Good.

GEORGIE: Why are you being so nice all of a sudden?

EDWARD: Look, I am a nice person. *(She laughs.)* I am! 10 percent of the time, I am a very nice person. *(He pats her face with the cloth again, then folds it neatly.)* You okay now?

GEORGIE: Yeah. Hey, Edward.

EDWARD: Yeah.

GEORGIE: What's she like? Lydia, I mean.

EDWARD: I'm not the person to ask. I don't like her.

GEORGIE: What, are you kidding? That makes you exactly the person to ask.

EDWARD: Lots of money, ancestors on the Mayflower, parents on Beacon Hill. That sort of thing.

GEORGIE: Yeah, yeah, yeah. Cut to the chase. What does she look like?

EDWARD: She's very pale. She's pretty, but pale and orderly. Quiet. I find her kind of sinister, to tell you the truth.

GEORGIE: You make her sound like Dracula.

EDWARD: Yes, she's very much like Dracula. Always meticulously dressed. You know, neat little dresses. Blouses with bows at the collar. Protruding

bicuspids. *(He bares his teeth. She starts to cry.)* Hey, hey, hey.
GEORGIE: Oh, perfect. He's gonna marry Dracula; that's just perfect. I'm sorry, I'm just –
EDWARD: Hey. It's okay.
GEORGIE: It's not okay. How can he do it?
EDWARD: It's what he thinks he wants.
GEORGIE: Well, why isn't it me?
EDWARD: I don't know. He's stupid.
GEORGIE: Don't talk down to me, Edward; I don't need you to act like I'm some sort of big baby here –
EDWARD: I'm not! I mean it. He's being really stupid.
GEORGIE: Yeah, right. *(Pause. She dries her eyes.)*
EDWARD: Look. I'm sorry I said those things, okay? I mean, those things I said before.
GEORGIE: No, it's okay. Some of it was true.
EDWARD: Still.
GEORGIE: Yeah. Hey, Edward.
EDWARD: Yeah?
GEORGIE: Can you put your arm around me for a second?
EDWARD: Georgie –
GEORGIE: Come on. I wouldn't ask except you've been nice for about two minutes or something and I'm afraid if I wait any longer, you'll, like, turn into yourself again.
EDWARD: You're not still doing this to get back at him?
GEORGIE: For heaven's sake. It's just a hug. *(He brushes her hair back from her face, and puts his arm around her. She hangs onto him for a moment, then pulls away a little. They sit, for a moment, with their arms around each other. She puts her head on his shoulder.)*
GEORGIE: This is nice. *(Pounding on the door. Georgie jumps then clings to Edward for a second.)*
EDWARD: Well. I wonder who that is.
GEORGIE: Oh, God. I can't handle this anymore.
EDWARD: Chin up. You can't give up now, sweetheart. *(The knocking becomes violent.)*
GEORGIE: Edward –
EDWARD: You're fine. If he gets out of line, just throw a pencil at him. *(He opens the door. Lydia is there.)* Oh, no.
LYDIA: *(Biting.)* Hello, Edward. How lovely to see you again. *(She crosses into the apartment and glares at Georgie.)*
EDWARD: Lydia. What a charming coincidence. We were just talking about you.
LYDIA: That is charming.
EDWARD: Where's Andrew?
LYDIA: Who cares?
EDWARD: Oh, I think several of us, at least... *(He looks out in the hallway but Andrew is nowhere in sight.)*

LYDIA: How about you? Do you care?
GEORGIE: Well, I don't –
LYDIA: Oh, please. I have a little trouble believing that!
GEORGIE: Wait a minute. I don't know who you are or what you think you're doing here, but –
LYDIA: Oh, I think you know who I am.
GEORGIE: Well, of course I know who you are! What are you doing here?
LYDIA: No. What are you doing here?
GEORGIE: I live here!
LYDIA: You know what I mean!
EDWARD: Excuse me, but where's Andrew?
LYDIA: Oh, where do you think he is? He's downstairs, shrouded in the shattered wreckage of his book, our marriage and my life.
EDWARD: Oh, Christ. *(He exits.)*
GEORGIE: Edward, hey! Hey, where are you going? Don't leave me here with her! Edward! *(But he is gone. Georgie turns and looks at Lydia, who is very steely indeed.)* Look. It's been great meeting you, but you know, I am having one ripper of a day, you know, so –
LYDIA: *Don't talk to me about bad days.*
GEORGIE: Listen –
LYDIA: No. No. You listen. *(She puts down her purse decisively, crosses to the door and shuts it.)*
GEORGIE: HEY –
LYDIA: I don't know you. You and I have never met. And you are wreaking havoc on my life. *(Lydia crosses back to her purse, reaches in and pulls out Georgie's jacket, blouse, slip, skirt, panty hose and shoes from the previous days. She folds these items and stacks them neatly as she speaks. Georgie watches, amazed.)* At first, I admired Andrew' interest in your welfare. He cares about people; he truly cares and I think that's wonderful. But these past few months, I must admit, I have become less interested in his interest. Not only do I listen to him talk about you incessantly, any time I come over to have dinner or spend the night here, I am bombarded by you. When you come home at night, we hear your little heels clicking on the ceiling. When you leave in the morning, we hear your little heels. When you go to bed we hear you brush your teeth, and talk on the phone, and listen to the radio and on certain evenings I could swear that we can even hear you undress. I am not enjoying this. For the past two months, I have been under the distinct impression that any time I spend the night here, I am actually sleeping with two people – Andrew and yourself. In fact, when you came home with Edward tonight, my first thought was, my God, the bed is already crowded enough; now we have to fit Edward in too? Now. I don't know what went on between you and Andrew.
GEORGIE: Nothing. Nothing at all.
LYDIA: Excuse me, but that clearly is not the case. And I want you out of my life! Is that understood?
GEORGIE: Where am I supposed to go?
LYDIA: I don't care! I'll find you a better apartment! *(She slams Georgie's shoe*

down on a bug.) It won't be difficult. *(They glare at each other for a moment.)*
GEORGIE: Well, that's true. Listen, I am really sorry but I am just not up to this right now, okay? I mean, if I get mad one more time tonight I might just die from it. So, can we chill out for a minute? You want a cup of tea or something?
LYDIA: Do you have anything stronger. Scotch? Is that scotch?
GEORGIE: Yes. It is.
LYDIA: I'll have scotch.
GEORGIE: Fine. *(She exits to the kitchen and reenters a second later with a glass. She pours Lydia a shot of scotch.)* Here. You knock that back, you'll feel much better.
LYDIA: Thank you. *(She drinks and looks around the apartment.)* That's an interesting outfit you have on.
GEORGIE: Excuse me?
LYDIA: I guess men really do like that sort of thing, don't they? You'd like to think some of them, at least one, or two, are above it, but that just doesn't seem to be the case. All of them, they're like Pavlov's dogs; you provide the right stimulus and the next thing you know, they're salivating all over you. Don't those shoes hurt?
GEORGIE: Yeah, as a matter of fact, they kind of do.
LYDIA: But I guess you don't wear them for comfort, do you? You wear them for other reasons. You wear them because they make your legs look amazing. *(She puts the second pair of shoes on and walks around the room for a moment and picks up a large book under the table.)* And I see you're also studying law. *(Georgie crosses and takes the book from her.)*
GEORGIE: No, I am not "studying law." I stole that from the library at work so I could figure out what the fuck was going on down there.
LYDIA: Really. How remarkable.
GEORGIE: Look –
LYDIA: Could I have another?
GEORGIE: Another?
LYDIA: Please. *(Georgie takes Lydia's glass from her and pours scotch into it, looks at her, and then continues to pour an enormous amount of scotch into the glass. She gives it back to her. Lydia looks at it, and knocks back a solid drink. Georgie stares.)*
LYDIA: God, I wish I still smoked.
GEORGIE: You used to smoke?
LYDIA: Two packs a day. It was disgusting.
GEORGIE: You know – you're very different from what I thought. It's weird, meeting you. It's just – weird.
LYDIA: Oh, really? Well, what did you think I'd be like?
GEORGIE: I don't know. I mean, you're very – forceful. I guess I thought you would be kind of formal and polite. Maybe like Dracula, or something.
LYDIA: Oh. Edward told you that; that's where you got that. He is so awful. Ever since I dumped him he's been telling everybody I'm some kind of vampire. He thinks it's witty.
GEORGIE: Wait a minute. You went out with him, too?

LYDIA: Didn't you know that?

GEORGIE: Man, what do those two do, trade off girlfriends once a year or something?

LYDIA: It's certainly starting to look that way.

GEORGIE: Wait a minute, that's not what I –

LYDIA: *(Overlap.)* Really, there's no need to explain. In fact, I would prefer not to know the details.

GEORGIE: I'm just trying to tell you –

LYDIA: And I'm trying to tell you: What I've had with both of them is substantially more real than whatever this is, and I don't want to know about it. All right? I just want it to stop. All right?

GEORGIE: Right.

LYDIA: As long as we understand each other.

GEORGIE: Oh, I understand you all right. This part, I think I got down solid.

LYDIA: Good.

GEORGIE: *(Finally angry.)* But what I don't have, you know – what I want to know is – if you're so fucking real, Lydia, then what the hell are you doing here? I mean, if you're so much better than me, then why even bother? You could just wait it out and I'll drift away like a piece of paper, like nothing, right? 'Cause that's what I am. Nothing. Right? So why the fuck are you up here, taking me apart?

LYDIA: I don't think I have to justify myself to you.

GEORGIE: Oh, yeah? Well, I think you do. All of you. You people. What an amazing fucking snow job you all are doing on the world. And I bought it! We all buy it. My family – they're like, all of a sudden I'm Mary Tyler Moore or something. I mean, they live in hell, right, and they spend their whole lives just wishing they were somewhere else, wishing they were rich, or sober, or clean; living on a street with trees, being on some fucking TV show. And I did it. I'm not myself anymore! I moved to Boston, I work in a law office, I'm the big success story. And they have no idea what that means. It means I get to hang out with a bunch of lunatics. It means I get to read books that make no sense. *(She pushes the law book off the table.)* It means that instead of getting harassed by jerks at the local bar, now I get harassed by guys in suits. Guys with glasses. Guys who talk nice. Guys in suits. Well, you know what I have to say to all of you? Shame on you. Shame on you for thinking you're better than the rest of us. And shame on you for being mean to me. Shame on you, Lydia.

LYDIA: *(Pause.)* I'm sorry.

GEORGIE: I think you'd better go.

LYDIA: Yes. Of course. *(Pause.)* I am sorry. I just – Andrew postponed our wedding tonight, and I'm a little – my life is in a bit of a shambles, tonight, and I know that's no excuse, but I'm just not myself. Please. Forgive me. *(She goes to the door.)*

GEORGIE: Oh, God. Wait a minute.

LYDIA: No. You're right. I've been behaving very badly. You're right. I'm sorry. *(She turns and opens the door.)*

GEORGIE: No, I'm the one. Come on, I'm being a jerk. He postponed the

wedding? Fuck me. I'm sorry, you said that before and it went right by me. I'm sorry. I got a bad temper, and – whatever. Just sit down, okay? *(Georgie brings her back into the room. Lydia pulls away.)*
LYDIA: Really, I think I'd best go. Please. Please don't be nice to me. I don't want to be friends with you.
GEORGIE: Yeah, I don't want to be friends with you either. I'm just saying, I didn't mean to, like, yell at you. I think you better finish your drink. *(She hands her scotch to her. Lydia looks at it for a moment.)* He's probably just nervous. Weddings make boys nervous.
LYDIA: I think it's worse than that. He – we haven't had sex in quite a while.
GEORGIE: You mean *none* of us are getting laid? No wonder we're all so uptight.
LYDIA: You mean you and Edward didn't –
GEORGIE: No.
LYDIA: No?
GEORGIE: No. I swear to God, I worked on him for four hours and I couldn't get him *near* the bedroom.
LYDIA: Edward? You couldn't – Edward?
GEORGIE: You didn't have that problem, huh?
LYDIA: As a matter of fact – never mind.
GEORGIE: He wanted it, too.
LYDIA: He always wants it. Well. If he wouldn't sleep with you, I think you must've really made an impression on him. *(They laugh a little.)* And I know you've made an impression on Andrew.
GEORGIE: *(Awkward.)* Oh. I don't know.
LYDIA: Please. Could we not? – *(Pause.)* I'd prefer not to pretend. I'd also prefer not to talk to you about it, but I just don't know who else to talk to.
GEORGIE: Hey –
LYDIA: I'm not crying! It's just, I can't talk to my family about this; they'll simply gloat. They never liked Andrew. He wasn't "good" enough. Is that unbelievable? He's the best man I've ever met, and he's not *good* enough for them. He doesn't make enough money. And they certainly don't like his politics. Edward was the one they liked. Well. You can imagine. You know what my father told me, when Andrew and I decided to get married: Never trust a man who thinks he can change the world. That's what he said! Can you imagine? I don't care. I mean, he voted for Reagan; I'm still mad at him about that, but – how can I tell them this? I always told them, they didn't understand, they just didn't understand. Andrew saved me. He is my best self; he makes me my best self. How can I tell them they were right?
GEORGIE: They're not.
LYDIA: No, I know. They're not. I know. It's just – I'm confused.
GEORGIE: Yeah. Me too. *(Pause.)* You want to dance? *(She crosses to the boombox and puts in a tape. Romantic music comes up, Frank Sinatra, "Strangers in the Night," or something like.)*
LYDIA: Excuse me?
GEORGIE: Come on. Dance with me.

LYDIA: What?

GEORGIE: It'll make you feel better. I'll lead and you can just dance –

LYDIA: Oh, no –

GEORGIE: Come on. Let me do this – *(She unties Lydia's bow and takes her in her arms.)*

LYDIA: I don't – aw, no – I don't dance –

GEORGIE: No, it's not silly. It's just nice. Haven't you ever danced with a girl before? It's nice. Come on. *(Georgie takes her by the arms and they begin to slow dance.)* I love to dance. It's so fucking romantic. You know? It always makes me want to have sex. Men are so dumb, they're so busy trying to get you in bed they can't even figure that out. I mean – I'm not making a pass at you.

LYDIA: I understand. *(Georgie nods, and they begin to dance more freely, Georgie leading and coaxing Lydia into the moves. As they turn through the room their movements become looser, more hilariously erotic. They laugh for a moment, and end up slow dancing. Suddenly, there are sounds of a loud struggle and pounding on the door.)*

EDWARD: *(Off.)* Georgie! Open the door! Georgie!

GEORGIE: Oh, what now?

ANDREW: *(Off.)* LET GO OF ME!

LYDIA: Oh, no – *(Both women start for the door, then stop and stare at each other.)*

GEORGIE: You know, we probably – probably we should just leave them out there. *(The struggle at the door sounds even more violent.)*

EDWARD: *(Off.)* GEORGIE OPEN THE GODDAMN DOOR! *(She goes to the door. Lydia turns off the music. Edward bursts in, dragging Andrew by the collar and sleeve. He throws him into the room.)*

EDWARD: Hi, girls. How's it going?

GEORGIE: Edward, what are you doing?

EDWARD: I'm trying to keep us all out of court. Now, I think it's about time we talked this out. Andrew?

ANDREW: What?

EDWARD: Start talking.

GEORGIE: Actually, I think that now is not a good time, Edward.

EDWARD: Georgie, I am not going to let him do this to you anymore.

ANDREW: Let me, excuse me, let me? Who put you in charge here?

EDWARD: Just talk to her, Andrew.

GEORGIE: I mean it, you guys. Lydia and I were doing just fine.

LYDIA: It's all right, Georgie –

ANDREW: No, it's not all right! I resent this! Who does he think he is, shoving everybody around?

EDWARD: I'm trying to help!

ANDREW: Help? You threatened to rape her, and now you think you can –

EDWARD: Wait a minute –

LYDIA: He what?

ANDREW: He threatened to rape her –

GEORGIE: You guys.

EDWARD: That is not exactly what –

LYDIA: Edward, for God's sake –

EDWARD: We were having a fight!

LYDIA: Oh, but really –

EDWARD: COULD WE NOT GO BACK TO THIS? I'M ALREADY PAST THIS POINT. *(Pause.)* Come on, Andrew. Deal with this woman.

ANDREW: Excuse me, but I don't need you to tell me what I have to do here –

EDWARD: Look, I'm on your side –

ANDREW: You are not on my –

EDWARD: Don't fight me, Andrew –

ANDREW: I will fight you if I want! *(He shoves him. Pause.)*

EDWARD: Don't you fucking shove me – *(He shoves him back. Georgie immediately leaps in between them.)*

LYDIA: ANDREW.

GEORGIE: EDWARD. *(She stands in between them for a moment as they glare at each other.)* I will not have this! *(She shoves them both away from each other.)* You are both driving me crazy. *(She storms into the kitchen. The other three stare at each other. Georgie reenters a moment later with a six pack of Diet Pepsi which she passes around silently.)*

EDWARD: What am I supposed to do with this?

GEORGIE: You're supposed to drink it, Edward. We are all going to just have a drink and calm down for a minute, okay? Drink it! *(Everyone pops their soda and drinks. Pause.)* Okay. So – could we not fight anymore? I mean, could we just like, finish our sodas and go to bed now?

EDWARD: Unfortunately, going to bed may just be the most complicated action we could contemplate at this moment in time.

ANDREW: Georgie, can I talk to you alone? Would the two of you mind if I talked to her alone for a second?

LYDIA: I'd mind.

EDWARD: Yes, I think I'd mind too.

ANDREW: Oh, come on –

GEORGIE: Edward, I thought you wanted to help.

EDWARD: I do want to help, but I'm also a little mad now, and besides which we all know what he's going to say anyway. Don't we?

LYDIA: I think we do.

EDWARD: So I think he should just say it. This involves all of us. So – just say it, Andrew.

ANDREW: Forget it.

EDWARD: No, come on. Say it.

GEORGIE: You guys –

EDWARD: You want to say it. Say it!

ANDREW: I don't want to say it.

EDWARD: Say it!

GEORGIE: Edward!

LYDIA: Please, Andrew. Just say it. *(Pause. Andrew looks at her.)* Please. It's not like I don't already know.

ANDREW: Fine. Fine. *(To Georgie.)* I love you. All right?

GEORGIE: All right. *(Pause.)*

LYDIA: Well, that is just *great*. *(She throws her drink at him.)*

ANDREW: Lydia –

LYDIA: I can't believe you said that! In front of me!

ANDREW: You told me to!

LYDIA: You're in love with her?

ANDREW: You said you knew!

LYDIA: You mean it, don't you? You're in love with her!

ANDREW: Well, of course I mean it. What else would I mean?

LYDIA: You could mean anything! I thought you meant that you thought you were in love with her! You jerk! You're in love with her! I mean, I can see sleeping with her, but falling in love with her?

GEORGIE: Watch it, Lydia.

LYDIA: I'm sorry –

ANDREW: I never slept with her –

LYDIA: Oh, please –

EDWARD: He didn't!

LYDIA: Well, you should've; it might've – you're in love with her?

ANDREW: Yes. *(Pause.)* I think we'd better call the wedding off altogether.

LYDIA: Yes, that would seem to be the next step, wouldn't it? You're in love with another woman; that could potentially interfere with our wedding plans.

ANDREW: Lydia, it's not you.

LYDIA: That much is clear, Andrew; I think I'm pretty straight on that point.

ANDREW: That's not what I – it's just me, okay? Things have not been great with us for a long time, and I'm just saying, it's not enough, you're not – *(He stops himself.)*

LYDIA: Go on. I'm not enough what? I'm not wild enough? I'm not sexy enough? I'm not passionate, I'm not needy, I'm not – I am just what I've always been, Andrew. What is suddenly not enough?

ANDREW: This is not the time or the place –

LYDIA: What kind of a life do you think you can have with her? We have a life together, we have – Georgie, I'm sorry, I don't mean this to be as insulting as it sounds, but honestly. Do you think this is going to work out? Andrew. Do you honestly think that?

ANDREW: I don't think anything. I'm just not going to lie about it anymore. *(Pause.)* I'm sorry.

LYDIA: It doesn't matter. I can learn not to love you. You learned not to love me, I can – could you take your glasses off, please? Just take them off. *(He takes them off and looks at her.)* There. You see? When you take them off, you look like a stranger, you look – I always think that when I see you in the morning. You look like a stranger without your glasses. Except you don't, really, I don't –

ANDREW: Lydia –

LYDIA: Could you please be quiet, please? *(Pause.)* It isn't working. Put your glasses on. *(He puts his glasses on. Pause. Lydia turns to Georgie.)* Well, Georgie, he's all yours. If you want him, you can have him.
GEORGIE: Thanks. Yeah, thanks a lot, Lydia. And Edward, thank you. Thank you for helping us clear all this up. We all feel much better now. *(She picks up her purse.)* And, Andrew, thank you for picking me up out of the gutter and teaching me how to talk and how to behave and how to read. I'm so glad to be a part of your world. I'm really just – this is working out just great. *(She walks out the door, slamming it behind them. They all stare at the closed door.)*
LYDIA: She's right. *(She goes to the door, opens it, leaves and slams it behind her. The men stare at the closed door.)*
EDWARD: Oh, great. They're teaming up. Now we're really in for it. *(He looks at Andrew. Blackout.)*

Scene 2

> *The next morning. The lights come up on Georgie's apartment, in much the same condition as the night before, except Edward is sprawled on the couch, sleeping, and Andrew is sprawled on the floor, tangled in blankets and a pillow. He turns and gets himself even more tangled up. He has not had an easy night. He sits up, frustrated, untangles himself from the blankets, and looks at Edward, who is sleeping soundly. Andrew looks at his watch, looks at Edward, picks up his pillow, crosses to Edward, and hits him with it. Edward jolts awake.*

EDWARD: What? What?
ANDREW: Get up.
EDWARD: Why? What time is it?
ANDREW: It's after ten.
EDWARD: Did Georgie come back?
ANDREW: No.
EDWARD: Man. This couch is really comfortable.
ANDREW: Oh, shut up.
EDWARD: Hey, I didn't tell you to sleep on the floor. You could have gone downstairs and slept in your own bed.
ANDREW: Excuse me, but since you wouldn't leave –
EDWARD: You could've slept in her bed.
ANDREW: I didn't want to sleep in her bed. It would have been...
EDWARD: Disappointing, under the circumstances?
ANDREW: Shut up.
EDWARD: You think she's got anything to eat around here? *(He stands and crosses to the kitchen. Andrew watches him, somewhat amazed.)*
ANDREW: How can you think about food at a time like this?
EDWARD: *(Off.)* It's ten o'clock in the morning. It's a great time to think about food.
ANDREW: Don't you have someplace to go? Something to do? A judge to

bribe? Some drug kingpin to get off on a technicality?

EDWARD: *(Reentering.)* Hey. Could you let me eat something before we go into this? Besides, it's Saturday. Courts are closed. *(He carries with him a box of cereal, which he pours into a bowl and starts to eat without milk.)*

ANDREW: That is just – what – how can you eat that without milk?

EDWARD: She doesn't have any milk. I mean, she has some, but it's alive. You don't want to pour it over your cereal. *(He hands Andrew a bowl and a spoon. Andrew watches Edward eat.)*

ANDREW: Why are you still here?

EDWARD: I don't know. Why are you still here?

ANDREW: I'm still here because you wouldn't leave.

EDWARD: Well, I'm still here because you wouldn't leave.

ANDREW: That makes no sense.

EDWARD: You seemed to think it made sense when you said it.

ANDREW: Edward –

EDWARD: What?

ANDREW: Leave. Just leave. This has nothing to do with you anymore. You've done enough damage. Leave.

EDWARD: *I've* done enough damage?

ANDREW: LEAVE! WOULD YOU JUST GET OUT OF HERE?

EDWARD: I'm not even going to respond to that. You know why? Because I'm getting a little tired of verbally beating the living daylights out of you.

ANDREW: Oh, is that what you've been doing?

EDWARD: As a matter of fact, it is. You and I fight, Andrew. This is the basis of our friendship. We fight, I win, and you lose. And it's getting old.

ANDREW: I lose?

EDWARD: You lose.

ANDREW: I lose.

EDWARD: That's right, buddy. So just eat your cereal and keep your mouth shut, because -

ANDREW: Lydia.

EDWARD: Excuse me?

ANDREW: I didn't lose then.

EDWARD: That had nothing to do with you. I mean, I admit that Lydia dumped me, but by then we were both sick of each other. That wasn't...

ANDREW: Wasn't it?

EDWARD: You didn't start seeing her until months after she and I... *(He stops himself. Looks at Andrew who looks back, deliberate. Pause.)*

Andrew: Lydia didn't want to hurt your feelings.

EDWARD: At the time, Lydia delighted in hurting my feelings. I don't believe you. If you were sleeping with Lydia while she and I were still together, I would have known.

ANDREW: Are you sure about that?

EDWARD: You were sleeping with her?

ANDREW: Yes.

EDWARD: You fucking creep. Don't you have any principles at all?

ANDREW: Did you actually say that? Mr. I Could Rape You If I Wanted -
EDWARD: Don't change the subject! You were sleeping with my girlfriend!
Christ, you're no better than I am!
ANDREW: It was your own fault!
EDWARD: You were sleeping with my girlfriend at the time she dumped me! I
think most people would agree I was the one getting screwed!
ANDREW: Don't play the victim. No one is going to believe you.
EDWARD: Yeah, well, don't you play the good guy. That's getting a little hard
to swallow, too.
ANDREW: You didn't want her anyway!
EDWARD: That's not the point! You were supposed to be my friend! Well,
fuck you. Just fuck you. I don't owe you shit. I'm getting out of here.
ANDREW: Thank God! (*Edward looks for his jacket, starts to put it on.*)
EDWARD: You know, just for the record, I did all of this for you.
ANDREW: What?
EDWARD: Yeah, that's right. As you'll recall, when you asked me to give
Georgie a job, all I knew was she was some wild thing with no experience at all.
Didn't even know how to *type*. But I gave her a job because you asked me to. And
then, okay, after that, I wasn't exactly great for a while, but –
ANDREW: Wasn't exactly great. Excuse me, wasn't –
EDWARD: But at least last night I figured out what was going on and tried to
stop it! I mean, I realized what an asshole I was being and I, I, I decided to
change and try to make up for everything. So –
ANDREW: Oh, please!
EDWARD: What? I did! I got you up here! I got you to admit how you felt about
her! I mean, at least I got you to stop lying to everybody. And maybe it didn't feel
so great, but at least now you have a chance at a real life instead of some –
whatever – with Lydia. So don't go whining to me about what a mess I made of
everything. If it wasn't for me you wouldn't have anything right now.
ANDREW: I don't have anything right now!
EDWARD: Oh, that is complete horseshit. I mean, get a fucking grip, would you?
Georgie adores you. You adore her. And all you can do is moan and gnash your
teeth! I mean, I realize that relations between the sexes are confused nowadays,
but they're not *that* confused. When she gets back here, you should just take her in
your arms and take her to bed.
ANDREW: Well, thank you for your advice, Mr. Sensitivity. Take her in your
arms and take her to bed. That's very delicate and perceptive of you.
EDWARD: Oh, for – Do you want her or not, Andrew? Because if you don't, I'll
take her, and this time, you won't get a second chance!
ANDREW: Forget it! I'm not giving her to you again! (*They stare at each other.*)
EDWARD: I can't believe you said that.
ANDREW: You said it, too.
EDWARD: Jesus. We really are a couple of assholes.
(*They sit for a moment, thinking about what assholes they have been.*)

ANDREW: I don't know what's the matter with me. I don't know who I am anymore.

EDWARD: (*Pause.*) You were sleeping with Lydia?

ANDREW: Just once. We both felt so guilty about it she had to break up with you before we could do it again. She was going to end it anyway.

EDWARD: I know. That was my fault. I completely fucked up everything with her. (*Pause.*) Don't tell her I said that.

ANDREW: Edward, she's probably never going to speak to me again.

EDWARD: Oh, right.

ANDREW: What are we going to do?

EDWARD: I don't know. But I have this terrible feeling that we're not entirely in control of this situation.

ANDREW: We never were.

EDWARD: Oh, sure we were. I mean, remember when we could just blame everything on women? Not a specific woman. Just, women in general. The whole idea of women.

ANDREW: Women.

EDWARD: It was so nice. Just blaming everything on them. We didn't have to think about anything. We didn't have to fight amongst ourselves, unless we wanted to. Because it wasn't our fault. It was women. Fuck 'em.

ANDREW AND EDWARD: Fuck Women!!

GEORGIE: (*At door*) Well, that *is* lovely. (*The men stand quickly. Georgie enters, carrying clothes, a bag of groceries and a book. She wears blue jeans, a sweater and her heals.*)

ANDREW: Georgie.

EDWARD: Georgie!

GEORGIE: Oh, man. I can't believe it. Are you guys going to torture me for the rest of my life?

ANDREW: We were just –

GEORGIE: I mean, what the fuck are you doing here? What the fuck is this? Well, fine. That's just fine. You think my whole life is your fucking property anyway. I guess it's no surprise to find you taking over my apartment. (*She crosses toward the kitchen, angry.*)

ANDREW: That's not what we were trying to do.

EDWARD: We were worried about you.

GEORGIE: Right. You guys probably spent the whole night deciding which one of you gets me.

ANDREW AND EDWARD: No! No, no, no, come on …

GEORGIE: You are both hopeless. (*She dumps things on the table and crosses to the kitchen with the groceries.*)

EDWARD: Where have you been?

GEORGIE: I was at Lydia's. (*She kicks her shoes off and starts to clean up, but not very well.*)

EDWARD: I was afraid of that.

GEORGIE: Yeah, we had a great time. We listened to records. Smoked cigarettes. Had conversation. You know, she talked, I listened. I talked, she listened. Very different from what the three of us have been doing, I gotta say.

EDWARD: Aw, come on, Georgie, We're trying to be sensitive, we really are, and you're just –

GEORGIE: Oh, now you're sensitive and I'm the pain in the ass. I love that -

ANDREW: All Right! Could we just not - do that, right away? I mean, could we just try to be civilized for - I don't know. Five minutes, maybe?

GEORGIE: Fine. The clock is ticking. Here, have a muffin. I'm going to make some tea. (*She hands a packet of muffins to Edward and goes to the kitchen. Edward concentrates on opening them. Andrew whacks him.*)

EDWARD: What?

ANDREW: Go.

EDWARD: Now? I want to find out what happens! (*Andrew stares at him.*)

EDWARD: Okay! I'll be in the bathroom. (*And he goes, taking the muffins. Georgie reenters and looks around.*)

GEORGIE: Where's Edward?

ANDREW: He had to go to the, uh, the bathroom.

GEORGIE: Sly, Andrew. Very sly. (*She takes more groceries out of the bag. Andrew picks a book off the table. As he speaks to her, she continues to move around the apartment, unpacking groceries, going to the kitchen, cleaning.*)

ANDREW: What's this?

GEORGIE: *Pride and Prejudice.* Lydia lent it to me. She says it's about a bunch of girls and their boyfriends. I thought it sounded good.

ANDREW: So. You and Lydia got along.

GEORGIE: You always told me I'd like her. I mean, I doubt we're going to be best friends or anything, but you know. The three of us, we should all have dinner sometime.

ANDREW: I don't think that's going to be possible.

GEORGIE: Well, it's up to you.

ANDREW: That's not - Georgie, could you stop - could you stand still, for a minute? Please. (*He takes her by the arm and holds onto her for a moment. They look at each other. She looks away. Carefully, he leans in to kiss her. She pulls away.*)

GEORGIE: I don't think you should do that.

ANDREW: I'm sorry. Yesterday, you seemed to want me to do that.

GEORGIE: Yeah, well, things were different yesterday. I was kind of fucked up. I mean, yesterday, I was actually going to screw someone I didn't much like just to prove some sort of stupid point that I can't even remember what it was. It's just lucky Edward isn't quite as bad as I thought he was. Neither is Lydia. She's a very forgiving person. You should call her, right now. I bet she'd be really glad to talk to you.

ANDREW: What are you doing?

GEORGIE: I'm telling you. I think you better call Lydia. (*Andrew and Georgie stare at each other.*)

ANDREW: You're changing your mind? (*Pause.*) You're going to do the decent thing and send me back to Lydia, the wronged woman whom you've come to respect, even care for -

GEORGIE: I'm not doing this for anybody but myself. I just can't take it anymore, Andrew. Between you and Edward, it's like, you both want - it's always about what you guys want. And I'm just like some thing just spinning in the middle of it all. I can't even think, you know?
ANDREW: If you're saying you're confused, that's fine. I'm confused, too. We'll work it out.
GEORGIE: I don't want to work it out. I mean, I'm confused, but I do know I don't want to be this person you keep trying to make me. I mean, all these things about me that really bug you, they aren't going anywhere. Let's just walk away from it, huh?
ANDREW: I finally decided to confront it! I can't walk away now!
GEORGIE: Look, I'm never going to be good enough for you.
ANDREW: You are good enough!
GEORGIE: There's always going to be something you're trying to fix -
ANDREW: I wasn't trying to fix you! All I ever wanted was to help you see what is here! What your life can be. You needed to change; you said so yourself! And you did change. Because of me. What did I do that was so terrible?
GEORGIE: Well, you did a lot of things that were terrible. And a lot of things that weren't. And I did, too; I'm not saying I'm perfect. A lot of the time, I'm just a fucking mess around you. I mean, when I'm with you, I'm always thinking about how to please you. How to make you happy. And then I hate myself when I don't. I need my life back.
ANDREW: I love you.
GEORGIE: (Pause.) You really should call Lydia. (Pause.)
ANDREW: Can I say one more thing?
GEORGIE: What.
ANDREW: I like your shoes.
GEORGIE: What?
ANDREW: I like your shoes. Actually, I always kind of liked them. You have nice legs.
GEORGIE: Look. I'm sorry, okay?
ANDREW: Me too.
GEORGIE: You did help me.
ANDREW: I know. (He exits.)
GEORGIE: Oh, fuck. (She sits down. Holds her head in her hands. Pause.)
EDWARD: (Off.) Can I come out now?
GEORGIE: (Pause.) Yeah. (Edward appears, his mouth full of foam, toothbrush in hand.)
EDWARD: (Tentative.) How are you?
GEORGIE: Not so great. (Pause.) Is that my toothbrush?
EDWARD: (Looking at it.) Is yours the red one?
GEORGIE: Mine's the only one, Edward. This is my apartment, remember? (She takes it from him and goes to the bathroom with it. Edward goes into the kitchen and gets a glass of water. He drinks, Georgie reenters trying not to cry. She starts to put groceries away. Edward stands in the door of the kitchen and watches her.)
EDWARD: Here, let me help you. (He starts to take them from her. She does not

let him..)
GEORGIE: I'm fine. I'm fine! (*Pause.*) I'm not fine.
EDWARD: It's okay, honey. Come on. I'll make you some tea. (*She lets him take the groceries.*)
GEORGIE: Look, you probably should go check on Andrew, I think he's -
EDWARD: I'll get around to him. I'm more concerned about you right now. (*He takes the rest of the groceries into the kitchen.*)
GEORGIE: I hope he goes back to Lydia.
EDWARD: I'd say it's anybody's guess what he'll do.
GEORGIE: I really like her.
EDWARD: She's all right.
GEORGIE: No, she's kind of great and you have to stop running around telling everybody she's a vampire. It's not funny and you're a jerk, okay?
EDWARD: Okay.
GEORGIE: Okay.
EDWARD: (*Pause.*) That's a nice sweater.
GEORGIE: It's Lydia's.
EDWARD: I know. I gave it to her. (*She stares at him.*) Oh, come on. I'm just trying to lighten the mood here. It's funny in a way, isn't it? Well, okay, it isn't but sort of it is. Never mind.
GEORGIE: No, you're right. It is kind of funny. You know, they were sleeping together before she dumped you.
EDWARD: Yes, I heard. Apparently, the whole world has heard. I don't know what the big deal is. It was only once.
GEORGIE: That's not what Lydia says.
EDWARD: What?
GEORGIE: Did he tell you that? It was only once?
EDWARD: How many times was it? Never mind. Don't tell me. I don't want to know. (*Cleaning, he picks up her shoes.*) These shoes really are beautiful.
GEORGIE: I'm throwing them out.
EDWARD: Oh, don't do that.
GEORGIE: They hurt my feet.
EDWARD: They're very beautiful.
GEORGIE: Look Edward –
EDWARD: Sorry. Sorry. Go ahead. Throw them away. Do whatever you want.
GEORGIE: Sorry. I'm sorry.
EDWARD: Hey, I'll make you breakfast. What did I do with those muffins?
GEORGIE: Listen Edward, thanks, but I think I've had about as much sensitivity from you as I can stand. Could you just take off? I mean, I didn't sleep much last night, and I'm beat.
EDWARD: Sure. You're sure you're okay?
GEORGIE: Yeah. I'm fine. I am. I'm fine.
EDWARD: Good. (*He crosses to the door. Turns back and looks at her.*) So what are you going to do now? Move into a convent?
GEORGIE: (*Pause.*) I knew that's what you were after.
EDWARD: I'm just asking.

GEORGIE: I should have known. You got so nice, so nice and helpful and reasonable. That's a sure sign that you want something.
EDWARD: I never made any bones about that.
GEORGIE: This whole concerned mother act –
EDWARD: I am concerned.
GEORGIE: Yeah, I picked that up.
EDWARD: He is all wrong for you.
GEORGIE: Edward –
EDWARD: I just hope you're not having second thoughts.
GEORGIE: I am not getting into this with you, Edward.
EDWARD: We're already in it. Aren't we? *(He smiles at her.)*
GEORGIE: Oh, no. *(She picks up one of her shoes and wields it as a weapon.)*
EDWARD: Come on, Georgie. I'm not the enemy.
GEORGIE: You sure about that?
EDWARD: Ninety percent.
GEORGIE: Edward – we don't have the most romantic relationship here.
EDWARD: Neither of us is exactly indifferent. Come on. I'm not Andrew.
GEORGIE: That much I got.
EDWARD: And I'm not talking about a one-night stand.
GEORGIE: I don't care what you're talking about –
EDWARD: Don't you think people can change?
GEORGIE: *(Pause.)* Yeah. Yeah, as a matter of fact, I do.
EDWARD: Then what are you afraid of?
GEORGIE: *(Pause.)* Nothing. I'm not afraid of anything. *(She throws down the shoe. Pause.)*
EDWARD: Good. *(Pause.)* Okay. You decide. And you let me know. *(He goes to the door.)*
GEORGIE: All right. All right. But if you want to try this, you gotta know, this isn't going to look anything like anything you've ever been in before. One kiss. For now, that's all you're getting.
EDWARD: I accept your terms.
GEORGIE: Fuck you.
EDWARD: Yeah, fuck you, too. *(She crosses and leans in to kiss him. Stops. Looks at him for a moment. Finally, she kisses him. She pushes him away. They look at each other.)*
EDWARD: Now what?
GEORGIE: Now we - negotiate.
EDWARD: All right.
GEORGIE: All right. Make me an offer. *(Both start to smile. Blackout.)*

END OF PLAY

JAR THE FLOOR
by Cheryl L. West

Playwright's Biography

Cheryl West is the author of several plays including *"Puddin n' Pete"*, *"Jar The Floor"*, and *"Before It Hits Home"*, a play that earned Ms. West the 1992 Helen Hayes Charles McArthur award for outstanding new play and the 1990 Susan Smith Blackburn Prize, an international award given to a woman who has written a work of outstanding quality for the English-speaking theater. *"Before It Hits Home"* had its premiere at the Arena Stage in Washington D.C. and its New York premiere at Second Stage in association with the New York Shakespeare Festival.

"Jar The Floor" had its West Coast premiere at Seattle's Empty Space Theatre and its East Coast premiere at the Arena Stage in Washington D.C., where it did record business and received four Helen Hayes nominations.

Her new play, *"Puddin 'n Pete"* premiered at the Chicago's Goodman Theatre in the February, 1993. For television, Ms. West is a consultant and writer for the upcoming PBS - Great Performance dramatic mini series, TRIALS and has also written a pilot for Twentieth Century Fox. Currently she is working on an original screenplay with Oprah Winfrey's Harpo Studio's.

Playwright's Note

I have found that as a work makes its journey, there are numerous questions about the route it takes. I don't mean to be a back seat driver but there are a few hints I'd like to offer as one takes the journey with these five women.

First off, they are a talky bunch. And yet it is not always what these women say, but how they say it. For example, MayDee is fond of horrific sarcasm delivered with an engaging, broad smile and nervous laughter. Though Lola talks a lot, she is equally creative with her silences. Raisa's timing may lean toward the bizarre, but what she says and when it's delivered is always and exactly on time. Vennie has learned biting sarcasm from her mother, but what she has that her mother lacks is a sense of humor. Clearly Vennie has had years to learn control yet, unlike MayDee, she is a master at defending herself without exposing any vulnerability.

The harder these women try not to be like each other, the more like they become. It is often said by children that when they have children they're going to behave differently as parents. They will be better. I submit that we're doing good if we're one step above our parents. To attempt more produces extremes. The women in Jar all think they're better than the generation before them and spend a lot of time convincing themselves of that fact. And in their zeal to be better, they lose sight of their own failings, their own contribution to each other's failings. And, yes, their actions are humorous, but to them it is not about fun, it is about jarring the floor in the midst of the very people who have the power to hurt them the most.

Raisa's cancer. Why was it included: Was I making fun? The answer, of course, is no. All the characters are concerned about image, looks, presentation: Vennie's hair, MaDear's "pretty like Lola" speech toward the end, and her feeling that she is ugly, nappy headed and too black; MayDee's precise grammar, the conservative, non revealing clothes; Lola's insistence on a youthful appearance at all costs. All of this and more the characters use to oppress themselves and each other. Raisa's presence, her physical appearance, is the most bold in challenging what's "presentable." Indeed, she is wearing her scar on the outside whereas most of the Jar women are struggling to keep their scars on the inside, hidden and aided by silence to remain hidden.

And, finally, the play is about making peace: with one's scars, with one's history, and, of course, with the embodiment of oneself – one's mother.

Enjoy!

CHARACTERS

MADEAR, 90, mother of Lola, grandmother of MayDee and great-grandmother of Vennie

LOLA, 65, daughter of MaDear and mother of MayDee and grandmother to Vennie

MAYDEE, 47, daughter of Lola, mother of Vennie and granddaughter of MaDear

VENNIE, 27, daughter of MayDee and granddaughter of Lola and great-granddaughter of MaDear.

RAISA, 28, friend of Vennie

NOTE: *All the women are Black except Raisa*

"*Jar The Floor*" was first presented in Champaign, Illinois, at Parkland College and was directed by Cheryl West.

ORIGINAL CAST

MADEAR...Ruth Latham
LOLA...Crystal Laws Green
MAYDEE...Margaret Porter-Wright
RAISA... Jackie Farber
VENNIE...Nonita Stiggers

TIME

MaDear's 90th birthday

SETTING

Most of the action takes place in the Lakeland kitchen and living room. There are three exits: one off from the living room with a long hallway leading to the bathroom and bedrooms, a kitchen exit that leads to the deck and a front door exit off from the living room. There's a full length mirror and a closet in the living room. The house is stylish and well decorated except for the piano. Its care and placement makes it appear as if it belongs in another house; it is covered and littered with papers and magazines.

Jar The Floor

Scene 1

*The living room. MaDear is sitting in her big chair in front
of a television that's turned up loud; she is sitting close, too
close. She is very involved in the story; at the same time she
is tearing at her braids, resulting in her hair sticking up all
over her head. There is a Bible on her lap.*

MADEAR: *(To the TV.) You* need yo behind beat. I oughtta take dis here stick
and beat yo sorry ass myself. Go on an git her, Jim. She don't deserve to live.
Lord Jesus, look behind you, look behind you, he's got a gun. *(Yelling.)* He's got a
a gun. *(TV gun shot heard.)* See, you just hard-headed, I tried to tell you...Didn't I
tell you he had a gun? *(MayDee enters.)*
MAYDEE: MaDear, you scared me. I thought somebody was holding you
hostage. How could you watch that garbage the first thing in the morning? It was
loud enough to wake the dead.
MADEAR: Man, you woke?
MAYDEE: Please don't start that, not this morning. I wish you'd stop moving
this chair. And what have you done to your hair?
MADEAR: Don't like how dat gal plait. She know I's tender-headed an she catch
my hair up an pull it so my eyes move way on de other side of my face...
*(MayDee moves MaDear's chair back from the TV, takes a lot of effort since
MaDear doesn't help in the least, even drags her feet.)*
MAYDEE: You only do that to your hair to upset Mama.
MADEAR: I cain't 'call dat gal's name.
MAYDEE: Lola, your daughter. *(Louder.)* LOLA! *(More to herself.)* Guess
they'll call soon.
MADEAR: What?
MAYDEE: My tenure. Remember? I told you they were supposed to call today.
You think I deserve tenure, don't you? That I'm a good teacher...
MADEAR: If you gotta go askin' me, it don't matter how good you is. Man's
comin to git me today. Chile fetch me my comb. Got to fix myself up, leave here
lookin decent... Man don't like me lookin' old. *(Using her cane, crosses to the
kitchen table.)* Did you hear me, Maydee? I'm goin home. I'm goin home...
MAYDEE: How about something different this morning? An omelette, broccoli
with mushrooms...
MADEAR: Man don't eat no mushrooms, says it keeps yo bowels from formin'
up right, come out wid little hoods on 'em an sometimes dem hoods get caught
and you needs you a button hook to try an pry 'em loose...
MAYDEE: Okay MaDear, no omelette. How about sausage and biscuits?
MADEAR: I don't eat no can biscuits made by no man name Hungry Jack.
MAYDEE: *(Crosses to table.)* Okay, well then it's corn flakes again. *(Puts the
cereal box and milk on the table.)* Knock yourself out.
MADEAR: You servin' me out de box? *(MayDee crosses to kitchen and back,*

puts the box in front of her.) I reckon I'm s'posed to eat wid my hands?
MAYDEE: How about a slice of melon?
MADEAR: It come out de garden?
MAYDEE: You know I don't have a garden. How many times do I have to tell you I don't have time to tend to a garden.
MADEAR: Well, you ain't killin' me wid no store bought fruit and vege'bles.
MAYDEE: *(Puts a slice of melon next to her bowl, cuts it up in little pieces.)* MaDear, today I would like you to try and stay sane. Understand? Sane! Can you do that for me? No talk about Papa, Man, Uncle. Nothing. You understand? *(Pouring cereal)* You're almost out of cereal. *(Crosses to refrigerator, writes on memo pad.)*
MADEAR: *(Takes out half empty jar of Vaseline from her robe pocket, holds it up.)* Needs Vaseline.
MAYDEE: What are you doing with all that Vaseline?
MADEAR: Dat's my business. And some hog head cheese.
MAYDEE: How many times do I have to tell you, they don't sell hog head cheese?
MADEAR: Den buy me a snout and I'll fix me some.
MAYDEE: *(Pulls up the window shade.)* Looks like Vennie will have a nice clear day in which to travel. I've made a lot of plans for this weekend. Did I show you the itinerary I had my secretary type up? Tomorrow I thought we'd go to the Bearden Retrospective exhibition. How I love his work. We're all going to have a great day today, aren't we? You, me, Mama and…my Vennie. *(MayDee crosses, kisses MaDear.)* Aren't we, Sweetie?
MADEAR: You gon' kiss at me all day?
MAYDEE: I sure hope that piece of car of Vennie's holds up.
MADEAR: Shouldn't bought no black car. I wouldn't be caught dead in no black car. If you gon' call yoself buyin' a car, you might as well buy yoself a white one. I gots me a white car back home, big shiny white car. *(Chuckles to herself, imitates driving.)* I puts on my red hat and I drives it everywhere, everywhere I wanna go.
MAYDEE: MaDear, you don't have a white car or any other car. You never learned to drive.
MADEAR: Don't you tell me 'bout what I learnt. I used to teach school. Drive my white car every day to de school house.
MAYDEE: And you never taught school. You were never a teacher…
MADEAR: Chil'ren everywhere. Mornin', Miss Dawkins. Every mornin, dey say "mornin', Miss Dawkins" and I say "mornin', chil'ren. Good mornin'." So don't tell me, nothin' a black car can do for me but carry me to a white one.
MAYDEE: MaDear, I was talking about Vennie. Vennie and her car.
MADEAR: Who?
MAYDEE: VENNIE LAKELAND. YOUR GREAT-GRANDDAUGHTER, MY DAUGHTER!
MADEAR: Well chile, now you ain't gotta shout. Nothin' wrong wid my hearin'. Man git Blackie. *(Starts taking off robe.)* Hitch up de wagon, we need to git on back home. We done stayed way too long in dis God forsaken place…

MAYDEE: *(Exasperated.)* MaDear, this is your home now. Remember? Papa is dead so we brought you up here. Papa's gone almost a year now...
MADEAR: Gal, you sho is talkin' silly. *(Throws her bowl on the floor, takes her cane and pounds the floor.)* Jar de floor, man. You ain't dead. You feel dat floor move? Don't you feel it? Don't you hear him?
MAYDEE: *(Crossing to table, wipes up the floor.)* Oh, MaDear...
MADEAR: I said did you feel dat floor move? I cain't hardly hold myself in dis here chair, feel like I'm gon' fly away to Jesus. *(Rakes her hand through MayDee's hair.)* Gal, you done pull most of yo hair out dere on de side, you nearly bald...
MAYDEE: I haven't. *(Going to the mirror.)* I just need another rinse.
MADEAR: Say rinse! Well, you can rinse if you want to, rinse yo hair right down de drain...*(Lola enters through back door carrying bags and an overflowing box. She is flashy but not totally at the expense of good taste.)*
LOLA: Morning everybody.
MADEAR: *(Muttering.)* And speakin of de drain...
LOLA: How's everybody this fine God sent beautiful morning? Hot as blue blazes out there. *(Kisses MayDee.)* Daughter look like somebody walked on your face last night and left they tracks.
MAYDEE: *(Still studying her hair.)* Thanks, Mama.
LOLA: *(Looking in the mirror behind MayDee.)* The right kind of color make that bald spot look like you got baby hair.
MAYDEE: What is this? I'm not going bald.
LOLA: It's okay, baby. Your father was bald at twenty, head smooth as a baby's behind. Pretended he still had hair too. Used to scratch his bald head every Sunday afternoon, just like clockwork. And every Sunday afternoon I'd tell him his hair sho was growing. Morning, Mama.
MADEAR: None of dem Smith boys ever had any hair. Heard tell dey didn't have hair no wheres 'bout dey body, not a lick.
LOLA: And where'd you hear that from Mama?
MADEAR: Don't you worry 'bout where, missy.
LOLA: Well, they told you a lie. That man was hairy like a gorilla. I never knew if I was having a nightmare or if it was just Smith turning over trying to get him a little bit. I'm so thankful baby you didn't come here looking like a little monkey, I'd been shaving your whole body every single day, thank you Jesus. *(Starts taking things out of her bag.)* Now quit fretting, MayDee. You lose all your hair just buy yourself a wig and keep on stepping. It's a sin to be so vain. *(Handing her some plastic containers.)* Here, put this cole slaw in the refrigerator and here the beans...candied yams...
MADEAR: Hair is a woman's glory.
LOLA: And that's a white woman's lie. By the time a colored woman get through rinsing, coloring, straightening, yanking, greasing that kitchen, trying to tame her some hair, she done gone to glory and back. I bet if you go to heaven right now, there'd be a bunch of nappy-headed black angels laughing their butts off singing free at last, free at last...
MAYDEE: Mama!

LOLA: I'm telling you the truth. We all gon' end up looking like them Jamaican mountain people before it's over. Saw it in a dream once. I fried some chicken too. Here. Don't put it in the refrigerator, just leave it on the stove...

MAYDEE: You didn't have to do all this cooking...

LOLA: Yes I did.

MAYDEE: I was going to make a pot roast...

LOLA: When?

MAYDEE: For dinner.

LOLA: And you ain't got on it yet?

MAYDEE: There's still time...

LOLA: I didn't wanna eat at midnight, that's why I went on 'head and cooked. Anyway my Pick-Me-Up like chicken better than pot roast...And what time that child getting here?

MAYDEE: Sometime this morning. There are several lectures this evening on campus I thought she might enjoy. And tomorrow I thought we'd go to an art exhibition after brunch...then maybe to the...

LOLA: So what time you schedule her to shit? That child is grown, MayDee. You need to stop planning her life out like that.

MAYDEE: I don't.

LOLA: Fine. I ain't in it. You like this little purse?

MAYDEE: Un-hun.

LOLA: It's a Louis Vuitton.

MAYDEE: It's nice.

LOLA: *(Crossing to couch, lights a cigarette.) You* think so? I think it's the ugliest thing. But all my club women buyin 'em, trying to buy 'em some class. *(MayDee brings her an ashtray.)* And you know Alberta, she had to go and outdo everybody. Went an bought herself a big ass briefcase and don't put nothing in it but bananas.

MAYDEE: Bananas?

LOLA: Yeah, she eats 'em round the clock for her potassium. You know who she is, look like a haint. Now she know she needed a briefcase like she needed a hole in her head. A Louis Vuitton with bananas in it! She won't even keep the minutes at the meetings. I told her she oughtta be the secretary, at least she'd have reason to carry that thing around. But no, told me she done retired from a woman's work. Ain't that something? She done retired! I told her every time she lay on her back underneath that ton of fun she married to, she doing a woman's work. Ain't big enough to hold nothing but some Kleenex and some small change. Paid all that money just to hold Kleenex. *(MayDee exits to change into robe.)*

MADEAR: How much you pay for dat bag, Sister?

LOLA: Ninety-five, I think.

MADEAR: Gal is you silly? Hope it was ninety five cents. A pillowcase been prettier.

LOLA: Glad I didn't buy you one.

MADEAR: You and me both happy 'bout dat.

LOLA: Oh, close your legs, Mama. *(Yelling.)* MayDee, I don't know why you let her sit around here all day long with her legs wide open.

MADEAR: Dey my legs. And dey don't close up no mo'. *(Fans her robe.)* My air is findin' its way.
LOLA: Your what? *(Closes MaDear's legs.)* Them legs would close if you wanted them to. AND KEEP YOUR HANDS FROM DOWN THERE. Anybody call?
MAYDEE: *(Entering, sprays the room with airspray.)* Who are you expecting this time?
LOLA: That's my business, dear heart.
MAYDEE: I told you before, my phone is not your answering service.
LOLA: I know that, sweetheart.
MAYDEE: Then why don't you have your so called "dates"...
LOLA: Shut up. Now you know I don't want her knowing my business...
MADEAR: Wouldn't be caught doin nothin I had to talk down to de floor 'bout.
LOLA: I swear she could hear a chinch piss on cotton. *(Yelling.)* To be ninety, you got good hearing old woman. You sure your phone is working? I knew I should've called and checked it out this morning. Every since MaBell got a divorce from AT&T ain't a phone worked steady since. Sometimes my phone just rings for the hell of it. *(Bangs the phone on its cradle.)*
MAYDEE: Mama, please...
LOLA: I ain't lying. I picks it up and it's still ringing. Since that nigger upstairs got cable ain't nothing worked right in my house. Got to look my spanking best day and night, no telling when my number is gon' be up living in that shack. That's why I'm so grateful Mama is here with you. It's so much safer!
MAYDEE: Boy, that's a new one.
LOLA: What?
MAYDEE: You don't live in a shack...
LOLA: Well, if I lived in a mansion like this, there would be no problem...
MAYDEE: Three bedrooms is hardly a mansion and you didn't have to rent that upstairs apartment, MaDear could've...
LOLA: Just 'cause I'm on a fixed income, you trying to make me feel bad. How 'bout that brother of mine, you don't see him volunteering to take her. He living up there in that fancy house with that no English speaking wife...
MADEAR: Doctor don't have no wife. He's comin' for me.
LOLA: He's not a doctor, Mama. Shit. He runs a maid service. He's a pimp in the cleaning business.
MAYDEE: Please, don't start. Not today. If she wants to believe...
LOLA: No. Un-Un. She don't allow me my lies, so why should I allow her hers. I get sick of you calling him the Doctor. His name is A.H. He ain't no MD. He liked to cut up animals and that's as far as his medical training went.
MADEAR: Gal, how you know? You ain't never been to my house.
LOLA: Here we go. Guess I ain't your daughter again. Which doorstep did you find me on today?
MAYDEE: *(Unwraps a piece of candy.)* You know I really wish you'd stop giving my number out.
LOLA: *(Overlapping, takes the candy out of her mouth.)* Give me that, your behind getting too big now...

Cheryl L. West 61

MAYDEE: I just wish you'd settle down with someone your own age...
LOLA: Settle! *(Gesturing toward MaDear.)* That's what settle looks like and I sho ain't ready for that.
MAYDEE: You'd rather chase after these boys? Let them use you as a business...
LOLA: Better used than going to waste. MayDee, don't you miss having somebody to hold, make you feel like a woman?
MAYDEE: Mama, I don't want to hold on to something I know can't handle the weight. I'm content...
LOLA: Content?!! What about being happy?
MAYDEE: I've always preferred the ease of contentment to the strife of happiness.
LOLA: Now that don't even make sense. I can't talk to you when you talking through them degrees of yours. There's no substitute for a good man...
MAYDEE: Learn to masturbate. It's safer, cleaner and more expedient.
LOLA: And why don't you shut your filthy mouth.
MADEAR: Better a filthy mouth den a filthy behind.
LOLA: Mama, Lola and MayDee talking. Understand? Two-way conversation, not three-way.
MAYDEE: *(Overlapping.)* Somebody your own age, like Mr. Brown. You two look so cute...
LOLA: MayDee, I left cute when I started walking.
MADEAR: You never walked. You went straight from crawlin' to switchin' yo behind.
LOLA: Yeah, I did have a walk, didn't I? Stop traffic. And dance, oh my land. Could've gone professional. Should've seen me kicking high, high, high at the Club DeLisa. Yes mam, star quality. The Parkway Ballroom, the RhumBoogie...sometimes I'd go seven days a week. Come on dance with me, MayDee. Dance with your old mother. *(Starts dancing.)*
MAYDEE: Mama, it's too early to be dancing.
LOLA: It's never too early. Dancing don't need no time permit. I got up this morning dancing. *(She swings MayDee around.)* Why don't you tickle them ivories a little...
MAYDEE: You know I don't play anymore.
LOLA: *(Plays a few keys on the piano.)* Just a few notes, baby.
MAYDEE: I said no.
LOLA: Then just dance with me... *(Lola swings MayDee again and then gets caught up in her own rhythm; MayDee watches her appreciatively as Lola sings.)* "Whatever Lola wants, Lola gets... and little man, little Lola wants you...Jump back, honey, jump back. Watch me now. Jump back honey, jump back." *(Dancing over to MaDear.)* Come on, Mama, you wanna dance?
MADEAR: You better git away from me gal wid all dat mess. You better git somewhere an find de Lord.
LOLA: You just can't let me be free. Between you and the Lord it's a wonder I'm able to greet the sun every morning.
MADEAR: You little split tail, don't you blaspheme de Lord.

MAYDEE: You're a wonderful dancer, Mama...
LOLA: I'd still be dancing regular if my feet weren't so bad...
MAYDEE: Mr. Brown doesn't seem to mind them.
LOLA: How you know what he minds?
MAYDEE: He adores you, Mama. He's your own age and I don't know why you...
LOLA: What, is he paying you or what?!!! His name been chasing out your mouth ever since I walked through that door...
MAYDEE: I just think...
LOLA: He's a nice enough man, that's not the problem.
MAYDEE: Then, what's the problem?
LOLA: Oh nothing.
MAYDEE: What?
LOLA: Didn't I say nothing? *(Crosses, away from MaDear, whispering.)* They cut his balls off. He had the cancer.
MAYDEE: Mama, he had prostate surgery. They didn't cut his testicles off.
LOLA: We keep good company but I ain't ready to get my pleasure through no ruba-dub-dub. I like something with a little more substance. You know what I mean?
MAYDEE: No.
LOLA: Shit, MayDee, you been running on empty too long. There's no rising in the flour. You understand now? *(Makes gesture.)* No RISING!!!
MAYDEE: Oh, Mama!
LOLA: I'm telling you the God's honest truth. That man ain't able. Wants to kiss and kiss, kiss... slobber... kiss... slobber. My whole body being baptized with his mouth. And you know me, I don't go in for no freaky deaky...
MAYDEE: At least he's affectionate. You can't ask for more than that.
LOLA: Yeah, he's affectionate alright, but so is a blanket if you wrap it right. *(Catches MaDear eavesdropping.)* Mama, why don't you go and get your clothes laid out.
MADEAR: Ain't wearin' clothes today.
LOLA: Well, then why don't you go watch TV in your room?
MADEAR: Ain't watching TV today.
LOLA: Then go in your room and just sit. I'll be in there directly to get you cleaned up and comb that head, look like the chickens been playing in it again.
MADEAR: I'm fine where I is. I ain't no child dats got to be sent to my room.
(Lola crosses, turns on the TV, then moves with some effort MaDear's chair closer to the TV; it takes a lot of effort since MaDear doesn't help in the least bit, even drags her feet.)
MAYDEE: I wish you all would stop moving that chair.
LOLA: When my surprise comes, we won't have to do this.
MAYDEE: What surprise? Mama, would you put that chair back. You're scratching the floor...
LOLA: It looks better here. Gives the room a lived-in effect and Lord knows this room could use some personality. And you might as well sell that piano, nothing but a dust collector. *(To MaDear.)* Now, Sweetie, you watch a little TV while me

and MayDee talk. Okay? *(MaDear doesn't respond. Lola crosses to kitchen area and as soon as she starts talking to MayDee, MaDear uses the remote to click off the TV but continues to stare at it as if it's on, all the while listening to their conversation. Periodically she looks over at them.)*
LOLA: I needs me some coffee.
MAYDEE: I'm not sure I want to hear this.
LOLA: You got anything in that bottom cabinet?
MAYDEE: It's a little early, don't you think?
LOLA: Yeah, we having us a morning drink. *(Retrieving the liquor from the cabinet, pours some in her cup.)* Coffee is for morning, we just stirring a little evening in it.
MAYDEE: Go ahead. Let's hear it.
LOLA: What I'm gon' tell you is gon' shock every bit of shit outta you. Gon' give you an enema right here on the spot.
MAYDEE: *(Laughing.)* I doubt it, Mama, but go ahead.
LOLA: Brace yourself. I hate to tell you this about your Mr. Brown, but he wanted me to do an unnatural act.
MAYDEE: Now this is getting good.
LOLA: Yes. Told me other women have no hesitation.
MAYDEE: Un-hun.
LOLA: He wanted me to… Lord Jesus my throat is closing up a mile a minute just thinking about it. Have mercy Father! He wanted me…Un, I'm so shamed.
MAYDEE: Mama, you trying to tell me he wanted you to have oral sex?
LOLA: Ooh, honey don't say it out loud!
MAYDEE: *(Laughs.)* It's just an alternative Mama. Myself, l happen to enjoy it better than intercourse.
LOLA: SHUT YOUR MOUTH AND THROW AWAY THE KEY!
MAYDEE: I'm serious. I can count the times on one hand where I've achieved orgasm through intercourse.
LOLA: Well, you ain't gon' catch me achieving that shit. I told him my mouth was a sanctuary, you hear me, a sanctuary. I couldn't have no man smelling me all up in my privates, all your fare-the-well wide open, exposed and let's face it, pussy ain't pretty.
MAYDEE: I think it's beautiful.
LOLA: Lord Jesus I'm getting dizzy. *(Getting up.)* I knew you was educated but I didn't know you was doing the freaky.
MADEAR: I wouldn't have no sin I had to pay for. And he's my husband!
LOLA: Mama, what you talking about?
MADEAR: *(Overlapping.)* HE'S MY HUSBAND, NOT YO HUSBAND. YOU HEAR DAT, SPLIT TAIL. HE'S MINE! MY HUSBAND.
MAYDEE: Could we all try and get along, at least for the day?
LOLA: I was trying, but she talking 'bout somebody's husband…
MAYDEE: Just for the day. Okay? Okay?
LOLA: *(Reluctantly.)* Okay. Okay. Okay already! *(Crossing to MaDear, false gaiety.)* And how's the birthday girl this morning? *(Kissing MaDear.)*
MADEAR: Every time you kiss me wid dem red lips I gits me a rash. Why I got

to pay for yo sins?

LOLA: Nobody asked you to pay for a damn...

MAYDEE: *(Interceding, swirls to model the robe.)* Mama, you like this robe? I got it on sale...

LOLA: I don't know why you spend good money on stuff like that. Not like you wearing it for anybody.

MAYDEE: I'm wearing it for myself.

LOLA: Um! Lord Jesus, to each his own. Let me show you all the things I got for the party. You wanna see, Mama? *(Taking things out of the box and bags.)* Crepe paper for streamers. Balloons... You wanna see the sign I made? *(Pulls out a colorful sign that reads: "Happy Birthday Viola, Mama, MaDear. We love you.")* You like it, Mama? *(No response, nor does she look at the sign.)* Did you hear me? *(Irritated.)* Mama, do you like the sign? It says happy birthday.

MADEAR: I can read.

MAYDEE: She likes it, don't you, MaDear?

MADEAR: De Doctor sent me a blue dress.

LOLA: He sent you that dress six months ago.

MAYDEE: It's a nice dress just like this sign Mama made for you.

MADEAR: My boy was sho nuff a gift from God.

LOLA: Good thing God gave him to you, nobody else would've wanted him.

(Phone rings. MayDee and Lola freeze.)

LOLA: Well, aren't you going to answer it?

MAYDEE: Maybe it's for you.

LOLA: It's not my house.

MAYDEE: So! That never mattered before.

LOLA: Well, I ain't one for answering other people's phones...

MADEAR: WILL ONE OF YA'LL ANSWER DE DAMN PHONE!

MAYDEE: *(Hesitates, picks up the phone, is shaky with anticipation.)* Hello? Oh...yes, operator, I will... *(MaDear starts talking to herself, what she says is not really audible, but clearly she's having a running conversation with herself or her imagination, it's a conversation with intense emotional range.)*

MAYDEE: *(In the phone.)* Vennie, what are you doing calling here? I thought you were on your way...

LOLA: *(Overlapping.)* Tell her don't tie up that phone. Your bill too high now, her calling and reversing them charges all the time.

MAYDEE: Well, it's a fine time to tell me...she's welcome, that's not the point...

LOLA: Who? Who?

MAYDEE: Okay... Can you tell me now? Vennie, I would just like a little preparation... Vennie, who do you think you're talking ...fine...fine... See you when you get here. *(Hangs up.)*

LOLA: Who she bringing?

MAYDEE: A friend.

LOLA: Female?

MAYDEE: Yeah.

LOLA: Figures.

MAYDEE: What's that supposed to mean?

LOLA: Nothing.

MAYDEE: Good. I know Vennie, she just didn't decide to bring somebody... She wants something. Said she had something important to discuss with me. All this secrecy. She couldn't tell me on the phone... Nooo, she has to wait until she gets here...

LOLA: With a friend.

MAYDEE: I got tickets to things. I hadn't planned on an extra person...

LOLA: Don't mean no harm, MayDee, she's your daughter and my granddaughter and I love her dearly, but I'm beginning to wonder about our Vennie, my little Pick-Me-Up.

MAYDEE: What?

LOLA: She like women a little too much, don't you think? Catch my drift?

MAYDEE: I'm glad she likes women. Means she likes herself.

LOLA: I likes myself, too, but I don't like no women. 'Member that time I caught her with that Johnson girl, both of 'em holding their dresses up, their little rabbits sticking out. Now, I didn't stay 'round to see what else they was 'bout to do...but if you ask me...

MAYDEE: Mama, she was ten years old!

LOLA: Ten and on fire. That stuff start in you young and once it gets started...whew! Look out. If you would've just let her have that baby...

MAYDEE: Now what's that got to do with anything?

LOLA: Plenty! A baby sets you on the straight and narrow path. Ain't no detouring. You's a mother and you knows you's a woman. She oughtta bring her behind back home so you can keep an eye on her.

MADEAR: I have to go to de bafroom.

LOLA: Then take your behind in there.

MADEAR: Gal, I should've killed you when you was born.

MAYDEE: MaDear, come on. I'll help you. *(MaDear exits.)*

MAYDEE: Do you have to antagonize her like that? You know she can't help herself. She can't help it if she's senile.

LOLA: She's not senile. Got more sense than the two of us put together. Stayed up, cooked, made that silly sign, bought all that food and decorations so she could have a good birthday. Does she appreciate it? Noooo. *(Yells toward the direction of the bathroom.)* DOES SHE APPRECIATE ALL I DO FOR HER? HAS SHE EVER APPRECIATED ANYTHING I EVER DID?

MAYDEE: I'm so tired of starting my mornings like this. It's either the TV blasting, her yelling and then there's your daily visit.

LOLA: Well, I don't have to come here. I call myself trying to help out. I come, give her a bath, comb her hair and try to help out as best I can while you at that big shot job teaching black people how to be black.

MAYDEE: Mama, I teach African-American Studies and Political Science...

LOLA: Call it what you want, but don't forget I sit here all day long, every day, playing nursemaid to somebody who'd rather die than act like I'm in the same room. Every day! From now on, I'll just keep my black ass home...

MAYDEE: *(Mumbling to herself.)* She's not my mother.

LOLA: What you say?

MAYDEE: Nothing.

LOLA: You said she's not your mother. That's what you said, didn't you? *(Mocking.)* "She's not my mother."

MAYDEE: Mama, look, my hair is falling out... I'm working around the clock, I have a grandmother who'd make Jesus Christ cry out for mercy...and I'm waiting on one of the biggest decisions of my life... Of course you wouldn't care...

LOLA: *(Dramatically pitiful.)* She's turned you against me, hasn't she?

MAYDEE: Can't do this today.

LOLA: She told me I wasn't gon' be no kinda mother. But I did the best I could, kept you clean, kept a man, even when I didn't want one, so you'd have a father...

MAYDEE: Thanks.

LOLA: Now what was that smart aleck remark for?

MAYDEE: Nothing.

LOLA: Don't tell me nothing. Every child needs a father. Wouldn't've known how to laugh without mine. Maybe Willie or Sam or Joe weren't the best fathers.

MAYDEE: Can say that again.

LOLA: At least they were there...more than I can say for that father who planted you in me. He never gave you a dime, not one red cent...

MAYDEE: I guess you think having four fathers is some type of blessing..

LOLA: At least they loved you. Willie wanted to legally adopt you, 'member? But I told him no out of respect for your real father.

MAYDEE: Can we talk about something else? Please?

LOLA: *(Overlapping.)* Willie was always taking up time, playing your little games with you. I'd feel so left out around the two of ya'll. Just hang in the doorway grinning till my mouth got all dried out, waiting for ya'll to notice me. What was that one game where you used to sit on his knee and he'd bounce you up and down and ya'll would clap hands...*(Sings and claps her hands.)* "Little pretty May, pretty as a picture..."

MAYDEE: I don't remember.

LOLA: Oh, yes you do. You would clap... *(Sings, claps her hands.)* "Nothing like her Mama 'cause she daddy's little girl, pretty as a picture, makes her Daddy..."

MAYDEE: Would you like to see the outfit I bought for Vennie?

LOLA: *(Overlapping.)* I remember I had to tell him to stop playing with you like that. You was going on fifteen and he still thought you liked that game...

MAYDEE: *(Mutters.)* He was the only one enjoying himself.

LOLA: Was scared all that bouncing up and down was gon' ruin your figure. Never did have much up there, I didn't want what you had to start dropping down.

MAYDEE: And a woman is nothing without a good figure, right? Maybe, if you had been any kind of mother, then maybe I wouldn't have needed a father so damn much.

LOLA: Why you cutting me to pieces today, huh MayDee? Just butchering my heart left and right. Sure as I'm born, she's turning you against me. She did the same thing with Papa! Now she's working her black magic on you.

MAYDEE: It's like you don't hear me. Did you hear me say my future hangs in the air? I'm not waiting for some gigolo stud to call...You've always been so self involved...you don't see anything beyond your own narcissistic reality.

LOLA: Well, you forgive me for my *(Tries to say the word, gets tangled in the pronunciation.)* narcis...narcis,...whatever the shit you called it. You try walking a mile on the roads I traveled. You try cleaning up behind white folks everyday and coming home to a daughter who sleeps with the kitchen knives and a nigger who acts like you ain't even there...

MAYDEE: Your choice. Not mine. Yours.

LOLA: I didn't have a choice. You had to eat.

MAYDEE: Right. You didn't do a damn thing for me.

LOLA: How you know 'bout choice? I did what I had to and I used what I had to do it with. Peddled ass...yes...

MAYDEE: I wish you wouldn't talk so crudely.

LOLA: Show me a woman who's never had to spread her legs, who didn't have to lay down somewheres first in order to rise up later with a loaf of bread in hand.

MAYDEE: I never did.

LOLA: Well good for you, Miss Thang. And while you feeling so superior try remembering how I kept your belly full, how you had a roof over your head...that you wore decent clothes...had toys, your own piano.

MAYDEE: I just want you to stop using me...stop making me sorry for being born.

LOLA: I ain't never made you sorry for being born. God, how did I raise a goddamn sponge for a daughter. Soak up every misery in the world and squeeze it right back in my face. I can't help it that you've spoiled Vennie silly...that you think every man comes dipped in horseshit, that you work like a dog and there's nobody there to slap you on the back twenty-four hours a day. You want a backslapper, MayDee, here buy yourself one. *(Opens her purse, takes out some bills).* I'll even throw in a few dollars and furnish you with a few names. *(Slaps the bills in MayDee's hands.)*

MAYDEE: I have to go help your mother. *(MayDee starts to exit, Lola grabs her.)*

LOLA: *(Pleading.)* MayDee, I do the best I can...You can't keep faulting me for doing the best I can. I know you the best thing ever came out of my life. *(MayDee throws the money at Lola's feet, exits.)* You waiting for this tenure, I'm waiting for this gigolo; different prize, MayDee, but the need's the same.

Scene 2

> *Several hours later. At the lights, MayDee is at the piano playing a classic, maybe from Beethoven, Bach. She is definitely enraptured by the music. MaDear is in her chair dressed in the blue flowered dress. Her hair is neatly braided and pinned on top of her head.*

LOLA: *(After a time, off, yelling.)* Somebody help me. My arms 'bout to fall off. MayDee.

MAYDEE: *(Quickly shuts the piano, to MaDear.)* Our little secret. I was just seeing if it still worked. *(No response from MaDear.)*

LOLA: MAYDEE!

MAYDEE: Coming.

(Lola enters wheeling an electric wheelchair that is overflowing with packages, including a large gift wrapped picture. She has changed clothes; the outfit is outlandish, red and complete with a matching boa, a glittering shawl.)

LOLA: Whew, thank you. You better stay young, MayDee, getting old is a bitch. Did I hear the piano? Vennie not here yet? I get me call?

MAYDEE: No. What is that?

LOLA: It's for Mama.

MAYDEE: Well, I knew it wasn't for me.

LOLA: It's a wheelchair for Mama.

MAYDEE: She doesn't need a wheelchair and an electric one at that.

MADEAR: What's dat you got dere, Sister?

LOLA: *(Takes packages out of chair.)* Here take these, MayDee. I got a surprise for you Mama. *(Rolling the wheelchair to MaDear.)* It's a wheelchair, an electric wheelchair. All you have to do is push this here button and you can ride till your behind gets tired.

MAYDEE: Mama, I don't believe you did this.

LOLA: What? *(MaDear crosses to wheelchair, gets slowly in the wheelchair, Lola and MayDee are too busy arguing to notice.)*

MAYDEE: What? Buying her a wheelchair, that's what!

LOLA: I didn't buy it, I rented it.

MAYDEE: But MaDear can walk.

LOLA: Barely.

MAYDEE: More than barely, Mama. You're going to make her a cripple before her time.

LOLA: I thought it would help out. Make her more independent.

MAYDEE: Help out? This house isn't big enough for another piece of furniture.

LOLA: It folds up, MayDee. Get up Mama. Let me show MayDee how your chair folds up. Got a little horn on it. Put it on myself. *(Lola squeezes the horn, it's an obnoxious sound.)*

MAYDEE: *(Yanking Lola's arm and pulling her toward the hallway.)* Come here.

LOLA: You 'bout to take my arm out the socket...

MAYDEE: Look down that hall. Do you see how narrow that hall is? *(Taking her down the hallway and out of sight.)* That wheelchair will block this whole hall up...all I need now is to add a traffic jam to my morning routine. I can see it now, MaDear beeping at me, nicks and scrapes all across my freshly painted walls...

MADEAR: *(Overlapping, pushes the button on the wheel chair and bumps into something.)* Oh Lordy, help me. *(She backs into something.)* MAYDEE COME GIT ME OUT DIS HERE CONTRAPTION...Whew ham mercy! *(Blows horn.)* Shit hold your horses... *(Lola and MayDee run back in the room.)*

LOLA: *(Stopping the chair.)* Now who told you to turn this on? You had no business turning this thing on. Why you have to be so fast? I was gon' show you how to operate it…

MADEAR: I knows how to do. I knows how to drive.

LOLA: The only thing you ever drove was Papa, drove him crazy!

MADEAR: You de one dat drove him crazy. Killed him wid all dat dancin'.

LOLA: *(A moment, hiding her hurt.)* Don't hit that button again. You hear me, Mama? You just sit in it. Don't you hit that button no more today.

MADEAR: You don't tell me…

MAYDEE: See what you've started. See! A wheelchair. I don't believe you.

LOLA: I was just trying to do something nice. Every damn thing I do turns to piss… *(She plops down on the couch and sulks, lights a cigarette.)*

MAYDEE: *(Waving the air.)* I wish you wouldn't do that in here.

LOLA: Why don't you say what you really mean? Mama, I wish you'd disappear.

MAYDEE: *(A moment.)* Mama. *(No response.)* Mama, look…it was a nice thought…but…

MADEAR: Nice way to kill a soul. A motor chair…

MAYDEE: I'm sorry. Come on. Let's not ruin things. It's MaDear's birthday. Okay, I'm not saying I'm sorry again. Let me show you the outfit I bought Vennie. *(Goes in the closet, retrieves a suit on a hanger, shows it to Lola.)* You like it?

LOLA: Vennie's not gon' wear that shit.

MAYDEE: This suit cost me a lot of money.

LOLA: Is that why you left the price on? Take the tags off, MayDee.

MAYDEE: What if I have to take it back? What if it doesn't fit?

LOLA: Cut the tags off, MayDee. I'll tell Vennie how much you paid for it.

MAYDEE: She's coming here for money. I can feel it.

LOLA: It's her money.

MAYDEE: It most certainly is not. I saved every last dime of that money. And I'm not giving up one red cent until she finishes… *(Catches herself.)*

LOLA: Finishes what?

MAYDEE: That money is for her to further her education.

LOLA: She done got one degree. Why you…

MAYDEE: *(Deliberately changes the subject.)* Can I see the picture, Mama?

LOLA: No. Leave that right where it is. It don't concern you.

MAYDEE: *(Picking up the picture.)* Boy, it's so big. This for MaDear?

LOLA: Gimme that. *(Taking the picture away.)* Didn't I tell you it didn't concern you?

MAYDEE: I don't know where we'd hang it? It's a little large.

LOLA: *(Her spirit returning.)* Right here. *(Crosses and starts to take down the picture already hanging.)* This is a perfect spot.

MAYDEE: I like that picture right where it is.

MADEAR: How you gon' hang somethin wid de paper on it?

LOLA: When I want the paper off, Mama, I'll take it off. Ok? *(MayDee takes the picture in hand and exits toward hallway.)* Where you think you going?

MAYDEE: To see how it looks in her room.

(Vennie and Raisa can be seen outside. They both have an odd sense of style and color. Vennie is especially decorated from head to toe, including blue eye contact

lenses and wild hair. Raisa has noticeably one breast.)
LOLA: *(Following behind her.)* Wait a minute. I bought that damn picture.
MAYDEE: *(Off.)* But it's my house.
LOLA: *(Off.)* Nobody asked you 'bout whose house it is.
(Lights up on outside.)
VENNIE: *(Looking around.)* I see nothing has changed.
RAISA: You sure they don't mind me coming?
VENNIE: No. They love company. Any opportunity to play family in front of an audience.
RAISA: Thought you were going to be charming today...
VENNIE: I did say that, didn't I? Okay. Here's the deal. Wanna get along with my people, compliment my grandmother on how young she looks. Debate politics with my mother. You don't have to worry about her, though, she'll love you.
RAISA: Really?
MAYDEE: *(Enters, crosses to door window.)* My God...
VENNIE: Un-hun. Look at you. Miss politically correct if I ever saw one. *(Fixes Raisa's blouse tenderly.)* You got guts, girl. Wish I had a little bit of it...
LOLA: *(Overlapping, entering, holding her forehead and the picture.)* Lord, MayDee, this picture was 'bout to fall on my damn head. If you aim to kill me, just do it straight out. I don't wanna meet my maker with a picture frame sticking out my forehead... I'm telling you the truth...
MAYDEE: Sorry.
VENNIE: *(Overlapping.)* And whatever you do, stay out of my great-grandmother's way...
LOLA: *(Overlapping.)* What you looking at so? She got her friend with her.
MAYDEE: Yes. *(Moving quickly from the window and turning Lola away.)*
RAISA: *(Overlapping.)* Do I look pale? *(Takes out compact, powders.)*
VENNIE: No more than usual. *(Raisa playfully hits at Vennie.)*
MAYDEE: *(Overlapping.)* Now, Mama, whatever you do, don't say anything to hurt Vennie's feelings. And no comments about her friend. You too, MaDear.
MADEAR: I ain't gotta talk no mo today. Sit right here in dis here motor chair.
LOLA: Well, I'm glad you like it, Mama.
MADEAR: I don't 'member sayin' I liked it.
RAISA: *(Overlapping.)* So we staying out here all day?
VENNIE: I wish.
MAYDEE: *(Overlapping.)* Remember, not a word...
VENNIE: *(Overlapping.)* Remember, not one word about the money.
RAISA: But...
VENNIE: Not one word. We're going to Europe.
LOLA: *(Overlapping.)* Not one word gon' pass through these lips, not one damn word. I ain't gon' say shit to neither one of 'em, just watch me. Now open the door and let us see this God forsaken child, she must look a sight. Go 'head, open the door. *(Takes a chair and lines it up next to MaDear's chair, sits, crosses her arms.)* Me and Mama gon' sit here like two peas in a pod.
MADEAR: *(Crosses her arms too.)* Two no-talkin' peas.
LOLA: That's right, Mama.

MAYDEE: O.K., I'm opening the door.
LOLA: For heaven's sake, don't be so dramatic, MayDee. Open the goddamn door! Now close your legs, Mama. *(Puts her arms around MaDear's knees, tries to hold them closed.)*
MADEAR: Gal, take yo hands offa my legs.
MAYDEE: *(Opens the door.)* Well, look who we have here. You finally made it.
VENNIE: Yes we did. *(Vennie and MayDee attempt to hug each other, finally they succeed with an awkward physical exchange.)*
MADEAR: *(Overlapping.)* MAN, IT'S A PURE WHITE WOMAN! *(MaDear puts a piece of her shawl in her mouth and Lola does the same.)*
VENNIE: Did you get your call?
MAYDEE: Not yet. Boy, look at this hair and these clothes.
VENNIE: Look great, don't I? You picked up more weight?
RAISA: *(Extending her hand to MayDee.)* Hi. I'm Raisa.
VENNIE: Yeah Mother, this is Raisa.
MAYDEE: Hello. Ra-za...
RAISA: Raisa.
MAYDEE: *(Trying not to stare.)* That's a pretty name. Well, put your things down. Make yourself at home, Raisa. It's so good to meet you. I don't get to meet many of Vennie's friends.
VENNIE: That's because I never had any. *(Noticing MaDear and Lola.)* Aren't you two a pretty picture? Mother must have you two under gag order again. What's this in your mouth? *(Takes the shawl out of their mouths.)* Mother, you didn't tell me MaDear was in a wheelchair. *(MaDear and Lola stare intently in Vennie's face, they look almost frightened of her, they both scoot back in their chairs.)*
MAYDEE: Well, that's because it just happened today.
LOLA: Vennie, what in the Sam Hell is wrong with your damn eyes?
MADEAR: *(Overlapping.)* Chile, you goin' blind? Yo eyes look like cat eyes. You know dey done turned a milky blue?
VENNIE: *(Laughing.)* Raisa, come on over. If you gon' spend the weekend with them, you might as well get your judgment out the way. *(Raisa walks over, behind her back MayDee is making wild gestures for MaDear and Lola to behave themselves.)*
RAISA: I'm Raisa.
MADEAR and LOLA: *(Staring at Raisa's chest.)* Good God A-mighty!
VENNIE: This is my grandmother Lola Bird and my great-grandmother Viola Dawkins.
RAISA: It's a pleasure to meet you. *(MaDear and Lola are dumfounded, are fixated on Raisa's chest.)* I can't believe you're Vennie's grandmother. You look so young. My grandmother is five years younger than you, but her face looks like the U.S. road map, blue veins and all. *(Laughs loudly, no one else laughs.)*
MAYDEE: Did you hear what Raisa said, Mama? You look so young.
RAISA: *(To MaDear.)* And I can't believe you're ninety today. It's an honor to meet you, Mrs. Dawkins. *(Pause.)* Would you like me to take off my shirt so you

might have a better look?
MAYDEE: Oh I don't think that's necessary...
RAISA: No, it's O.K. It's part of my therapy. You know, accepting myself...
MAYDEE: *(Overlapping.)* Vennie, why don't you show Raisa your room? I'm sure you're tired. Maybe you want to freshen up a bit.
VENNIE: We're fresh...
RAISA: *(Overlapping.)* No, it's really O.K. I don't mind talking about it. I think it's good to talk about it. I rather that than people acting like it's not there or it's there but it's not...well, you know what I mean...
MAYDEE: *(Overlapping.)* Why don't you take...
RAISA: *(Overlapping.)* My hair finally grew back, thank God...
MAYDEE: *(Overlapping.)* You must need your breast...rest... *(Mortified at her mistake.)* Vennie, why don't you show Raisa where your room is.
RAISA: *(Overlapping.)* It's really good for me, takes the guessing out of conversation, don't you think?
VENNIE: *(Overlapping.)* We just got here. So why am I getting relegated to the room already? This is a party, isn't it? *(Starts dancing and snapping her fngers, loud.)* I told Raisa this was a good-time house, didn't I? P-A-R-T-Y. *(Sings to MaDear.)* "Happy birthday, you sho look good to me. I need your loving like a blind man needs to see..."
MAYDEE: *(Picking up their bags.)* I'll just take these things to your room.
VENNIE: Cool. I get the point. Come on Raisa. *(To Ma Dear and Lola.)* You all better start talking, may not see me for a while.
MAYDEE: What's that supposed to mean?
RAISA: We have surprises for all of you.
MAYDEE: Oh, how nice. Thank you.
VENNIE: If ya'll don't stop staring and start talking, you ain't getting nuttin' from me.
MAYDEE: Anything.
VENNIE: Nuttin'.
MAYDEE: Baby, that's a double negative.
VENNIE: I know that. I majored in English, remember?
MAYDEE: So you did. Too bad you didn't... *(They glare at each other.)*
RAISA: It was nice meeting you...all of you. *(Pulls Vennie away.)*
VENNIE: As usual, Mother, it's so good to be home. *(Vennie and Raisa exit.)*
MAYDEE: *(Watches Raisa and Vennie exit, then:)* I've never been so embarrassed. You two staring at her like she was a damn alien.
LOLA: *(Finding her voice again.)* That gal ain't got but one tit!
MAYDEE: So!
LOLA: So? She ain't wearing nothing. Did you see she only had one tit?
MADEAR: And dat one tittie bigga den two of mine put together!
LOLA: In all my days, I ain't never seen nothing like it.
MAYDEE: Aesthetically, it might not be that pleasing to the eye...
LOLA: Aesthetically?!!! And let's not mention the eyes.
MAYDEE: They're contact lenses. A lot of my students are wearing them.
LOLA: And you still teach 'em? You teaching 'em how to be black and all they

learning is how to glow in the dark. Lord Jesus, what is this world coming to?

MAYDEE: Mama...

LOLA: MayDee, I can deal with that. If Vennie wants to wear blue film on her eyes, that's her business, but that, what's her name...

MAYDEE: Raisa.

LOLA: Whatever her name is...

MADEAR: Raisin...

LOLA: Now that don't make no sense.

MAYDEE: Yes it does. You might find it offensive, but politically she has a point.

LOLA: MayDee, now don't talk silly. This ain't got nothing to do with no politics! Shoot! Politics is Jessie, the late Harold Washington, bless his soul...now they was politics. Politics ain't about being the walking wounded.

MAYDEE: It is politics. Her breast is gone, so why should society mandate she purchase something artificial so we're not offended by the...

LOLA: She don't have to purchase something artificial. I'll cut her a kitchen sponge and stick it up there. Put her on a brassiere and you wouldn't know the difference.

MADEAR: No sense wearin' a harness if you ain't got nuttin' to hitch...

LOLA: Mama, me and MayDee the ones discussing this...

MAYDEE: What if it was an arm or a leg...

LOLA: That's different. You can't help that...

MAYDEE: Mama, I know it's hard for you to put yourself in somebody else's place, but what if...what if it was you who had lost a breast?

LOLA: Look, I'm as Christian as the next person, but when something bad happen to you, you ain't supposed to walk around displaying it for the whole world to see. Lord knows I've seen my share of the knife, but you don't see me walking around naked showing everybody...Now how I look, *(Mocking gestures like she's shaking someone's hand.)* Nice to meet you. My name is Lola Bird *(Lifts up her skirt and parades around and repeats.)* Nice to meet you, my name is Lola Bird. And I'm in therapy.

MADEAR: Now dat ain't a pretty sight. Sit yo tail down gal.

MAYDEE: Mama, put your dress down. And please hush before she hears you.

LOLA: It's highway robbery. That's why white folks so crazy now...

MADEAR: Dey always been crazy...

LOLA: Going to therapy, telling some stranger all they business. AND PAY HIM GOOD MONEY! Pay him good money to tell 'em to introduce theirselves by taking they shirts off. Therapy my behind...

MAYDEE: There's nothing wrong with therapy.

LOLA: Shit. Not here. She might as well have been naked. I'm sorry, MayDee, but if Vennie gon' be that way she could have least gotten herself a nice black girl with two breasts, now I could deal with that. And offering to show us. Did you hear her offer to take her shirt off? She was gon' show us.

MADEAR: Yeah. I was waitin'.

LOLA: Now don't that beat all. Mama's done gon' freaky too. It must be this house. *(Starts searching the floor of the house.)* MayDee, something is seeping through the pores of this house. I declare it is. My horoscope told me to beware of cosmic forces today...

MADEAR: *(Loud.)* SISTER, SISTER, COME HERE.

LOLA: What is it now, Mama?

MADEAR: WHEW, FETCH ME A TOWEL. MY BREASTS DONE FILLED UP WID MILK! OOOHHH!! *(Cupping her breast, opens her dress, takes part of the shawl and stuffs it by her breast, presumably to catch the milk.)*

LOLA: Mama, don't start that. I done had enough shocks on this day.

MAYDEE: *(Overlapping.)* You smell something? Oh shit. I forgot the rolls in the oven. *(Races over to the oven, removes the rolls that are burned.)* Burned.

MADEAR: *(Still holding her breasts.)* Man, dis gone be some kinda birthday. Burnt food, Vennie done got cat eyes an a white gal wid one tittie and you an me gon' have us a baby. Milk flowin' just like de Mississippi. Whew...

(Lights.)

END OF FIRST ACT

Act II

> *At the lights, MaDear is in her wheelchair and, as usual, she's having a conversation with herself. Raisa enters whistling.*

RAISA: *(Entering.)* Where's everybody?

MADEAR: In the shed out back.

RAISA: I'm Raisa, again.

MADEAR: Pleased to make yo acquaintance, Miss Raisin.

RAISA: Would you like your surprise now? *(Opens the bag, pulls out oversized t-shirts.)* Let's see, now which one is yours? I did the screens myself. I'm an artist. At least I'm trying to be one. Yeah, here it is. This one's for you. *(She holds a shirt that reads, "Ninety and Still Kicking.")* Do you like it?

MADEAR: I bet you wish you'd died.

RAISA: *(Taken aback for a moment, pause.)* Yes. There were moments I thought I had.

MADEAR: Dey want me to b'lieve Man is dead.

RAISA: Your husband?

MADEAR: He lef me. He lef me here all by myself. Who gon' take care of dis baby? De only reason I stay wid him is dese chil'ren. He got other women in dat shed out back. I sees 'em…drankin' an doin' the devil's dance…he dance wid 'em…ain't never danced wid me, just jumps on top of me…Man, you hurt me…you hurt me.

RAISA: I'm sorry. I'm so sorry.

MADEAR: Dey hurt you too, dey did, didn't dey? You got you a bad wound?

RAISA: You wanna see? *(Kneels, slowly opens her shirt.)*

MADEAR: Oh. *(Taken aback by the scar, but then tenderly touches it.)*

RAISA: I never thought I'd miss anything so much. The scar's not very pretty.

MADEAR: Chile, you ain't got nuttin' to be shamed of. Some folks wear dey scars on de inside…you jus wearin' yours on de outside.

RAISA: I guess. *(Getting up and buttoning her shirt.)*

MADEAR: I'm tellin' you dat scar ain't nuttin' to be shamed of. It's yo history. Just like dis belly. *(Unsnaps her dress, shows Raisa her profuse stretch marks.)* All my babies lef dey mark… Go 'head touch 'em, dey ain't gon' bite you. *(Raisa touches her belly.)* You show me a woman dat ain't gotta scar somewhere an I'll show you a woman dat ain't lived nuttin' but a lie. It's dem inside scars, dem de ones you gotta watch out for. Dey'll tear you up tryin' to git loose. I know. But yours, it's breathin' good…yes, sir…breathin' real good. *(Closes her dress.)* You got chil'ren?

RAISA: A son.

MADEAR: And he yo pride an joy, ain't he?

RAISA: Un-hun. We wanted another child, a girl, but after I got sick…

MADEAR: Ain't never wanted no fast gal 'round up in my house. Ain't no house big enough for two women. You must not been married long…

RAISA: Almost six years. But we been together almost twenty. *(Seeing MaDear's quizzical look.)* He was my brother's best friend so we kind of did what was expected, spit on each other in grade school, kiss in high school and marry in college...

MADEAR: Today's my anniver'sry. Seventy years today. Blessed wid one son, he comin' for me today...Un-hun. You got somebody comin for you?

RAISA: No. My husband and I are separated.

MADEAR: Say what?

RAISA: He had a hard time...you know adjusting... *(Some gesture to her missing breast.)*

MADEAR: Ain't dat 'bout nuttin'? Dey took yo tittie an he too fool he gon' let de tittie take him 'long wid it. I wouldn't have another man if he sprouted wings and flew.

RAISA: It's really not his fault. It's bad enough trying to make ends meet, raise a child, he's in law school, and I was working two jobs just so we could make ends meet...and then I up and get sick...

MADEAR: De marriage vow say through sickness and in health.

RAISA: Yeah, it does, doesn't it? But sometimes you just want to be wanted...that kind of want that doesn't have anything to do with a vow. Kept buying me nightgowns...all different kinds, silk ones, lace ones, the granny kind, every time I turned around he was bringing home a new one...

MADEAR: Man ain't never bought nuttin' for me to wear...

RAISA: Well, you can bet Mark didn't buy the gowns for me...I never slept in a gown the whole time we were married...His favorite saying was: "honey, nothing's changed." But look at me. Don't I look like a changed woman? But I got Vennie, bless her heart...

MADEAR: Got cows to milk and my garden needs tendin' and my chickens need seein' after...I gots to git home...Man'll be comin in from de fields wantin' his dinner...and I ain't got nothin' cooked and my daughter, she done lef me...*(Very confused.)* I gits so cold...I don't wanna die here Miss Raisin...I can hear it comin'... Don't you hear it?

RAISA: Mrs. Dawkins...

MADEAR: *(Grabbing Raisa's hand.)* I cain't jus sit here and let it git me. I know you hears it, Miss Raisin...don't let it git you. You hear it?

RAISA: I hear it, Mrs. Dawkins. I hear it... Don't worry I'm not going to let it get me. I'm going to Europe, buy me some mean Italian shoes, red ones... I want to hear another language, don't even care if I understand it...I just want to hear it...sit in one of those little cafes all day philosophizing, smoking cigarettes, drinking coffee, eating croissants with cheese and butter, pure decadence! You know what I really want, it'll sound silly...I want to pretend I'm famous, you know a...a renowned artist...Think I could fool 'em? *(Pause.)* Found a new spot on my liver...they said it's Chemo time, but I said, no it's Raisa's time...I've always wanted to go to Europe...and Vennie says we're going...I can't tell her this but I'm not really counting on it...I'm just dreaming...

MADEAR: *(Suddenly.)* Will you take me home? I cleans good. I'll do wash an tend yo chil'ren, and I won't git in de way of yo business...you can count on

Viola…won't be no trouble…no trouble at all. I'm beggin' you, Miss Raisin, I just wanna see my home again.

RAISA: Why don't I help you put on your new shirt? Watch your head. *(She gently puts the shirt over MaDear's head, fixes it on her.)* There. Don't you look nice. Ninety and still kicking. You must stay true to your shirt, I say you gotta go out kicking. Come on, let me see how high you can kick…

MADEAR: Gal, I cain't kick. My legs are weighted down…

RAISA: I bet you can kick. *(She kneels down and starts lifting MaDear's feet and legs.)* See, you still have some kick left in you. Come on, aim for the old kisser here. Ooh, and the left jaw takes a dive…Ooh, and there goes the right…*(With Raisa's assistance MaDear starts kicking toward Raisa's face, both are clearly enjoying themselves.)*

(Vennie enters yawning from the hallway. Watches Raisa and MaDear for a minute, decides to join in.)

RAISA: *(Overlapping.)* You got me on the ropes. And she's down *(Raisa falls down, counts.)* 1-2-3…wait a minute…wait a minute…slowly but surely, she's getting up…up…she's up. *(Sits up and resumes the game.)* And the Senior Dawkins kicker strikes again…down for the count…

VENNIE: *(Joins them.)* If you could see how you two look.

MADEAR: *(Suddenly and viciously hits at Vennie.)* Git away from here, split-tail. We's playin' dis game. *(Vennie backs off obviously hurt. MaDear starts laughing, gestures for Raisa to kick her feet up, just then Lola and MayDee enter through the back door carrying chips and dip.)*

LOLA: What in the Sam Hell…Mama, put your legs down.

RAISA: I'm sorry, we were just playing.

LOLA: I leave the room for one minute and ya'll start using my Mama for entertainment.

MAYDEE: I can't remember the last time I saw MaDear laugh out loud.

LOLA: What you mean?!!!! Mama and me, we laugh every day while you at school, don't we Mama? You just keep me in stitches. *(False exaggerated laugh.)* Hee, Hee. I thought I was getting a hernia one day I laughed so hard…

MAYDEE: Vennie, is something wrong?

VENNIE: No. Why does something always have to be wrong?

MAYDEE: I asked you a simple question…

VENNIE: I was just standing here. You automatically assume…

LOLA: Pour me a drink, Vennie. A little CC and wet it with soda and a little lime slice, baby.

MAYDEE: The usual for me.

VENNIE: What about for MaDear?

LOLA: Nothing for her.

MADEAR: Pour me a taste outta dat brown jar. Dat's my medicine.

LOLA: Mama, now you know that ain't your medicine, that's liquor. ALCOHOL.

MADEAR: Don't tell me 'bout what I know.

MAYDEE: It's her birthday. A little taste wouldn't hurt.

LOLA: O.K., but don't look at me when she starts talking silly.

VENNIE: Raisa?

RAISA: Nothing for me. We forgot to give them their shirts. Do you like it, Mrs. Dawkins?

MAYDEE: It's very nice. Do you like it, MaDear?

MADEAR: I'm kickin'.

VENNIE: Raisa did the screens. I did the slogans. *(To MayDee.)* This one's for you.

MAYDEE: Thank you. *(Reading it.)* "Tenure by Popular Demand." That's catchy...

VENNIE: Put it on...

MAYDEE: Oh no, not till I hear something.

VENNIE: You'll get it. You never fail.

MAYDEE: *(Pointedly.)* I try not to.

LOLA: Where's mine?

VENNIE: Right here. *(Hands it to Lola.)*

(Lola reads it silently, folds it up and places it to the side.)

VENNIE: Don't you like it?

LOLA: Yes, baby. MaLola likes everything you do. It's very nice.

VENNIE: You didn't show anybody.

MAYDEE: Let's see it, Mama.

LOLA: Later.

RAISA: Maybe you would've like another color...

VENNIE: *(Picking up the shirt, showing everyone, reading.)* "The best damn Grandmother."

MAYDEE: *(Laughing.)* Now I know why she didn't want to show it.

VENNIE: I thought you'd love this.

LOLA: I said it was nice. I just don't know when I'll have occasion to wear it.

VENNIE: Tonight. These are our party t-shirts. MaDear, you gon' wear your shirt?

MADEAR: Couldn't beat it off me. A little more outta my jug dere baby.

LOLA: Mama, you don't need anything else to drink...

MAYDEE: Sure we'll put them on, won't we, Mama?

LOLA: Speak for yourself.

MAYDEE: *(Crossing to the phone.)* Well, I guess I'll just unplug this here telephone for the rest of the day...

LOLA: *(Grabbing the shirt.)* Just what I always wanted. I'm a tie mine up here on the side...

VENNIE: I have another surprise in the car.

MAYDEE: Oh?

VENNIE: It's for MaDear. *(Vennie exits, there's a long silence, much clearing of the throat as they all decide what to talk about.)*

LOLA: So...

RAISA: I'm really enjoying myself.

LOLA: Don't take much to amuse you, do it?

MAYDEE: Mama.

LOLA: So how long you known our Vennie?

RAISA: A few months. She's great. She's been a real friend. After I left my husband...
LOLA: You got a husband?
MAYDEE: I hope you like chicken...
RAISA: (Overlapping.) Yes...And a five-year-old son...
LOLA: So, your husband know you and Vennie friends?
MAYDEE: Mama...
RAISA: (Overlapping.) Yes and no...
MAYDEE: What else did you say you cooked?
RAISA: I mean he's met her...
LOLA: Oh. Same time you met her?
RAISA: Oh no. I met Vennie at a bar. See, I had never been to a woman's bar before so I thought what the hell...first time I left the house natural like...
MAYDEE: Without the prosthesis.
RAISA: Yeah. So I thought what better place to free myself. So I did. When I walked in everybody started staring and I started to get a little scared but I sat down anyway. Vennie was singing, (Sings.) "Everybody plays the fool, sometimes...no exception to the rule." And boy could I relate...
LOLA: I bet you could.
RAISA: So finally, when she was on break, all these people were around but she looked kinda, I don't know...kinda lonely, so finally I introduced myself. Right away, just by the way she looked at me, I knew I'd found a friend. She bought me a drink. I got so giddy... You ever been scared and excited all at once?...
LOLA: Yes, men do that to me.
RAISA: Well, Vennie did it for me that night. She tells the worst one tit jokes. We closed the place, her making up tit jokes. Then we started making fun of everybody else's tits...
LOLA: So you two just hang out in women's bars now making fun of people's titties?
RAISA: Oh no. We go to all kinds of bars, wherever Vennie is playing. She's been my saving grace, couldn't have gotten through these last few months without her.
VENNIE: (Enters.) Did I miss something?
RAISA: No, I was just boring them with how we met.
LOLA: Yeah, it was some story...
VENNIE: MaDear, I started these so you could have a little garden out back. I remember the first time you let me work in the garden. You remember? I was so scared that a snake was gon' get me...
MADEAR: You ain't never wanted to work in de garden. All you knew to do was turn up yo tail... And he was mine.
LOLA: Mama that's Vennie. You stop being ugly now.
VENNIE: Doesn't she know me?
LOLA: Of course she know you. She just putting on.
VENNIE: I got peppers and onions, tomato plants...and collard greens...And I thought we could plant them together.
MADEAR: Dey don't allow no garden here. Back home I gots me a big

garden...Everythang planted I planted. I planted dem wid dese here hands...Man, show 'em my garden...show 'em, Man...
LOLA: Mama, we got company now, no need for you to talk foolish...What your friend Raisa gon' think...you talking out your head like that...
RAISA: I understand...My grandmother went through the same thing...
LOLA: Well, we don't like to encourage her.
MAYDEE: I wish you would've consulted me first about this garden. It was a nice thought but...
VENNIE: *(Overlapping.)* What's there to consult? The yard is huge.
MAYDEE: And costly to keep up. Mama, you still going to do my hair?
LOLA: Yeah, get a towel. *(MayDee exits.)*
VENNIE: I wasn't intending on planting a farm.
MAYDEE: *(Off.)* That's not the point.
VENNIE: What's the point then?
LOLA: The point is a garden needs a lot of attention. It's a lot of work.
VENNIE: Grandma, I know that.
LOLA: What you call me?
VENNIE: MaLola.
LOLA: That's better. I don't know what's gotten into you. Grandma! The idea!
MAYDEE: Vennie, no one has time to take care of a garden...
VENNIE: MaDear doesn't ask for much. If she can't be in Mississippi, the least you all can do is try and create it for her here.
LOLA: Create Mississippi!
MAYDEE: *(Entering.)* I'm not sure I want Mississippi in Park Forest, Illinois...
LOLA: Well I'm sure. I ain't never wanted it. I didn't care too much for Mississippi when I was in Mississippi. I'm telling you the truth.
MADEAR: Dat's yo home, gal. I birthed you an weaned you...
LOLA: And don't a day go by when you ain't reminding me...
MAYDEE: *(Overlapping.)* We'll discuss this garden thing later. Until then, Raisa honey, why don't you do me a favor and set those things by the back door on top of the garbage can?
RAISA: Sure. *(Exits out back.)*
MAYDEE: By the way, Vennie, I got you a little something. *(Goes to the closet, retrieves the outfit with much flourish.)* Saks was having a big sale...
VENNIE: *(Looks at the outfit, Lola starts to look upwards, whistles.)* You got to be kidding. I'm not wearing this sh...
LOLA: Vennie, watch that mouth. *(To MayDee.)* I told you.
VENNIE: You could've at least taken the tags off.
LOLA: I thought you...
MAYDEE: I wasn't sure if it would fit. *(Raisa enters.)*
VENNIE: Mother, this ain't happening. Maybe you should wear it or get your money back.
LOLA: *(Noticing how hurt MayDee looks.)* Well, let's see. I think with the right kind of jewelry... *(Takes off her necklace, puts it up next to the outfit.)* Get some big earrings and a pretty silk scarf... then...
VENNIE: Have to accessorize it beyond recognition...

LOLA and VENNIE: Accessorize it to death. *(They both laugh.)*

MAYDEE:*(Covering the outfit.)* I'm glad I can be a source of humor for you two-

RAISA: I like it. I think it's classy.

VENNIE: Then you wear it. *(Raisa gives Vennie a pointed look.)* Okay, Mother, thank you. It's a nice outfit. I'll wear it to Church or if I'm invited to meet the President. Just kidding.

MAYDEE: I didn't mean it for every day wear. I thought we could go shopping and maybe get some shoes...

LOLA: If you want me to do your hair...

MAYDEE: Why don't you put it with your things.

VENNIE: Why don't I just hang it back in the closet for now?

MAYDEE: Oh. Okay. By the way, did you get that other package I sent you a few weeks back?

VENNIE: Which one? You send me one every other week.

MAYDEE: Would it be too much to ask for you to call or send a note...

VENNIE: You never give me a chance. You send me something and you call me the same day you mail it to ask me if I received it. *(MayDee sits and Lola starts oiling and scratching her scalp.)*

MAYDEE: I can't remember. Did I send you some catalogs, some packets on financial aid?

VENNIE: Did you send me something on financial aid? Mother, you been sending me...

LOLA: Why you still sending her stuff about school? She finished. And I want you to know, young lady, I'm still mad that I didn't get to go to no graduation. Bought me a new dress and everything. Next thing I know your Mama telling me you decided not to go through the ceremony...now that hurt me...

MAYDEE: Don't you think she would be a great teacher Mama? *(Raisa and Vennie start decorating the room with party flavors.)*

VENNIE: I told you I don't want to teach.

MADEAR: *(Re-enacting an imaginary classroom.)* Good mornin' Mrs. Dawkins. Mornin' chil'ren. Dis is our lesson for today...

MAYDEE: *(Overlapping, trying to ignore MaDear.)* You don't have to teach. Just have it, something to fall back on.

VENNIE: If I have something to fall back on, then I'll never learn to stand up.

MAYDEE: See? See what I mean? That was quite a profound statement, dear. And that's what I'm saying, you have a good mind, a splendid mind, doesn't she, Mama?

LOLA: I don't get in between you all's business.

VENNIE: Why do we get into this every time I come home?*(Lola starts oiling MayDee's scalp.)*

MAYDEE: *(Sarcastic.)* Every time? What? Once a year, you manage to make an appearance? And of course it's usually because you want something. Of course this time you may surprise me...

VENNIE: Look Mama, I'm going to sing. That's what I want to do. That's what I'm going to do. By hook or by crook...

LOLA: Then sing in the shower. Sing in church. You could come go with me on

Sunday. Plenty opportunities to sing, but you gotta eat, gotta have a place to live...

MADEAR: I sing for de Lord. *(Starts singing.)* "I'm on de battle field for my Lord, yes I'm on de battlefield..."

LOLA: Mama, please. *(Crosses to MaDear, opens the bible and firmly puts it in her lap.)* We can sing later. Here.

MAYDEE: If you're so bent on this music career, then take some classes. Train yourself properly. Perhaps you could move back home, stay here until you get on your feet. The University has a fine program...I'm sure we can stay out of each other's way...

RAISA: Mrs. Lakeland, have you heard Vennie sing?

LOLA: Of course...

MAYDEE: Yes, I've seen her, several times.

VENNIE: But not in a while.

RAISA: The crowds love Vennie.

LOLA: Crowds don't last and they'll make sure you don't either.

RAISA: But she's so good. She dances...

LOLA: Well now she gets that from me 'cause her mother got two left feet that wouldn't know right if she pointed them there. But now ain't nobody can beat her on that piano. MayDee used to could make that piano sing.

MAYDEE: A long time ago.

LOLA: Paid good money for her to take them lessons. Good money. Took extra jobs when I could so she could keep going with them lessons.

MAYDEE: We were talking about Vennie...

LOLA: Scrape and scratch...scrimping so she could keep up with her lessons and the more she played white, the harder I had to work...

MAYDEE: Music is music. It has no color.

LOLA: Yes it does...green! Them teachers said you were gifted. Even had you convinced black music was trash, but I went along, wanted you to make it, kept the house quiet so she could practice.

MAYDEE: I appreciate that, Mother...

LOLA: Did without so she could keep up with them lessons. One year I didn't even have boots, snow up to my neck. As long as she was happy...

MAYDEE: I learned early how fickle the entertainment business could be... If I had been white, maybe things would have been different.

VENNIE: Nowadays you don't have to be white to make it.

LOLA: Says who? Now don't talk stupid, Miss College graduate. White people still control everything, no offense Raisa. But just 'cause they control everything don't mean you can't negotiate you a piece of that pie. Just got to have a little gumption, a little spine, something your mama didn't seem to have...

MAYDEE: Vennie, it's not that I mind you singing...

VENNIE: Thanks. I'm glad you don't mind me living my own life.

LOLA: *(Brushing MayDee's hair a little too hard.)* One audition, one freakin' audition, spent my last dime on you a new outfit and she come home crying, crying her eyes out... I thought somebody had beat you silly...

MAYDEE: I just don't want to see you hurt...

LOLA: Life is full of hurts. You dust yourself off and get on back out there. You just don't lay down and be a welcome mat for the next foot that's ready to go up your ass...

MAYDEE: Sometimes it's not that easy, Mama.

LOLA: Sure it ain't, 'specially if gon' keep telling yourself how hard everything is. Certainly was a helluva lot easier for you than it was for me.

MAYDEE: *(Old seething anger and bitter pain.)* Being the poor little nigger with no grace in her back trying to play classical was not easy, Mama. I got so tired of them asking me if I knew how to play something black. *(European accent.)* "You people have so much rhythm, why don't you play what you know?" I played what I knew...Debussy, Bach, the Liszt Sonata, the Chopin Barcarole. Gifted alright but I was still a nigger playing in the wrong league. *(To Vennie.)* And I will not let that happen to you. I will not see you hurt...

VENNIE: You can't direct my life...

LOLA: Vennie, your mother is not gon' be here forever. And, Lord knows, my days are numbered. We only trying to help. We wouldn't be so bothered if we didn't love you...

VENNIE: Then stop loving me so much. Just chill.

LOLA: What? Chill? *(Threatens her with the hairbrush.)* I'll chill right on your behind. You ain't too old to hit the floor.

MADEAR: Spare de rod, spoil de child.

MAYDEE: And I can't keep sending you envelopes. You know what I'm talking about, Vennie Lakeland...

VENNIE: I never asked.

MAYDEE: Nor refused.

LOLA: What kind of shit is chill? Never heard of no damn chill...

MAYDEE: Mama, please.

VENNIE: You all are embarrassing me.

MAYDEE: Well, I don't mean to...

LOLA: I'm a do more than embarrass you. Your Mama's telling you the truth. She works hard for her money.

MADEAR: And de truth shall set you free...

LOLA: That's right, Mama.

MAYDEE: I just want the best for you, baby.

LOLA: We both want the best for you...

MAYDEE: Mama, would you please let me talk...

LOLA: Then talk. I ain't stopped you from talking. I barely opened my mouth since Vennie walked through that door. You the one that's going on and on about the past...

MAYDEE: As I was saying. I don't want to see you playing one night stands the rest of your life...

LOLA: In women's bars at that...

MAYDEE: Making fifty here and twenty-five there...

VENNIE: I make more than that...

LOLA: Then look like you'd buy something decent to put on your behind.

MAYDEE: But you can do better...

VENNIE: What if I don't want to do better?

LOLA: You oughtta wanna do better by them clothes you wear. A college graduate and still living poor as a church mouse.

MAYDEE: It's not the clothes that I object to. I know the styles change...

LOLA: A raggedy woman will never attract a man...

VENNIE: Who says I want to attract a man?

MAYDEE: Can we stay on the subject?

LOLA: See! What I tell you? You 'member that Johnson gal?

MAYDEE: Mama, please.

VENNIE: What I'd like is for you to let me live my life as I see fit. Poor, raggedy, whatever.

LOLA: And you want to live it without a man, don't you. Don't you?

MAYDEE: She doesn't need a man...what I'm concerned about...

LOLA: See, and you wonder why she's like she is.

VENNIE: Like what? And what is all this talk about men? Nobody in this room is with a man.

LOLA: Speak for yourself...

MADEAR: (Overlapping.) I got me a man.

VENNIE: (Overlapping.) Mama hasn't had a man since before I was born.

MAYDEE: Vennie! I don't appreciate you discussing my business...

VENNIE: But it's okay to discuss mine.

LOLA: Now she gotta point there, MayDee...

MAYDEE: Well, let's just discuss the gigolo...

LOLA: Hey now, anybody care for some dip?

VENNIE: If I meet a man I like, then cool. We'll deal. It's not complicated. If I don't it ain't gon' make me crazy.

MAYDEE: (Correcting.) Going to...

VENNIE: What?

MAYDEE: Going to make me crazy, not gon' make...

VENNIE: See, this is why I don't come home.

LOLA: But you call here everyday and collect...

MAYDEE: I really would like us to have a good day, after all it's MaDear's birthday... We can discuss this later...

VENNIE: You started it.

MAYDEE: Started what? What did I start this time?

VENNIE: What you start every time I come home Mother... Pick, pick, pick. My clothes ain't right, my hair ain't right, my grammar ain't right...sum it up, I ain't right...

LOLA: Whine...whine...whine...grow up, Vennie.

MAYDEE: That's not true.

VENNIE: (Sarcastically, but delivered calmly with a smile.) Oh, yeah it is. See, Raisa, I'm something to be bought for, organized and then displayed so others can marvel at how wonderful MayDee Lakeland is...how she overcame such obstacles to get her Ph.D, raise me single handedly, made sure I participated in every activity, karate, dance, art, piano...

RAISA: Vennie, I don't think...

VENNIE: Do we have an itinerary this weekend, Mother? Come now, didn't the secretary outline what activities Mother dear is going to do with daughter dear this weekend? Certainly you didn't leave our time together to chance. 'Cause then maybe you would have to enjoy me. And that would be too much like right, wouldn't it Mother? S'pecially given that you don't even like me.

MAYDEE: (Pause, embarrassed to have this conversation in front of Raisa, MayDee laughs.) You're just like your grandmother, such a sense of humor. I love you Vennie, don't you know that? Whatever you do.

VENNIE: What I know is being your daughter hurts...bad, or should I say badly -

MAYDEE: You don't mean that. (Exits with hair stuff.)

LOLA: Now look what you done. You done gone and hurt your Mama's feelings. I don't know what's wrong with this generation. They wanna blame they mothers for every damn thing...

VENNIE: I'm sorry.

MAYDEE: (Enters.) I'm not hurt...

VENNIE: I wasn't blaming you...

MAYDEE: Really, I'm not hurt. If that's how you feel...

LOLA: (Crosses to MaDear, maybe pats her or fixes her shawl.) Look like every week Oprah got some crazy on her program that's killed somebody or raped somebody or can't keep a job or got some other kind of problem and who they say is the cause? They mother! It's a damn shame that the woman responsible for bringing you into this world got to hear you rise up one day and blame her for every ill that comes your way...bunch of ungrateful S-O-B's ...makes the hair on the back of my ass rise...

MAYDEE: Mama, please!

LOLA: Don't Mama me. It gets on my last nerve. The day you decided to use psychology on that child instead of a good ass whippin' was her day of ruin...

MAYDEE: All I was doing was trying to get her to think about her future...

VENNIE: I'm sorry. I'm sorry. I'm sorry. I'm sorry. How many more sorry's is it going to take?

RAISA: (Laughs loudly, everyone turns around and looks at her.) This is just like being home. This could be my mother's living room.

LOLA: Oh, your people have money, too?

MAYDEE: Mama...

RAISA: No, I meant how my mother rakes me over the coals, she does the same thing, except she grabs her chest and has heart palpitations. (Acting out her mother with heavy accent.) "You wanna kill me...why don't you just put a knife to my chest? Here, here's the bread knife, the same one I used to cut up your little sandwiches with. Here take it and take my heart right along with it. For this we survived the depression, spent our life savings to send you to college, for you to paint pictures of fruit baskets and naked men...Miss Artist. Feh!" (Collapses laughing.)

MAYDEE: (Crossing to Lola, in a show of unity, puts her arm around Lola's shoulder.) Well, we're a little different. We've always supported Vennie and her dreams. I worked three jobs...sometimes it was four, wasn't it Mama?

LOLA: Sometimes I think you was working five jobs.

MAYDEE: I wanted to make sure Vennie always had the best.

LOLA: And I took care of my little Pick-Me-Up when her mother was too busy working to be a real mother to her...Ain't that right, Baby? Sometimes I had to be both mother and father...

MAYDEE: And I never, ever like the idea of using guilt to control my daughter...

LOLA: No. No, we ain't what you would call a guilt family...

VENNIE: *(Laughs.)* You all are real comedians. You two don't even listen to each other...

LOLA: I heard every word your mother said and I very much agree.

MAYDEE: I simply said.

VENNIE: That's why I don't think I want children. It does a job on your vision.

RAISA: I know it did a job on mine. I planned to be real open, everything my mother was, I planned to be the opposite. But the first time my son had an erection I panicked. I started screaming. *(Screaming.)* "Stop that, stop that right now. Don't you touch your penis and testicles." Scared the poor lamb half to death, he 'bout fell back in the tub. Well, at least I used the proper words...penis and testicles... *(No one knows how to follow up.)*

LOLA: *(Finally.)* Umph! How old you say your son was?

RAISA: Five.

LOLA: And his pee pee getting hard?

(The phone rings, pandemonium.)

VENNIE: I'll get it.

LOLA: *(Overlapping.)* No, I'll get it.

MAYDEE: *(Overlapping.)* No, I'll get it. I bet it's the call. I'll get it.

MADEAR: *(Overlapping, repeats.)* It's the man... It's de man callin' for me... It's de man...

LOLA: *(Overlapping, pulling MayDee back.)* If it's for me, tell him...tell him...

MAYDEE: Would you let go of me? *(Picks up the phone.)* Hello. Oh, yes, Dean Claudet...

MADEAR: *(Wailing.)* I gots to git home.

LOLA: Mama, this is your home.

MADEAR: Dis ain't my home. *(Continues to cry loud and hit at them the more they try to console her.)* Dis ain't my home.

LOLA: Stop that crying now. This is your home, Mama. Some people don't even have a place to lay their head, ain't got a pot to piss in and here you are living nice, like a queen...got your own room, your own TV and you still complaining, we could have you in a home somewhere...

RAISA: *(Overlapping.)* Should I get her some water?

LOLA: No. Don't pay her no mind. She does this all the time. Just trying to get some attention...she's like a child...

MADEAR: *(Louder.)* Dis ain't my home. *(Screaming.)* Dis ain't my home. *(MaDear keeps screaming and wailing.)* Dis ain't my home. Man, dis ain't my home...Dis ain't my home...

LOLA: Mama, stop that screaming. Stop showing out now. I told you she didn't need anything to drink.

VENNIE: *(Overlapping, stroking.)* MaDear, sssh, it's okay. It's okay... Sssh, Mother's on the phone.

LOLA: *(Overlapping.)* Did you hear me, Mama? Stop that screaming. Stop it right now. I'm a spank you...I'll spank your little legs if you don't stop that noise...

MAYDEE: *(Overlapping, hand over the phone.)* MADEAR, SHUT UP RIGHT NOW!

VENNIE: *(Yells at MayDee.)* DON'T TELL HER TO SHUT UP.

LOLA: Go 'head and take your call. *(Puts her hand over MaDear's mouth.)* I got it covered... *(MayDee goes back to her call.)*

VENNIE: Why do you all treat her like this? You have her sitting around here like some museum piece...

LOLA: Now you wait a minute, young lady. You wait just a minute! You bring your hippie looking behind home once a year...Ain't never had to wash her behind... *(MaDear bites Lola's hand.)* Ouch! Shit. You bit me...Mama, you bit me...

MADEAR: MISS RAISIN, COME ON. LET'S GO...WE GOTTA MAKE A BREAK FOR IT...

RAISA: Miss Dawkins, I...

LOLA: *(Overlapping.)* Mama, you ain't going nowhere. And you bit me. I should take those teeth out your mouth right now. You can sit there and gum yourself silly for the rest of the day...Father, deliver me. *(Raises her arms to the ceiling.)* Just give me a sign... any sign...

VENNIE: I oughtta take her back with me...

LOLA: *(Up to the ceiling.)* That's close, but not quite. *(MayDee, overlapping, hangs up the phone, walks slowly toward MaDear, everybody freezes, no one can read her intentions.)*

LOLA: *(Using her body to shield MaDear.)* Now, MayDee, Mama can't help herself...she's the only Mama I got...One door closes baby, another one'll open... I declare it will...

VENNIE: *(Using her body to shield Lola.)* Mother, maybe next year.

MAYDEE: *(Crosses to MaDear, gives her a big kiss.)* You know I love you, old woman. Let's go plant that garden right now. Everybody, I have arrived! *(Picks up the t-shirt, hugs it happily to her chest, starts dancing around, everyone hugs and is equally excited.)* I have arrived...

VENNIE: Yeah...Me too, Mother. Raisa and I are going to Europe. Just came home to say goodbye and maybe get the rest of my money... Okay? *(MayDee, Lola and MaDear stare at Vennie as the lights go down. Lights.)*

Scene 4

Music is loud. At the lights, Vennie and Raisa are teaching Lola a new dance, a dance in the Hammer-time vein. Lola is not quite getting it, but she thinks she is. She is wearing her new shirt over her clothes.

VENNIE: You have to use your arms more. Like this. *(Demonstrates.)*
LOLA: What you think I'm doing, shit. S'cuse me Raisa. *(She tries again.).*
RAISA and VENNIE: *(Chanting.)* You got it... Go head... Go head...
MAYDEE: *(Overlapping, off.)* Can you turn that down? Can you turn that down? *(Enters, is fuming, stares at them for a moment, then clicks off the music.)*
LOLA: Hey.
MAYDEE: Didn't you hear me say it was too loud?
VENNIE: We didn't hear you.
MAYDEE: I guess not.
LOLA: Me and these girls were just having a little fun. I like this Raisa. She ain't no shortstop on this dancing.
RAISA: I used to not dance at all. Vennie taught me.
LOLA: Well you's a credit to your race now. Come on let's show MayDee. MayDee put the record back on.
MAYDEE: I will not.
LOLA: Come on, just for a minute. It's so cute...
VENNIE: Forget it, MaLola. We were having too much fun. A misdemeanor in this house.
MAYDEE: That's it. Raisa, if you'll excuse us.
RAISA: Sure. *(She exits.)*
LOLA: Let me get on back to this cake. I was counting them candles...Was on forty, I think... I don't know if all ninety gon' fit...*(Starts counting candles for the cake. Vennie starts to exit.)*
MAYDEE: Not so fast.
VENNIE: Almost made it.
LOLA: I'm so glad about you getting that call. Who would've ever thought I'd raise a college professor...Pick-Me-Up, Baby, you wanna help me count?
MAYDEE: I'm very upset.
LOLA: MayDee, maybe you should take one of your pills and have a little nap. We'll call you when we get everything ready...
MAYDEE: Mama, did you hear me? I said I'm...
LOLA: Shit, MayDee , you're always upset... All we was doing was having a little fun. I'm so glad my baby's home. My Pick-Me-Up...
MAYDEE: She is not your Pick-Me-Up. She happens to be my daughter... mine... And I have not had one moment alone with her since...
LOLA: Well, shit...let me outta here. You only got to tell me once when I'm not wanted. I'll go sit with the crazy one...ya'll call us when we allowed back in the front of the house. *(She exits. Silence for a moment.)*
VENNIE: So. I thought you said all you had to say earlier. You're not giving me the money. You don't care if I go across the street, let alone to Europe. I can sink or swim because it's not your boat...did I leave anything out?...
MAYDEE: Stop it.
VENNIE: Stop what?
MAYDEE: You're right. I don't like you.
VENNIE: And? What am I supposed to do, cry? Tell me something I don't

already know...

MAYDEE: You are selfish, arrogant and spoiled rotten...And I don't like it. I don't like that I had anything to do with creating what you are at this moment... If I could do it over again I probably wouldn't have bothered...

VENNIE: I wish you hadn't. Would've saved us both some trouble. I could've done nicely without being reminded every day how much a bother I was. I mean, you kept me busy, I'll give you that...Keep the child busy...guaranteed to help you forget she exists...

MAYDEE: Oh, so we're going to play my favorite game, poor deprived Vennie. It must be hard having such a meanie for a mother. A mother who tried to expose you to...

VENNIE: Yeah, you exposed me, alright. I had a great time being carted off or should I say dropped off...Vennie and her activities...You ever remember going to any of 'em with me? You ever want to hear about 'em when I got home? Even more basic, were you ever home?

MAYDEE: I had to work. You had to eat...

VENNIE: Yeah, by myself. If it hadn't been for MaLola, I wouldn't had nothing...

MAYDEE: *(Automatically corrects.)* Anything.

VENNIE: Sorry. Anything. This lecture over?

MAYDEE: I was home when I could be...And who made sure you had a home?

VENNIE: You, Mother.

MAYDEE: I didn't want to be gone all the time Vennie, but I didn't have a choice...

VENNIE: Yeah, right... Can I go now?

MAYDEE: All this was for you...You kept me working, kept me wanting to do more...I wanted you to be proud of me...

VENNIE: I am. I just don't know you.

MAYDEE: You can have the money.

VENNIE: I don't want it.

MAYDEE: I was just holding on to it...maybe you would finish your education. I been saving that money since you were five, Vennie... I wasn't saving it for you to throw away...

VENNIE: My career is throw away?

MAYDEE: I didn't say that. But going all the way to Europe on a chance is... is ...stupid! I give you the money and what's going to happen...you'll throw it all away on this...this pipe dream...

VENNIE: I said I didn't want the money...

MAYDEE: *(On a roll.)* You know how many singers there are? Every black girl in the world wants to be a singer. Hundreds. How many going to make it? Maybe one. Two at the most. And believe me, sweetheart, you ain't that special to be one of 'em. You better prepare yourself for something besides singing.... I'm just not going to do it, Vennie. That money was for your future. I saved thirty thousand dollars for your damn future. I wore the same coat for six years, stockings with holes in 'em, didn't know what it was to own more than one pair of shoes...got off one job and ran to the next...

VENNIE: *(Overlapping.)* And ran to the next. You act like you did it all…My father…

MAYDEE: Father! You really do live in a dream world, don't you? Your father bought you boots one year, a Halloween costume the next, and a tricycle, a grand total of what, fifty dollars…Your father! Only thing he was ever good at was disappearing.

VENNIE: Disappearing! You drove him away, like you drive everybody away.

MAYDEE: Yeah, so what's your excuse? *(Pause.)* Look, I don't have anything against your father, Vennie. We were both young. He did me a favor, got me out of the house…

VENNIE: Yeah. Yeah. I've heard this before…

MAYDEE: I never wanted you to make the same mistake…

VENNIE: Oh you made sure of that. No little crumb-snatchers 'round here.

MAYDEE: *(Pause.)* You know…I never wanted to be a mother but when I found out I was pregnant…I had this inkling, maybe you'd be a girl…and that gave me joy…If I had to have a child, I prayed, please make it a daughter…I knew…

VENNIE: Knew what, mother?

MAYDEE: I knew I'd love you…I thought I'd finally have something special…I knew how much a daughter could love her mother. Sure I made mistakes, Vennie, but I kept working, hoping that if I just worked hard enough…one day you'd forgive me…and grab a hold to that future that I never had…a future I worked like a dog to give you…No, I didn't want you to be a mother at sixteen, saddled to some man…struggling, hating yourself, hating me because I didn't protect you… I wanted…

VENNIE: I…I…I…Always I. What you want. Always for you, isn't it?

MAYDEE: You damn straight. I'm your mother. I'm entitled. Why do you think any parent puts up with the shit you children dish out? Because we like it?!! No, it's because one day we're hoping that you'll wake up and stop treating us like jackasses, one day, one glorious day you'll prove to us that every sacrifice we made was worth it. If you don't want to do it for yourself, then yes, dammit, do it for me.

VENNIE: I can finish school later…

MAYDEE: Bullshit, Vennie. Six years and three schools later, you still haven't finished. You don't like the teachers…you don't like the school…you don't like their politics…so you just up and quit. *(Lola has entered, unbeknownst to Vennie and MayDee.)* One semester left and you quit. Again. Just like you do every job. On some damn principle. What do you have to to show for my twenty-five thousand two hundred and thirty something dollars?…Nothing. No paper, no graduation…no skills, nothing. If you going to Europe, baby, you going on a wing and a prayer because you aren't getting a dime from me. You got some kind of gall even asking…come in here with some cheap ass t-shirts and some half dead weeds and what was Raisa for, your poster child?…

VENNIE: *(Deeply wounded.)* You just have to attack anything that's special to me, don't you? That poster child happens to be my best friend. Actually she's my only friend. As you say, I'm not very likeable, but for some reason she likes me, for me.

MAYDEE: Well good. Maybe her liking will transport the both of you wherever you plan to go.

LOLA: MAYDEE!

VENNIE: I'm out of here... *(Vennie starts to walk away.)*

LOLA: *(To Vennie.)* Don't you move a step. You woman enough to dish it out, you better stand there and be woman enough to take it in. What I heard true? You lied to me, Vennie? You never graduated?

VENNIE: No.

LOLA: *(Very hurt.)* That was some of my money in that thirty-thousand. I sacrificed...

VENNIE: I tried to tell you...

LOLA: You didn't try that hard. MaLola didn't wanna see this day... I don't care if you wanna sing or sell pussy, but you was supposed to get that piece of paper first. I told everybody you graduated...that I had me two graduates...And you lied to me...you was this family's hope...and you lied to me, Vennie...ain't nothing left for me now but Jesus...

VENNIE: I'm sorry, MaLola.

MAYDEE: You're sorry?!! You tell her, you sorry? What about me? Shit. I'm your mother. Most of that money was mine. She put in a thousand, maybe two, but the other twenty-seven was mine, my sweat, my sacrifice. Mine! And you have the nerve to turn around and tell *her*, you sorry...

LOLA: MayDee, calm down...

MAYDEE: No, Mama. Don't tell me to calm down. And you got your nerve sitting there like you so disappointed. *(Sarcastically.)* Your sacrifice. Your two graduates. You may have made me but you didn't make this graduate. Where were you when I was trying to go to school? Huh? Where was your sacrifice then? Both of you make me sick.

LOLA: You wait just a minute, heifer. I helped you when I could... Damn near raised this child...

MAYDEE: Yeah, anything to make up for not raising your own. Too busy letting your men have fun with her. *(Lola slaps MayDee. MayDee raises her hand to slap her back.)*

LOLA: Go 'head. I dare you.

VENNIE: *(Getting in the middle of them, crying.)* Stop. Stop. Please stop. Please. *(To MayDee.)* Oh Mama...I didn't know... *(Reaches to hug MayDee who immediately turns and moves away.)*.

LOLA: *(Crossing to the cake, dismissively.)* Wasn't nothing to know. *(Starts counting the candles. There is a moment of silence as each wrestles with the pain of it all.)*

VENNIE: *(More to herself than anyone in particular.)* I'm sorry...Maybe I shouldn't've come home...No matter what I do I always seem to screw things up...(Somewhat frantically starts straightening the room.)* We're supposed to be having a party...we got the cake going...what else do we need?...
Mama...MaLola... *(No response.)* Please... *(Raisa wheels MaDear in. Raisa has decorated MaDear's hair with flowers.)*

RAISA: Did we hear somebody mention a party...Doesn't the birthday girl look beautiful?

VENNIE: *(Grateful for the diversion.)* Yes. Yes. MaDear, you look beautiful. *(Kisses her.)* I love you. We all love you. Don't we? *(No response.)* We've had such good news today. Mother getting tenure. I told you all the way here that she was going to get it, didn't I Raisa? And look at this cake MaLola got for you...

RAISA: *(In collusion, working with Vennie to dissipate the tension.)* Wow. *(Eyeing the cake.)* Look at this. Quite a few candles here, Mrs. Dawkins. *(To Lola.)* Can I help?

MAYDEE: *(Not looking at Lola, softly.)* Did you ever cry over me, Mama?

LOLA: Leave me be, MayDee.

MAYDEE: I always wondered, when I started peeing in the bed again, didn't you even get just a little suspicious...

LOLA: *(A little loud.)* Forty-one, forty-two, forty-three...forty-four...

MAYDEE: *(Overlapping.)* I mean, how many thirteen-year-olds start wetting the bed again. Huh?

VENNIE: Mother, I don't think...

MAYDEE: Stay out of this, Vennie...

LOLA: *(Louder.)* Forty-five, forty-six...

MAYDEE: How many sleep with knives? Huh, Mama? Answer me that.

LOLA: Don't do this, MayDee. I didn't know...

MAYDEE: Because keeping that man was more important...

MADEAR: *(Very agitated.)* My anniversary. Man was mine...

LOLA: Don't start that, Mama...please... Vennie, take her in the back...

MADEAR: *(To Vennie.)* Git away from me, gal. You thought you had him. We was fine till you came along, me, brother and man...I fixed you. I got dem straps an I cut 'em up... *(Starts tearing at her clothes.)*

VENNIE: What's MaDear talking about?

LOLA: MayDee, I didn't know. Baby, really, I didn't. He was just being a father, you always needed more attention...I never thought...

MAYDEE: Why didn't you? Why didn't you think?

LOLA: *(Pitiful.)* If you ever cared anything about me, MayDee, you'd stop this right now...

MAYDEE: He hurt me, Mama...He hurt me...

LOLA: Baby, I don't know what I did to you today, but...

MAYDEE: Why can't you just say it? It wasn't my fault. It wasn't my fault...

LOLA: You done bent me, don't knock me down, MayDee, not in front of my baby...Pick-Me-Up...

MAYDEE: She's not your baby!

VENNIE: *(Comforts Lola.)* MaLola...it's okay...

LOLA: *(Pleading to Vennie.)* I didn't know, Pick-Me-Up...I put him out...I didn't know...your Mama was all I had...I didn't know...She was *my* baby...I love her...MaLola loves you...I didn't know...

MAYDEE: Oh stop it. Those tears are about forty years too late.

VENNIE: *(To MayDee.)* Why do you have to punish everybody?

MAYDEE: Why don't you ask your grandmother that?

VENNIE: Mother, she can't undo it...

MADEAR: *(Overlapping.)* Cut it to pieces...ridin' on his hip...Tore it up...Yo place was in de house wid me, not wrapped 'round him. I got dem straps and I cut 'em up, ridin' on his hip. He wasn't for you. He was for me. I married him, he wasn't yo's...

LOLA: SHUT UP, MAMA!

MAYDEE: *(Overlapping.)* If you wouldn't holler at her... *(Soothing.)* MaDear, everything's okay...everything's fine...

MADEAR: I sees you, split-tail...you in dat shed out back wid my husband...

LOLA: He was teaching me to dance, that's all Mama. He was teaching me to laugh. You made it so we had to sneak. You wouldn't let me dance, you wouldn't let me laugh, you wouldn't let me do a damn thing except work and hide out somewhere. He wasn't just yours, he was my Daddy and I loved him...

MAYDEE: Stop hollering at her.

LOLA: *(Overlapping, totally losing what little control she has left, the result is a sobbing that is literally choking the words out of her.)* And he loved me. He knew you didn't... He made those straps, dammit, so he could carry me 'cause you never carried me nowhere. I was a child, Mama...you understand? A child. Why couldn't you just love me a little?

MADEAR: Split-tail, I sees you...

LOLA: My name is not split-tail. It's not Sister. It's Lola. Lola, Mama.

MADEAR: *(Pitiful.)* Man, man, you love me?

LOLA: Mama, please...He's gone. Let him rest in peace...

MAYDEE: MaDear, you want your presents? Let's open some presents, that'll make you feel better.

VENNIE: *(Retrieving the picture.)* Yeah. How 'bout this big one? MaLola?

MADEAR: *(Suddenly.)* Catch dis baby. Sister, come over here and catch dis baby. Help me.

LOLA: You ain't having no more babies, Mama. You didn't want the ones you had...Why don't you tell 'em that, you gon' tell 'em something. Tell 'em 'bout all the ones you got rid of... *(To MayDee.)* You think I was no count as a mother...well, this chick here got me beat hands down...

MAYDEE: You're so hateful. MaDear would never do that.

LOLA: Grow up, MayDee. You take the hand you deal. If you gon' find any happiness in this life, don't tally up your mistakes till you on your way outta here. So don't tell me what she won't do. Today I didn't think you'd talk to your child like you did, and I sure didn't think you'd ever raise your hand to me. So don't tell me 'bout what somebody will or won't do. 'Cause they'll surprise you every time.

VENNIE: *(Crosses to Lola, hands her the picture.)* This for MaDear, isn't it? *(The request is not without some pleading.)* Can you give it to her now? *(Pause.)* Please, MaLola...Please...For me?

LOLA: *(Looks at Vennie for a long moment, the years of special communication between them rules out, finally Lola takes the picture.)* Mama, see this present, it's for you. It's from me... and A.H. *(MaDear looks up at the mention of A.H.)* We both thought you'd like it.

MAYDEE: But Uncle didn't...

LOLA: *(Pointedly, to MayDee.)* Oh, didn't I tell you? I should have said this

present was brother A.H.'s idea. Here let's take the paper off...
RAISA: Wow, who is it?
MAYDEE: I've never seen this before.
LOLA: (Overlapping, proudly.) That's me when I was a baby and that's Mama and her mother. See Mama?
MADEAR: (Cowers, grabs a hold of Lola.) Don't let her git me. I got to hide under de porch. I got to hide...help me, Sister...
LOLA: Mama, it's just a picture.
MADEAR: I ugly as sin...ugliest in her litter (Her mother's voice.) "Viola, come here right now. Bring yo black ugly behind here." I so black...I so ugly and nappy headed. I so's scared of her...Help me...Don't let her git me...
LOLA: (Trying to comfort her.) I ain't gonna let her get you, Mama.
MADEAR: (Crying.) Help me. I ain't right. Help me, Sister. I ain't right.
LOLA: I ain't gon' let nobody get you. See, she got a smile on her face. (MaDear looks timidly.) You see? (MaDear timidly touches the picture for a quick second.)
MADEAR: Momo...
LOLA: Yes, she loves you. Just like I do...Come on, let Lola clean you up, get you ready for your party. (Lola and MaDear exit with MaDear still repeating.)
MADEAR: (Mumbling as she exits.) I ain't right, help me...got to hide... I got to hide...
(An awkward silence. MayDee has turned away from Vennie and Raisa. Vennie looks at her mother, gets ready to exit, but Raisa stops her, almost shoves her in MayDee's direction.)
VENNIE: Mother... (No response from MayDee. Vennie is ready to give up, turns to Raisa; Raisa gestures for her to try again. But before Vennie can say anything, MayDee addresses Raisa.)
MAYDEE: (With her usual formality.) Raisa, I'm truly sorry that you had to witness such antics...I apologize for my behavior and that of my family...
RAISA: Oh, this was nothing. Visit my house sometimes, talk about walking a tightrope...every hour somebody's falling off. But somebody's always there to catch 'em. As mother would say, love looks forward, hate looks back, but family has eyes all over its head.
VENNIE: What?
RAISA: Don't ask me. She talks in parables all the time.
MAYDEE: Your mother sounds like a very wise woman.
VENNIE: (Appreciating the picture.) Maybe we should do one of these...while we still have MaDear. The four of us. I mean it's not like we ain't family. (Quickly corrects herself.) I mean aren't... aren't family...aren't...aren't... (MayDee smiles at Vennie. Takes the picture and positions it over the piano, Vennie helps her.)
MAYDEE: Raisa?
RAISA: Yes?
MAYDEE: Do you love your mother?
RAISA: Yes.
MAYDEE: How come?
RAISA: Well...um...I don't know. She's my mother...

MAYDEE: Right. Just because she's your mother. And Daughter, you're going to have to learn to love me for that very same reason.
VENNIE: I never said I didn't love you...
MAYDEE: So you didn't. *(A pause, as MayDee waits for Vennie to reassure her that she indeed does love her, no response from Vennie is forthcoming, finally.)* We'll just make this dream on your dime. I've decided to retire from motherhood. Maybe I'll take what used to be your "future" money and carve me out a little present. How does that sound?
VENNIE: Mother, this isn't for me, not totally...
MAYDEE: But it is your life and your choice...totally...
VENNIE: You're not going to stop me, Mother. I'm going. I'll find a way.
MAYDEE: No doubt. You're my daughter. I know whatever you decide, you'll survive. *(Takes tableware out.)* Why don't you two make yourself useful. *(Vennie gets ready to say something.)* Give me a break. Just do it...please. Your mother is going to make herself a nice stiff drink, put her feet up...and try to figure out how many ways a little money can say I love you...
VENNIE: What did you say?
MAYDEE: Nothing. *(Overlapping, phone rings.)*
LOLA: I'll get it. I'll get it. *(Comes flying in the room.)* It's for me. I said I got it. *(In the phone.)* Hello...Oh, Jimmy...That's okay... No, I'm glad you finally called...Yes...
MADEAR: *(Overlapping, can be heard before she's seen.)* Man? Man, is dat you callin' for me? Man? I'm comin'. I'm comin'. *(Entering. She has draped Lola's boa on her shoulder and is wearing Lola's hat and carrying Lola's purse. She has smeared lipstick across her face, and is tapping her cane on the floor as if she's looking for something.)* See, I'm ready...Man, you ain't dead. You didn't leave me. *(Crying.)* You didn't leave me here all by myself...Jar de floor...See, I'm pretty now...like Lola Bit. You gon' dance wid me, Man? *(Attempts a step or two.)* See, I can dance now...I ain't ugly no mo, Man... I'm pretty like Lola...Momo say nobody love me...but...I ain't ugly no more. I'm pretty like Lola...Come on now, Man, jar de floor...please...I know you didn't leave me...jar de floor... *(Lola stops talking, Vennie begins to stomp her foot, softly at first and then louder. MayDee eventually joins in. Lola hangs up the phone, joins in and then Raisa.)*
MADEAR: I know you's wid me, Man. You didn't leave me here all by myself... *(The stomping continues, she turns around and looks at them as if she's seeing them for the first time.)* I cain't half hear ya'll chil'ren. Let me feel you. *(The stomping builds as the heartbeat between the generations resounds loudly.)* Ya'll chil'ren better jar de floor. Yes Lord, jar dat floor. *(Lights.)*

THE END

THE BALTIMORE WALTZ
by Paula Vogel

Playwright's Biography

Playwright, screenwriter and professor Paula Vogel has headed Brown's Playwriting Workshop since 1985. Vogel has taught playwriting at Cornell University, The University of Alaska, The Writer's Voice in New York, and Trinity Conservatory in Providence, Rhode Island.

Her most recent playwriting credits include productions of *The Baltimore Waltz*, originally produced at Circle Repertory, at the Tarragon Theatre in Toronto, the Yale Repertory Theatre, Portland Stage, and The Magic Theatre. *And Baby Makes Seven* will be produced by the Circle Repertory Company in the Spring of 1993. Her other plays include *Desdemona, The Oldest Profession*, and *Meg*.

Vogel is a member of Circle Repertory Company and is on its Board of Directors. Her most recent awards include an 1991-92 Obie for Best Play for *The Baltimore Waltz*, which also won the AT&T New Play Award 1991-92; a Yaddo Fellow(May 1992); a Rockefeller Foundation Bellagio Fellow (Summer 1992); a McKnight Fellow (1992-92); a Radcliffe Bunting Fellowship; and a National Endowment for Arts Playwriting Fellowship (1980, 1990-91). Vogel was also the 1992 recipient of the Rhode Island Governor's Arts Award.

Playwright's Note

In 1986, my brother Carl invited me to join him in a joint excursion to Europe. Due to pressures of time and money, I declined, never dreaming that he was HIV positive. This is the letter he wrote me after his first bout with pneumonia at Johns Hopkins Hospital in Baltimore, Maryland. He died on January 9, 1988.

As executor of his estate, I give permission to all future productions to reprint Carl's letter in the accompanying program. I would appreciate letting him speak to us in his own words.

The Baltimore Waltz – a journey with Carl to a Europe that exists only in the imagination – was written during the summer of 1989 at the MacDowell Colony, New Hampshire.

Paula Vogel

March 1987

Dear Paula:

I thought I would jot down some of my thoughts about the (shall we say) production values of my ceremony. Oh God – I can hear you groaning – everybody wants to direct. Well, I want a good show, even though my role has been reduced involuntarily from player to prop.

First, concerning the choice between a religious ceremony and a memorial service. I know the family considers my Anglican observances as irrelevant as Shinto. However, I wish prayers in some recognizably traditional form to be said, prayers that give thanks to the Creator for the gift of life and the hope of reunion. For reasons which you appreciate, I prefer a woman cleric, if possible, to lead the prayers. Here are two names: Phebe Coe, Epiphany Church; the Rev. Doris Mote, Holy Evangelists. Be sure to make a generous contribution from the estate for the cleric.

As for the piece of me I leave behind, here are your options:

1) open casket, full drag.

2) open casket, bum up (you'll know where to place the calla lilies, won't you?).

3) closed casket, interment with the grandparents.

4) cremation and burial of my ashes.

5) cremation and dispersion of my ashes in some sylvan spot.

I would really like good music. My tastes in these matters run to the highbrow: Faure's "Pre Jesu" from his Requiem, Gluck's "Dance of the Blessed Spirits" from Orfeo, "La Virgina Dell'Angeli" from Verdi's Forza. But my favorite song is "I Dream of Jeannie," and I wouldn't mind a spiritual like "Steal Away." Also, perhaps, "Nearer My God to Thee." Didn't Jeannette MacDonald sing that di-vinely in "San Francisco"?

Finally, would you read or have read A.E. Housman's "Loveliest of Trees"?

Well, my dear, that's that. Should I be lain with Grandma and Papa Ben, do stop by for a visit from year to year. And feel free to chat. You'll find me a good listener.

Love, Brother

* * * * * * * * * * * * * *

To the memory of Carl –
because I cannot sew.

Ron Vawter:

"...I always saw myself as a surrogate who, in the absence of anyone else, would stand in for him. And even now, when I'm in front of an audience and I feel good, I hearken back to that feeling, that I'm standing in for them."

Breaking the Rules, David Savran

Paula Vogel   101

CHARACTERS

ANNA
CARL, her brother
THE THIRD MAN/DOCTOR, who also plays:
>   Harry Lime
>   Public Health Official
>   Airport Security Guard
>   Garcon
>   Customs Official
>   The Little Dutch Boy at Age 50
>   Munich Virgin
>   Radical Student Activist
>   Concierge
>   Dr. Todesrocheln
>   and all other parts.

"The Baltimore Waltz" premiered at the Circle Repertory Company. It was directed by Anna Bogart and had the following cast:

ORIGINAL CAST

ANNA..Cherry Jones
CARL...Richard Thompson
THIRD MAN...Joe Mantello

SETTING

The Baltimore Waltz takes place in a hospital (perhaps in a lounge, corridor or waiting room) in Baltimore, Maryland.

NOTES

The lighting should be highly stylized, lush, dark and imaginative, in contrast to the hospital white silence of the last scene. Wherever possible, prior to the last scene, the director is encouraged to score the production with music – every cliche of the European experience as imagined by Hollywood.

ANNA might be dressed in a full slip/negligee and a trench coat. CARL is dressed in flannel pajamas and a blazer or jacket. The stuffed rabbit should be in every scene with CARL after Scene VI. THE THIRD MAN should wear latex gloves throughout the entire play.

The Baltimore Waltz

Scene I

Three distinct areas on stage: Anna, stage right, in her
trench coat, clutching the Berlitz Pocket Guide to Europe;
Carl, stage left, wearing pajamas and blazer; The Third
Man/Doctor in his lab coat and with stethoscope, is
center.

ANNA: *(Reads from her book. Her accents are excrable.)* "Help me please."
Dutch: "Kunt U mij helpn, alstublieft?" "There's nothing I can do." French: – "I
have no memory." *(Reading.)* "Il n'y a rien a faire." "Where are the toilets?" "Wo
sind die Toiletten?" I've never been abroad. It's not that I don't want to – but the
language terrifies me. I was traumatized by a junior high school French teacher
and, after that, it was a lost cause. I think that's the reason I went into elementary
education. Words like bureau, bidet, bildungsroman raise a sweat. Oh, I want to
go. Carl – he's my brother, you'll meet him shortly – he desperately wants to go.
But then, he can speak six languages. He's the head librarian of literature and
languages at the San Francisco Public. It's a very important position. The thought
of eight-hundred-year-old houses perched on the sides of mountains and rivers
whose names you've only seen in the Sunday Times crossword puzzles – all of
that is exciting. But I'm not going without him. He's read so much. I couldn't
possibly go without him. You see, I've never been abroad – unless you count
Baltimore, Maryland.
CARL: Good morning, boys and girls. It's Monday morning, and it's time for
"Reading Hour with Uncle Carl" once again, here at the North Branch of the San
Francisco Public Library. This is going to be a special reading hour. It's my very
last reading hour with you. Friday will be my very last day with the San Francisco
Public as children's librarian. Why? Do any of you know what a pink slip is?
(Carl holds up a rectangle of pink) It means I'm going on a paid leave of absence
for two weeks. Shelley Bizio, the branch supervisor, has given me my very own
pink slip. I got a pink slip because I wear this – *(He points to a pink triangle on
his lapel.)* A pink triangle. Now, I want you all to take the pink construction paper
in front of you, and take your scissors, and cut out pink triangles. There's tape at
every table, so you can wear them too! Make some for Mom and Dad, and your
brothers and sisters. Very good. Very good, Fabio. Oh, that's a beautiful pink
triangle, Tse Heng. Now before we read our last story together, I thought we
might have a sing-along. Your parents can join in, if they'd like to. Oh, don't be
shy. Let's do "Here we go round the Mulberry Bush." Remember that one? *(He
begins to sing. He also demonstrates.)*
"Here we go round the Mulberry Bush, the Mulberry Bush, the Mulberry Bush;
Here we go round the Mulberry Bush, so early in the morning."
"This is the way we pick our nose, pick our nose, pick our nose; This is the way
we pick our nose, so early in the morning."

Third verse! *(He makes a rude gesture with his middle finger.)*
"This is the way we go on strike, go on strike, go on strike; this is the way we go on strike, so early in the –"
What, Mrs. Bizio? I may leave immediately? I do not have to wait until Friday to collect unemployment? Why, thank you, Mrs. Bizio. Well, boys and girls, Mrs. Bizio will take over now. Bear with her, she's personality-impaired. I want you to be very good and remember me. I'm leaving for an immediate vacation with my sister on the east coast, and I'll think of you as I travel. Remember to wear those pink triangles. *(To his supervisor.)* I'm going. I'm going. You don't have to be rude. They enjoyed it. We'll take it up with the union. *(Shouting.)* In a language you might understand, up-pay ours-yay!
ANNA: It's the language that terrifies me.
CARL: Lesson Number One: Subject position. I. Je. Ich. Ik. I'm sorry. Je regrette. Es tut mir leid.
ANNA: But we decided to go when the doctor gave us his verdict.
DOCTOR: I'm sorry.
CARL: I'm sorry.
DOCTOR: There's nothing we can do.
ANNA: But what?
CARL: How long?
ANNA: Explain it to me. Very slowly. So I can understand. Excuse me, could you tell me again?
DOCTOR: There are exudative and proliferative inflammatory alterations of the endocardium, consisting of necrotic debris, fibrinoid material, and disintegrating fibroblastic cells.
CARL: Oh, sweet Jesus.
DOCTOR: It may be acute or subacute, caused by various bacteria: streptococci, staphylococci, enterococci, gonococci, gram negative bacilli, etc. It may be due to other micro-organisms, of course, but there is a high mortality rate with or without treatment. And there is usually rapid destruction and metastases.
CARL: Anna –
ANNA: I'm right here, darling. Right here.
CARL: Could you explain it very slowly?
DOCTOR: Also known as Loffler's syndrome, i.e., eosinophilia, resulting in fibroblastic thickening, persistent tachycardia, hepatomegaly, splenomegaly, serious effusions into the pleural cavity with edema. It may be Brugia malayi or Wuchereria bancofti – also known as Weingarten's syndrome. Often seen with effusions, either exudate or transudate.
ANNA: Carl –
CARL: I'm here, darling. Right here.
ANNA: It's the language that terrifies me.

Scene II

CARL: Medical Straight Talk: Part One.

ANNA: So you're telling me that you really don't know?

DOCTOR: I'm afraid that medical science has only a small foothold in this area. But of course, it would be of great benefit to our knowledge if you would consent to observation here at Johns Hopkins –

CARL: Why? Running out of laboratory rats?!

ANNA: Oh, no. I'm sorry. I can't do that. Can you tell me at least how it was...contracted?

DOCTOR: Well – we're not sure, yet. It's only a theory at this stage, but one that seems in great favor at the World Health Organization. We think it comes from the old cultus ornatus –

CARL: Toilet seats?

ANNA: Toilet seats! My God. Mother was right. She always said –

CARL: And never, ever, in any circumstances, in bus stations –

ANNA: Toilet seats? Cut down in the prime of youth by a toilet seat?

DOCTOR: Anna – I may call you Anna? – you teach school, I believe?

ANNA: Yes, first grade. What does that have –

DOCTOR: Ah, yes. We're beginning to see a lot of this in elementary schools. Anna – I may call you Anna? With assurances of complete confidentiality – we need to ask you very specific questions about the body, body fluids, and body functions. As mature adults, as scientists and educators. To speak frankly – when you needed to relieve yourself – where did you make wa-wa?

ANNA: There's a faculty room. But why – how –

DOCTOR: You never, ever used the johnny in your classroom?

ANNA: Well, maybe once or twice. There's no lock, and Robbie Matthews always tries to barge in. Sometimes I just can't get the time to – surely you're not suggesting that –

DOCTOR: You did use the facilities in your classroom? *(The Doctor makes notes from this.)*

CARL: Is that a crime? When you've got to go, you've got to –

ANNA: I can't believe that my students would transmit something like this –

DOCTOR: You have no idea. Five-year-olds can be deadly. It seems to be an affliction, so far, of single schoolteachers. Schoolteachers with children of their own develop an immunity to ATD...Acquired Toilet Disease.

ANNA: I see. Why hasn't anybody heard of this disease?

DOCTOR: Well, first of all, the Center for Disease Control doesn't wish to inspire an all-out panic in communities. Secondly, we think education on this topic is the responsibility of the NEA, not the government. And if word of this pestilence gets out inappropriately, the PTA is going to be all over the school system demanding mandatory testing of every toilet seat in every lavatory. It's kindling for a political disaster.

ANNA: *(Taking the Doctor aside.)* I want to ask you something confidentially. Something that my brother doesn't need to hear. What's the danger of transmission?

DOCTOR: There's really no danger to anyone in the immediate family. You must use precautions.

ANNA: Because what I want to know is...can you transmit this thing by...by doing – what exactly do you mean by precautions?

DOCTOR: Well, I guess you should do what your mother always told you. You know, wash your hands before and after going to the bathroom. And never lick paper money or coins in any currency.

ANNA: So there's no danger to anyone by...what I mean, Doctor, is that I can't infect anyone by–

DOCTOR: Just use precautions.

ANNA: Because, in whatever time this schoolteacher has left, I intend to fuck my brains out.

DOCTOR Which means, in whatever time is left, she can fuck her brains out.

Scene III *Carl and the Doctor.*

CARL: *(Agitated.)* I'll tell you what. If Sandra Day O'Connor sat on just one infected potty, the media would be clamoring to do articles on ATD. If just one grandchild of George Bush caught this thing during toilet training, that would have been the last wehad heard about the space program. Why isn't someone doing something?! I'm sorry. I know you're one of the converted. You're doing...well, everything you can. I'd like to ask you something in confidence, something my sister doesn't need to hear. Is there any hope at all?

DOCTOR: Well, I suppose there's...always hope.

CARL: Any experimental drugs? Treatments?

DOCTOR: Well, they're trying all sorts of things abroad. Our hands are tied here by NIH and the FDA, you understand. There is a long-shot avenue to explore, nothing, you understand, that I personally endorse, but there is an eighty-year-old urologist overseas who's been working in this field for some time –

CARL: We'll try anything.

DOCTOR: His name is Dr. Todesrocheln. He's somewhat unorthodox, outside the medical community in Vienna. It's gonna cost you. Mind you, this is not an endorsement.

ANNA: You hear the doctor through a long-distance corridor. Your ears are functioning, but the mind is numb. You try to listen as you swim towards his sentences in the flourescent light in his office. But you don't believe it at first. This is how I'd like to die: with dignity. No body secretions – like Merle Oberon in "Wuthering Heights." With a somewhat becoming flush, and a transcendental gaze. Luminous eyes piercing the veil of mortal existence. The windows are open to the fresh breeze blowing off the moors. Oh. And violins in the background would be nice, too. *(Music: violins playing Strauss swell in the background.)*

Scene IV *The Phone Call.*

THE THIRD MAN: Lesson Number Two: Basic dialogue. The phone call. Hello. I would like to speak to Mr. Lime, please.

CARL: Entschuldigen Sie, bitte – operator? Operator? Hello? Guten Tag? Kann

ich bitte mit Herrn Lime sprechen? Harry? Harry? Wie geht es dir?! Listen,
I...can you hear...no, I'm in Baltimore...yeah, not since Hopkins...no, there's–
well, there is something up. No, dear boy, seriously – it's my sister. ATD.
THE THIRD MAN: ATD? Jesus, that's tough, old man. You've got to watch
where you sit these days. She's a sweet kid. Yeah. Yeah. Wait a second.
(Offstage.) Inge? Inge, baby? Ein Bier, bitte, baby. Ja. Ja. You too, baby. *(Pause.)*
Okay. Dr. Todelsrocheln? Yeah, you might say I know him. But don't tell
anybody I said that. There's also a new drug they've got over here. Black market.
I might be able to help you. I said might. But it's gonna cost you. *(Cautiously,
ominously.)* Do you still have the rabbit?
CARL: I'll bring the rabbit.
THE THIRD MAN: Good. A friend of mine will be in touch. And listen, old
man...if anybody asks you, you don't know me. I'll see you in a month. You
know where to find me.
THE THIRD MAN and CARL: *(Simultaneously.)* Click.

Scene V

THE THIRD MAN: Lesson Number Three: Pronouns and the possessive case. I,
you, he, she and it. They and We. Yours, mine, and ours.
VOICE OF ANNA: There's nothing I can do. There's nothing you can do.
There's nothing he, she or it can do. There's nothing we can do. There's nothing
they can do.
ANNA: So what are we going to do?
CARL Start packing, sister dear.
ANNA: Europe? You mean it?
CARL: We'll mosey about France and Germany, and then work our way down to
Vienna.
ANNA: What about your job?
CARL: It's only a job.
ANNA: It's a very important job! Head of the entire San Francisco Public –
CARL: They'll hold my job for me. I'm due for a leave.
ANNA: Oh, honey. Can we afford this?
CARL: It's only money.
ANNA: It's your money.
CARL: It's our money.

Scene VI

THE THIRD MAN: Lesson Four: Present tense of faire. What are we going to
do? Qu'est-ce qu'on va faire?
ANNA: So what are we going to do?
CARL: We'll see this doctor in Vienna.
ANNA: Dr. Todelsrocheln?

CARL: We have to try.

ANNA: A urologist?

CARL: He's working on a new drug.

ANNA: A European urologist?

CARL: What options do we have?

ANNA: Wait a minute. What are his credentials? Who is this guy?

CARL: He was trained at the Allgemeines Krankenhaus during the Empire.

ANNA: Yeah? Just what was he doing from, say, 1938 to 1945? Research?

CARL: It's best not to ask too many questiosn. There are people who swear by his work.

ANNA: What's his specialty?

CARL: Well, actually, he's a practitioner of uriposia.

ANNA: He writes poems about urine?

CARL: No. He drinks it.

ANNA: I'm not going.

CARL: Let's put off judgment until we arrange a consultation...my god, you're so messy. Look at how neat my suitcase is in comparison. You'll never find a thing in there.

ANNA: I refuse to drink my own piss for medical science. *(Carl grabs a stuffed rabbit and thrusts it in Anna's suitcase.)*

ANNA: What are you doing?

CARL: We can't leave bunny behind.

ANNA: What is a grown man like you doing with a stuffed rabbit?

CARL: I can't sleep without bunny.

ANNA: I didn't know you slept with...stuffed animals.

CARL: There's a lot you don't know about me.

Scene VII

THE THIRD MAN: Lesson Five: Basic dialogue. At the airport. We are going to Paris. What time does our flight leave? Nous allons a Paris. Quelle est l'heure de depart de notre vol? *(The Third Man becomes an Airport Security Guard.)*

AIRPORT SECURITY GUARD: Okay. Next. Please remove your keys and all other metallic items. Place all belongings on the belt. Next. *(Carl and Anna carry heavy luggage. Carl halts.)*

CARL: Wait. I need your suitcase. *(He opens Anna's luggage and begins to rummage around.)*

ANNA: Hey!

CARL: It was a mess to begin with. Ah – *(He retrieves the stuffed rabbit.)* There.

ANNA: Are you having an anxiety attack?

CARL: You hold it. *(He and Anna stamp, sit and stand on the baggage. Carl manages to relock the bag.)*

ANNA: What is wrong with you?

CARL: X-rays are bad for bunny.

AIRPORT SECURITY GUARD: Next. Please remove all metallic objects. Keys. Eyeglasses. Gold Fillings. Metallic objects?

CARL: Go on. You first. *(Anna passes through, holding the stuffed rabbit. Carl sighs, relieved. Carl passes through. The Airport Security Guard stops him.)*
AIRPORT SECURITY GUARD: One moment, please. *(The Airport Security Guard almost strip searches him. He uses a metallic wand which makes loud, clicking noises. Finally, he nods. He hands Anna and Carl their bags, still suspiciously looking at Carl.)*
ANNA: Okay, bunny – Paris, here we come!

Scene VIII

THE THIRD MAN: *(Simultaneously with Carl's next lines.)* Lesson Six. Direct pronouns. I am tired. And my sister looks at herself in the mirror.
CARL: Sixieme Lecon: Pronoms – complements directs. Je suis fatigue. Et ma soeur – elle se regarde dans la glace. *(Carl climbs into a double bed with the stuffed rabbit. Anna stares into a mirror. The Third Man, apart, stands in their bedroom.)*
THE THIRD MAN: The first separation – your first sense of loss. You were five – your brother was seven. Your parents would not let you sleep in the same bed anymore. They removed you to your own bedroom. You were too old, they said. But every now and then, when they turned off the lights and went downstairs – when the dark scared you, you would rise and go to him. And he would let you nustle under his arm, under the covers, where you would fall to sleep, breathing in the scent of your own breath and his seven-year-old body.
CARL: Come to bed, sweetie. Bunny and I are waiting. We're going to be jet-lagged for a while. *(Anna continues to stare in the mirror.)*
ANNA: It doesn't show yet.
CARL: No one can tell. Let's get some sleep, honey.
ANNA: I don't want anyone to know.
CARL: It's not a crime. It's an illness.
ANNA: I don't want anybody to know.
CARL: It's your decision. Just don't tell anyone…what…you do for a living. *(Anna joins Carl in the bed. He holds her hand.)*
ANNA: Well, there's one good thing about travelling in Europe… and about dying.
CARL: What's that?
ANNA: I get to sleep with you again.

Scene IX

CARL: Medical Straight Talk: Part Two. *(The Third Man becomes a Public Health Official.)*
PUBLIC HEALTH OFFICIAL: Here at the Department of Health and Human Services we are announcing Operation Squat. There is no known cure for ATD right now, and we are recognizing the urgency of this dread disease by

recognizing it as our 82nd national health priority. Right now ATD is the fourth major cause of death of single schoolteachers, ages 24 to 40...behind school buses, lockjaw and playground accidents. The best policy, until a cure can be found, is of education and prevention. *(Anna and Carl hold up posters of a toilet seat in a circle with a red diagonal slash.)* If you are in the high risk category – elementary school teachers, classroom aides, custodians and playground drug pushers – follow these simple guides. *(Anna and Carl hold up copies of the educational pamphlets.)*

PUBLIC HEALTH OFFICIAL:
Do: Use the facilities in your own home before departing for school. *Do:* Use the facilities in your own home as soon as you return from school.
Do: Hold it.
Don't: Eat meals in public restrooms.
Don't: Flush lavatory equipment and then suck your digits.
If absolutely necessary to relieve yourself at work, please remember the Department of Health and Human Services ATD slogan: Don't sit, do squat.

Scene X

> *Music: accordian playing "La vie en rose." Anna and Carl stroll.*

CARL: Of course, the Left Bank has always been a haven for outcasts, foreigners and students, since the time that Abelard fled the Ile de La Cite to found the university here –
ANNA: Oh, look. Is that the Eiffel Tower? It looks so...phallic.
CARL: And it continued to serve as a haven for the avant-garde of the Twenties, the American expatriate community that could no longer afford Montparnesse –
ANNA: My god, they really do smoke Gauloise here.
CARL: And, of course, the Dada and Surrealists who set up camp here after World War I and their return from Switzerland – *(The Third Man, in a trench coat and red beret, crosses the stage.)*
ANNA: Are we being followed?
CARL: Is your medication making you paranoid? *(Pause.)* Now, over here is the famous spot where Gertrude supposedly said to her brother Leo – *(The Third Man follows them.)*
ANNA: I know. God is the answer. What is the question? – I'm not imagining it. That man has been trailing us from the Boulevard St. Michel.
CARL: Are you getting hungry?
ANNA: I'm getting tired.
CARL: Wait. Let's just whip around the corner to the Cafe St. Michel where Hemingway, after an all-night bout, threw up his shrimp heads all over Scott's new suede shoes – which really was a moveable feast. *(The Third Man is holding an identical stuffed rabbit and looks at them.)*
ANNA: Carl! Carl! Look! That man over there!

CARL: So? They have stuffed rabbits over here, too. Let's go.
ANNA: Why is he following us? He's got the same –
CARL: It's your imagination. How about a little dejeuner? (Anna and Carl walk to a small table and chairs.)

Scene XI

GARCON: *(With a thick Peter Sellers French accent.)* It was a simple bistro affair by French standards. He had le Veau Prince Orloff, she le boeuf a la mode – a simple dish of haricots verts, and a medoc to accompany it all. He barely touched his meal. She mopped the sauces with the bread. As their meal progressed, Anna thought of the lunches she packed back home. For the past ten years, hunched over in the faculty room at McCormick Elementary, this is what Anna ate: on Mondays, pressed chipped chicken sandwiches with mayonaisse on white; on Tuesdays, soggy tuna sandwiches; on Wednesdays, velveeta cheese and baloney; on Thursdays, drier pressed chicken on the now stale white bread; on Fridays, velveeta and tuna. She always had a small wax envelope of carrot sticks or celery, and a can of Diet Pepsi. Anna, as she ate in the bistro, wept. What could she know of love?
CARL: Why are you weeping?
ANNA: It's just so wonderful.
CARL: You're a goose.
ANNA: I've wasted over thirty years on convenience foods. *(The Garcon approaches the table.)*
GARCON: Is everything all right?
ANNA: Oh God. Yes – yes – it's wonderful.
CARL: My sister would like to see the dessert tray. *(Anna breaks out in tears again. The Garcon shrugs and exits. He reappears a few minutes later as The Third Man, this time with a trench coat and blue beret. He sits at an adjacent table and stares in their direction.)*
ANNA: Who is that man? Do you know him? *(Carl hastily looks at The Third Man.)*
CARL: No, I've never seen him before. *(The Third Man brings the stuffed rabbit out of his trench coat.)*
ANNA: He's flashing his rabbit at you. *(Carl rises.)*
CARL: Excuse me. I think I'll go to les toilettes.
ANNA: Carl! Be careful! Don't sit! *(Carl exits. The Third Man waits a few seconds, looks at Anna, and then follows Carl without expression.)* What is it they do with those rabbits? *(A split second later, the Garcon reenters with the dessert tray. Anna ogles him.)*
GARCON: Okay. We have la creme plombiere pralinee, un bavarois a l'orange, et ici we have une Charlotte Malakoff aux Framboises. Our specialite is le gateau de crepes a la Normande. What would mademoiselle like? *(Anna has obviously not been looking at the dessert tray.)*
ANNA: *(Sighing.)* Ah, yes. *(The Garcon smiles.)*

GARCON: Vous etes Americaine? This is your first trip to Paris?
ANNA: Yes.
GARCON: And you do not speak at all French?
ANNA: No. *(The Garcon smiles.)*
GARCON: *(Suggestively.)* Bon. Would you like la specialite de la maison?

Scene XII

CARL: Exercise: La Carte. La specialite de la maison.
Back at the hotel, Anna sampled the Garcon's specialite de la maison while her
brother browsed the Louvre. *(Anna and the Garcon are shapes beneath the covers
of the bed. Carl clutches his stuffed rabbit.)*
Jean Baptiste Camille Corot lived from 1796 to 1875. Although he began his
career by studying in the classic tradition, his later paintings reveal the influence
of the Italian style.
ANNA: *(Muffled.)* Ah! Yes!
GARCON: *(Also muffled.)* Ah! Oui!
CARL: He traveled extensively around the world, and in the salon of 1827 his
privately lauded techniques were displayed in public.
ANNA: Yes – oh, yes, yes!
GARCON: Mais oui!
CARL: Before the Academy had accepted realism, Corot's progressive paintings,
his clear sighted observations of nature, revealed a fresh almost spritely quality of
light, tone and composition.
ANNA: Yes – that's right – faster –
GARCON: Plus vite?
ANNA: Faster –
GARCON: Encore! Plus vite!
ANNA: Wait!
GARCON: Attends?
CARL: It was his simplicity, and his awareness of color that brought a fresh wind
into the staid academy –
GARCON: Maintenant?
ANNA: Lower – faster – lower –
GARCON: Plus bas – plus vite – plus bas –
CARL: He was particularly remembered and beloved for his championing the
cause of younger artists with more experimental techniques, bringing the
generosity of his advancing reputation to their careers.
ANNA: Yes – I – I – I – I –!
GARCON: Je – je! Je! ! Je! *(Pause.)*
CARL: In art, as in life, some things need no translation.
GARCON: Gauloise?
CARL: For those of you who are interested, in the next room are some stunning
works by Delacroix.

Scene XIII *Back at the Hotel.*

CARL: Lesson Seven: Basic vocabulary. Parts of the body. *(Carl, slightly out of the next scene, watches them. Anna sits up in bed. The Garcon is asleep beneath the sheet.)*
ANNA: I did read one book once in French. Le Petit Prince. Lying here, watching him sleep, I look at his breast and remember the Rose with its single, pathetic thorn for protection. And here – his puckered red nipple, lying poor and vulnerable on top of his blustering breast plate. It's really so sweet about men. *(She kisses the Garcon's breast. The Garcon stirs.)*
GARCON: Encore?
ANNA: What is the word – in French – for this? She fingers his breast.
GARCON: For un homme – le sein. For une femme – la mamelle.
ANNA: Sein?
GARCON: Oui. sein.
ANNA: *(She kisses his neck.)* And this?
GARCON: Le Cou.
ANNA: Et ici?
GARCON: Bon. Decollette – *(Anna begins to touch him under the sheet.)*
ANNA: And this? *(The Garcon laughs.)*
GARCON: S'il vous plait…I am tickling there. Ah. Les Couilles.
ANNA: Culle?
GARCON: Non. Couilles. Le Cul is something much different. Ici c'est le cul.
ANNA: Oh, yes. That's very different.
GARCON: *(Taking her hand under the sheet.)* We sometimes call these also Le Quatrieme Etat. The Fourth Estate.
ANNA: Really? Because they enjoy being "scooped"?
GARCON: Bein sur.
ANNA: And this?
GARCON: Ah. Ma Tour Eiffel. I call it aussi my Charles DeGalle.
ANNA: Wow.
GARCON: My grandfather called his Napoleon.
ANNA: I see. I guess it runs in your family.
GARCON: *(Modestly.)* Oui. Grand-mere – qu'est-ce que c'est le mot en anglais? Her con – here – ici – do you know what I am meaning?
ANNA: You're making yourself completely clear –
GARCON: We called hers the Waterloo de mon grand-pere – *(Anna digs under the sheet more.)*
ANNA: And this? *(The Garcon is scandalized.)*
GARCON: Non. There is no word en francais. Pas du tout.
ANNA: For this? There must be –
GARCON: Non! Only the Germans have a word for that. *(Carl enters and casually converses with Anna. Startled, the Garcon covers himself with the sheet.)*
CARL: Hello, darling. Are you feeling better? *(Carl walks to the chair beside the bed and removes the Garcon's clothing.)*
ANNA: Yes, much. I needed to lie down. How was the Louvre? *(The Garcon*

carefully rises from the bed and takes his clothing from Carl, who is holding them out. He creeps cautiously stage left and begins to pull on his clothes.)
CARL: Oh, Anna. I'm so sorry you missed it. The paintings of David were amazing. The way his paintbrush embraced the body – it was just incredible to stand there and see them in the flesh.
ANNA: Ah yes – in the flesh. *(She smiles at the confused Garcon.)*
CARL: Well, sweetie. It's been a thoroughly rewarding day for both of us. I'm for turning in. How about you? *(The Garcon is now fully dressed.)*
ANNA: Yes, I'm tired. Here – I've warmed the bed for you. *(She throws back the sheet.)*
CARL: Garcon – l'addition!
ANNA: *(To the Garcon.)* Merci beaucoup. *(Anna blows him a kiss. The Garcon takes a few steps out of the scene as Carl climbs into bed.)*

Scene XIV

THE THIRD MAN: Anna has a difficult time sleeping. She is afflicted with night thoughts. According to Elizabeth Kubler-Ross, there are six stages the terminal patient travels in the course of her illness. The first stage: Denial and Isolation. *(The Third Man stays in the hotel room and watches Carl and Anna in the bed. They are sleeping, when Anna sits upright.)*
ANNA: I feel so alone. The ceiling is pressing down on me. I can't believe I am dying. Only at night. Only at night. In the morning, when I open my eyes, I feel absolutely well – without a body. And then the thought comes crashing in my mind. This is the last spring I may see. This is the last summer. It can't be. There must be a mistake. They mixed the specimens up in the hospital. Some poor person is walking around, dying, with the false confidence of my prognosis, thinking themselves well. It's a clerical error. Carl! I can't sleep. Do you think they made a mistake?
CARL: Come back to sleep – *(Carl pulls Anna down on the bed to him, and strokes her brow. They change positions on the bed.)*
THE THIRD MAN: The second stage: Anger. *(Anna sits bolt upright in bed, angry.)*
ANNA: How could this happen to me! I did my lesson plans faithfully for the past ten years! I've taught in classrooms without walls – kept up on new audio-visual aids – I read Summerhill! And I believed it! When the principal assigned me the job of the talent show – and nobody wants to do the talent show – I pleaded for cafeteria duty, bus duty – but no, I got stuck with the talent show. And those kids put on the best darn show that school has ever seen! Which one of them did this to me? Emily Baker? For slugging Johnnie MacIntosh? Johnnie MacIntosh? Because I sent him home for exposing himself to Susy Higgins? Susy Higgins? Because I called her out on her nosepicking? Or those Nader twins? I've spent the best years of my life giving to those kids – it's not –
CARL: Calm down, sweetie. You're angry. It's only natural to be angry. Elizabeth Kubler-Ross says that –

ANNA: What does she know about what it feels like to die?! Elizabeth Kubler-Ross can sit on my face! *(Carl and Anna change positions on the bed.)*
THE THIRD MAN: The third stage: Bargaining.
ANNA: Do you think if I let Elizabeth Kubler-Ross sit on my face I'll get well? *(Carl and Anna change positions on the bed.)*
THE THIRD MAN: The fourth stage: Depression. *(Carl sits on the side of the bed beside Anna.)*
CARL: Anna – honey – come on, wake up.
ANNA: Leave me alone.
CARL: Come on, sweetie...you've been sleeping all day now, and you slept all yesterday. Do you want to sleep away our last day in France?
ANNA: Why bother?
CARL: You've got to eat something. You've got to fight this. For me.
ANNA: Leave me alone. *(Carl lies down beside Anna. They change positions.)*
THE THIRD MAN: The fifth stage: Acceptance. *(Anna and Carl are lying in bed, awake. They hold hands.)*
ANNA: When I'm gone, I want you to find someone.
CARL: Let's not talk about me.
ANNA: No, I want to. It's important to me to know that you'll be happy and taken care of after...when I'm gone.
CARL: Please.
ANNA: I've got to talk about it. We've shared everything else. I want you to know how it feels...what I'm thinking...when I hold your hand, and I kiss it...I try to memorize what it looks like, your hand...I wonder if there's any memory in the grave?
THE THIRD MAN: And then there's the sixth stage: Hope. *(Anna and Carl rise from the bed.)*
CARL: How are you feeling?
ANNA: I feel good today.
CARL: Do you feel like travelling?
ANNA: Yes. It would be nice to see Amsterdam. Together. We might as well see as much as we can while I'm well –
CARL: That's right, sweetie. And maybe you can eat something–
ANNA: I'm hungry. That's a good sign, don't you think?
CARL: That's a wonderful sign. You'll see. You'll feel better when you eat.
ANNA: Maybe the doctor in Vienna can help.
CARL: That's right.
ANNA: What's drinking a little piss? It can't hurt you.
CARL: Right. Who knows? We've got to try.
ANNA: I'll think of it as...European lager.
CARL: Golden Heidelberg. *(Carl and Anna hum/sing the drinking song from "The Student Prince.")*

Scene XV

THE THIRD MAN: And as Anna and Carl took the train into Holland, the seductive swaying of the TEE-train aroused another sensation. Unbeknownst to Elizabeth Kubler-Ross, there is a seventh stage for the dying. There is a growing urge to fight the sickness of the body with the health of the body. The seventh stage: lust. *(Anna and Carl are seated in a train compartment. Carl holds the stuffed rabbit out to Anna.)*
ANNA: Why?
CARL: Just take it. Hold it for me. Just through customs.
ANNA: Only if you tell me why.
CARL: Don't play games right now. Or we'll be in deep, deep do-do. *(Anna reluctantly takes the stuffed rabbit and holds it.)*
ANNA: You're scaring me.
CARL: I'm sorry, sweetie. You're the only one I can trust to hold my rabbit. Trust me. It's important.
ANNA: Then why won't you tell me – ?
CARL: There are some things you're better off not knowing.
ANNA: Are you smuggling drugs? Jewels?
CARL: *(Whispers.)* It's beyond measure. It's invaluable to me. That's all I'll say. *(In a louder tone.)* Just act normal now.
CUSTOMS OFFICIAL: Uw paspoort, aistublieft. *(Anna and Carl give him their passports. Carl is nervous. Anna smiles at the Customs Official a bit lasciviously.)* Have you anything to declare?
ANNA: *(Whispering.)* Yes – captain, I'm smuggling contraband. I demand to be searched. In private. *(The Customs Official blushes.)*
CUSTOMS OFFICIAL: Excuse me?
ANNA: Yes. I said – waar is het damestoilet?
CUSTOMS OFFICIAL: Oh...I thought... *(The Customs Official giggles.)*
ANNA: Yes?
CUSTOMS OFFICIAL: First left. *(The Customs Official returns their passports.)* Have a very pleasant stay. *(Anna waves bunny's arm goodbye. The Customs Official looks at her, blushes again and retreats. Carl relaxes.)*
CARL: You're good at this. Very good.
ANNA: When in Holland, do like the Dutch...Mata Hari was Dutch, you know.

Scene XVI

CARL: Questions sur le Dialogue. Est-ce que les hommes Hollandais sont comme les Francais? Are Dutch men like the French? *(Anna and The Little Dutch Boy at Age 50. He wears traditional wooden shoes, trousers and vest. His Buster Brown haircut and hat make him look dissipated.)*
THE LITTLE DUTCH BOY AT AGE 50: It was kermis-time, the festival in my village. And I had too much bier with my school friends, Piet and Jan. Ja. Soo – Piet thought we should go to the outer dyke with cans of spray paint, after the

kermis. So we went.

Here in Noord Brabant there are three walls of defenses against the cruelty of the North Sea. The first dyke is called the Waker – the Watcher; the second dyke is de Slaper – the Sleeper; and the last dyke, which had never before been tested, is known as the Dromer – the Dreamer.

And when we got to the Dreamer, Piet said to me: "Willem, you do it." Meaning I was to write on the walls of the Dreamer. This is why I was always in trouble in school – Piet and Jan would say, "Willem, you do it," and whatever it was – I would do it.

Soo – I took up a can of the paint and in very big letters, I wrote in Dutch that our schoolmaster, Mijnheer Van Doorn, was a gas-passer. Everyone could read the letters from far away. And just as I was finishing this, and Piet and Jan were laughing behind me, I looked – I was on my knees, pressed up against the dyke – and I could see that the wall of the Dreamer was cracking its surface, very fine little lines, like a goose egg when it breaks from within.

And I yelled to my friends – Look! And they came a bit closer, and as we looked, right above my head, a little hole began to peck its way through the clay. And there was just a small trickle of water. And Jan said: "Willem, put your thumb in that hole." And by that time, the hole in the dyke was just big enough to put my thumb in. "Why?" I asked of Jan. "Just do it," he said. And so I did.

And once I put my thumb in, I could not get it out. Suddenly we could hear the waves crashing as The Sleeper began to collapse. Only the Dreamer remained to hold off the savage water. "Help me!" I yelled to Jan and Piet – but they ran away. "Vlug!" I cried – but no one could hear me. And I stayed there, crouching, with my thumb stuck into the clay. And I thought what if the Dreamer should give in, too. I thought how the waves would bear my body like a messenger to the Village. How no one would survive the Flood. Only the church steeple would remain to mark the place where we had lived. How young we were to die. *(Pause.)*

Have you ever imagined what it would be like to be face to face with death?

ANNA: Yes – yes, I have.

THE LITTLE DUTCH BOY AT AGE 50: And have you ever prayed for deliverance against all hope?

ANNA: I – no. I haven't been able to get to that stage. Yet.

THE LITTLE DUTCH BOY AT AGE 50: But the Dreamer held. And finally there came wagons with men from the village, holding lanterns and sand and straw. And they found me there, strung up by my thumb, beside the big black letters: Mijnheer Van Doorn is een gas-passer. And they freed me and said I was a hero, and I became the boy who held back the sea with his thumb.

ANNA: Golly. You were very brave

THE LITTLE DUTCH BOY AT AGE 50: I was stupid. Wrong place, wrong time.

ANNA: How long ago did this happen?

THE LITTLE DUTCH BOY AT AGE 50: *(Sadly.)* Let us just say it happened a long time ago.

ANNA: You've faced death. I wish my brother were here to meet you.

THE LITTLE DUTCH BOY AT AGE 50: Where is he? Wo ist dein bruder?

ANNA: Oh, he stayed in Amsterdam to see the Rijksmuseum and the Van Gogh Museum.

THE LITTLE DUTCH BOY AT AGE 50: And you did not go? You should see them, they are really fantastic.

ANNA: Why? What's the use? I won't remember them, I'll have no memory.

THE LITTLE DUTCH BOY AT AGE 50: So you are an American?

ANNA: Yes.

THE LITTLE DUTCH BOY AT AGE 50: So, do you want to sleep with me? All the women touristen want to sleep with the little Dutch boy who put his thumb in the dyke.

ANNA: Do you mind so much?

THE LITTLE DUTCH BOY AT AGE 50: *(Shrugs.)* Nee. It's a way to make a living, is it niet?

ANNA: *(Quietly.)* Let's go then.

Scene XVII

CARL: Repetez. En Francais. Where is my brother going? Ou va mon frere? Bien.

ANNA: I had just returned from my day trip and left the Centraal Station. The sun sparkled on the waters of the canal, and I decided to walk back to the hotel. ...Just then I saw my brother. *(Carl enters in a trench coat, sunglasses, holding the stuffed rabbit.)* I tried to catch up with Carl, dodging bicycles and pedestrians. And then, crossing the Amstel on the Magere Brug, he appeared. *(The Third Man enters, in a trench coat, sunglasses, and with black gloves, holding a stuffed rabbit.)* I trailed them from a discrete distance. *(The Third Man and Carl walk rapidly, not glancing at each other. Carl stops; The Third Man stops a few paces behind. Carl walks; The Third Man walks. Carl stops; The Third Man stops. Finally, they face each other and meet. Quickly, looking surreptitiously around, Carl and The Third Man stroke each other's stuffed rabbits. They quickly part and walk off in opposite directions. Anna rushes to center stage, looking in both directions.)* I tried to follow the man in the trench coat, and crossed behind him over the Amstel, but I lost sight of him in the crowd of men wearing trench coats and sunglasses. I want some answers from my brother. Whatever trouble he's in, he has to share it with me. I want some answers back at the hotel. He's going to talk.

Scene XVIII

CARL: Questions sur le dialogue. You must learn. Sie mussen lernen. *(Anna enters the empty hotel room. On the bed, propped up on pillows, lies a stuffed rabbit.)*

ANNA: Carl? Carl? Are you back? Carl? *(Anna stops and looks at the stuffed rabbit.)*

CARL: *(From the side.)* You were not permitted to play with dolls; dolls are for girls. You played with your sister's dolls until your parents found out. They gave

you a stuffed animal – a thin line was drawn. Rabbits were an acceptable surrogate for little boys. You named him Jo-Jo. You could not sleep without him. Jo-Jo traveled with you to the seashore, to the hotel in New York City when you were seven, to your first summer camp. He did not have the flaxen plastic hair of your sister's Betsey-Wetsy, but he had long, furry ears, soft white on one side, pink satin inside. He let you stroke them. He never betrayed you. He taught you to trust in contact. You will love him always. *(Anna moves towards the stuffed rabbit.)*
ANNA: My brother left you behind, did he? Alone at last. Okay, bunny, now you're going to talk. I want some answers. What have you got that's so important? *(Just as Anna reaches for the stuffed rabbit, The Third Man (in trench coat, sunglasses and black gloves) steps out into the room.)*
THE THIRD MAN: *(Threateningly.)* I wouldn't do that, if I were you. *(Anna screams in surprise.)* Now listen. Where is your brother? I have a message for him. Tell him he's running out of time. Do you understand? *(Anna, scared, nods.)* Good. He'd better not try to dupe us. We're willing to arrange a swap – his sister for the rabbit. Tell him we're waiting for him in Vienna. And tell him he'd better bring the rabbit to the other side. *(The Third Man leaves. Anna, shaken, sits on the bed and holds the stuffed rabbit. She strokes it for comfort. Carl enters, in a frenzy. He carries his stuffed rabbit. Anna stares as Carl tosses the decoy rabbit away.)*
CARL: Don't ask me any questions. I can't tell you what's happening. Are you able to travel? Good. We have to leave Amsterdam tonight. There's a train in an hour. We'll go to Germany. Are you packed?

Scene XIX

ANNA and THE THIRD MAN: *(Simultaneously.)* Wann geht der nachste Zug nach Hamburg? *(German band music swells as Anna and Carl sit in their railroad compartment, side by side. Anna, pale,holds the stuffed rabbit in her lap.)*
CARL: Ah, Saxony, Bavaria, the Black Forest, the Rhineland…I love them all. I think perhaps now would be a good time to show the slides.
ANNA: I'm so sorry. I hate it when people do this to me.
CARL: Nonsense. People like to see slides of other people's trips. These are in no particular order. We'll only show a few, just to give a taste of the German countryside.
ANNA: Carl took over two hour's worth of slides.
CARL: If you'll just dim the lights, please. *(The Third Man wheels in the projector and operates it throughout the travelogue.)*
CARL: Well. Bonn's as good a place to start as anywhere. This is the view from our snug little hotel we stayed in. The gateway to the Rhine, the birthplace of Beethoven, and the resting place of Schumann.
(Slide: the view of downtown Baltimore from the Ramada Inn near Johns Hopkins Hospital, overlooking the industrial harbor.)
ANNA: Looks a lot like Baltimore to me.

CARL: My sister jests. As you can see in the slide, one night we splurged and stayed in a rather dear inn near the Drachenfels mountains, where Lord Byron had sported.
(Slide: a close-up of the balcony railing looking into the Ramada Inn hotel room.)
ANNA: *(Dead-panned.)* This is the room I slept in while I stayed with my brother Carl.
(Slide: gutted ruins of inner-city Baltimore near the Jones-Fall Expressway; rubble and obvious urban blight.)
CARL: Alas, poor Koln. Practically wiped out by airplane raids during World War II, and yet, out of this destruction, the cathedral of Koln managed to survive – one of the most beautiful Gothic churches in the world, with a superb altar painted by the master artist of Koln, Stefan Lochner.
(Slide: an impoverished storefront church, a black evangelical sect in Baltimore.)
Let's see – what do we have next?
(Slide: a Sabrett's hotdog cart with its blue and orange umbrella in front of Johns Hopkins Hospital.)
Oh, yes. Let's talk about the food. Whereas I snapped mementoes of the regal pines of the Black Forest, Anna insisted on taking photos of everything she ate.
ANNA: I can remember things I feel.
CARL: Well, then, let's talk about the food. Germany has a more robust gustatory outlook than the delicate palate of France. The Germans positively celebrate the pig from snout to tail. I could not convince Anna to sample the Sulperknochen, which is a Rheingau concoction of ears, snout, tail and feet.
ANNA: Ugh.
(Slide: a close-up of vender placing a hot-dog on a bun and lathering it with mustard; there are canned sodas in a wide variety.)
CARL: And of course, everything is washed down with beer.
(Slide: Anna sipping a Bud Lite.)
ANNA: It was delicious.
CARL: Enough of food. May we talk about culture, sister, dear? Next slide, please.
(Slide: the Maryland National Armory; the state penitentiary.)
Ah, Heidelberg. Dueling scars and castles. Spectacular ruin which serves as the locale for open-air concerts and fireworks...
(Slide: the Baltimore smokestack.)
...and by a quaint cable car, you can reach the peak at Konigstuhl, 2,000 feet high, with its breathtaking view of the Neckar Valley.
(Slide: the Bromo Seltzer tower in Baltimore.)
(Slide: the interstate highways viewed from the tower.)
Every cobblestoned street, every alleyway, was so pristine and clean.
(Slide: the row-houses on Monument Street.)
(Slide: a corridor of Hopkins Hospital, outside the basement laboratories.)
Wasn't it, Anna:?
ANNA: *(Dead-pan.)* Yes. Sterile.
(Slide: a hospital aide washing the floor.)
CARL: Even the Black Forest looked swept. We splurged once again and stayed

at the Waldhorn Post here, outside of Wildbad.
(Slide: exterior of Johns Hopkins Hospital.)
The hotel dates back to 1145 – the chef there is renowned for his game dishes.
(Slide: Anna in front of a vending machine dispensing wrapped sandwiches in the Hopkins Hospital cafeteria.)
ANNA: I wasn't too hungry.
CARL: I was ravenous.
(Slides: Route 95 outside the harbor tunnel; the large toll signs are visible.)
Let's see – the Romantic Road...Die Romantishe Strasse...a trek through picture-book Bavaria and the Allgau Alpen...Fussen to Wurzburg.
ANNA: Honey, perhaps they've seen enough. It's hard to sit through this many –
CARL: Wait. Just one more. They've got to see Neuschwanstein, built by mad King Ludwig II. It's so rococco it's Las Vegas.
(Slide: the castle at Disneyland.)
I believe that Ludwig was reincarnated in the twentieth century as Liberace. Wait a moment, that's not the castle.
ANNA: Yes, it is.
CARL: *(Upset.)* It looks like – how did that get in here?
ANNA: I don't know which castle you're referring to, but it's definitely a castle.
(Slide: a close-up of the castle, with a large Mickey Mouse in the picture.)
CARL: That's not funny, Anna! Are you making fun of me?
ANNA: Don't get upset.
(Slide: Donald Duck has joined Mickey Mouse with tourists.)
CARL: I went to Europe. I walked through Bavaria and the Black Forest. I combed through Neuschwanstein! I did these things, and I will remember the beauty of it all my life! I don't appreciate your mockery !
ANNA: It's just a little –
CARL: You went through Germany on your back. All you'll remember are hotel ceilings. You can show them your Germany –
(He rushes off, angry.)
ANNA: Sometimes my brother gets upset for no apparent reason. Some wires cross in his brain and he – I'm sorry. Lights, please. *(The Third Man wheels the projector off-stage.)*
I would like to show you my impressions of Germany. They were something like this –

Scene XX *In Munich.*

> *Anna is under the sheet beside the Munich Virgin, who is*
> *very young.*

ANNA: Are you comfortable?
MUNICH VIRGIN: Ja, ja...danke.
ANNA: Good. Have you been the bellhop here for a long time?
MUNICH VIRGIN: Not so very long a time. My vater owns the hotel, and says I

must learn and work very hard. Soon I will be given the responsibility of the front desk.

ANNA: My. That's exciting. *(Pause.)* Are you cold?

MUNICH VIRGIN: Nein. Just a...klein nervos. My English is not so very good.

ANNA: Is this your first time? You always remember your first time. *(Pause.)* I'm very honored. *(Pause.)* Listen. I'm a schoolteacher. May I tell you something? A little lesson? When you're a much older man, and you've loved many women, you'll be a wonderful lover if you're just a little bit nervous ...like you are right now. Because it will always be the first time.

MUNICH VIRGIN: You are a very nice woman.

ANNA: The human body is a wonderful thing. Like yours. Like mine. The beauty of the body heals all the sickness, all the bad things that happen to it. And I really want you to feel this. Because if you feel it, you'll remember it. And then maybe you'll remember me.

Scene XXI

> *Anna and the Munich Virgin rise. Carl gets into the bed
> with his stuffed rabbit. Anna gets ready to leave.*

THE THIRD MAN: Conjugations of the verb "verlassen." To leave, to abandon, to forsake. The present tense.

CARL: Are you leaving me alone?

ANNA: Yes. Just for a little while. I need to take a walk. I'm restless. It's perfectly safe.

CARL: Okay, sweetie. Don't be too long. Bunny and I are ready for bed.

ANNA: I won't stay out long. I'll be right back.

THE THIRD MAN: The future tense of the verb "verlassen."

CARL: Will you be leaving me alone again tonight? I'm ready for bed.

ANNA: I will be leaving you alone. Just for a little while.

CARL: Who will it be tonight? The bellhop? The desk clerk? Or the maitre d'?

ANNA: Don't be mean. You said you didn't make judgments.

CARL: I don't. I just want to spend time with you.

ANNA: I'll be back in time for a bedtime story.

THE THIRD MAN: The past tense of the verb "verlassen."

CARL: Again? Again? You left me alone last night. And the night before.

ANNA: I can't help it. I've been a good girl for the past thirty years. Now I want to make up for lost time.

CARL: And what am I supposed to do while you're out traipsing around with every Thomas, Deiter und Heinrich?

ANNA: Hug bunny.

THE THIRD MAN: There are three moods of the verb "verlassen": the indicative, the imperative, and the subjunctive. Anna and Carl are never in the same mood.

CARL: Leave me alone.
ANNA: Carl, don't be like that.
CARL: Why? It doesn't matter what I want. You are going to leave.
ANNA: I never stay out very long.
CARL: All I can say is if this establishment charges us for room service, they've got some nerve –
ANNA: I've got to take what opportunities come along –
CARL: I wish you wouldn't go –
ANNA: Please understand. I don't have much time. I spend as much time with you as I can, but while I still have my health...please?

Scene XXII

THE THIRD MAN: As children they fought.
CARL: We never fought, really.
ANNA: Not in a physical way. He was a sickly child.
CARL: She was very willful.
ANNA: No rough-housing. But he knew all of my weak points. My secret openings. He could be ruthless.
CARL: She'd cry at the slightest thing.
ANNA: He has a very sharp tongue.
CARL: But when one of you is very, very sick, you can't fight. It's not fair. You've got to hold it in. We never fight.
ANNA: But we had a doozy in the hotel room in Berlin.
CARL: Well, my god, Anna, even though you're sick, I have the right to get angry.
ANNA: We'd been traveling too long. We were cranky. The rooms were closing in.
CARL: I'm just saying that we should spend a little more time together. I don't get to see you alone enough. You're always restless.
ANNA: Fine. You go out without me for a change.
CARL: I'm going out for a walk.
ANNA: *(Starting to weep.)* I don't care.
CARL: When she was little, this would be the time I'd bribe her. With a comic book or an ice cream. I always had pennies saved up for these little contigencies.
ANNA: But sometimes, for the sake of my pride, I would be inconsolable. I would rush off and then feel just awful alone. Why didn't I take the bribe? *(To Carl.)* I'm going out.
CARL: To fuck?
ANNA: No, dear. The passive voice is used to emphasize the subject, to indicate the truth of the generalization. I'm going out. To get fucked.

Scene XXIII

Music: Kurt Weill. Anna goes over to a small cabaret table.
There is a telephone on the table. The Radical Student
Activist sits at another identical table, smoking, watching
her.

ANNA: I'm going to enjoy Berlin without him. I'll show him. I'm going to be carefree, totally without scruples. I'll pretend I've never taught first-graders. *(Beat.)* I'm going to have a perfectly miserable time. *(The Radical Student Activist picks up the telephone. The telephone at Anna's table rings.)* Oh my goodness. My miserable time is calling me. *(Anna picks up the phone.)* Yes?
RADICAL STUDENT ACTIVIST: Are you alone, Fraulein?
ANNA: Well, uh, actually – yes, I am.
RADICAL STUDENT ACTIVIST: Gut. Du willst mal richtig durchgefickt werden, ja?
ANNA: I'm sorry. I don't speak a word of German. *(The Radical Student Activist laughs.)*
RADICAL STUDENT ACTIVIST: Ja. Even better. I said, would you like to get fucked?
ANNA: Do you always come on to single women like that?
RADICAL STUDENT ACTIVIST: Would you like it better if I bought you tall drinks with umbrellas? Told to you the stories of how hard a time my parents had during the war? Tell you how exciting I find foreign women, how they are the real women, not like the pale northern madchen here at home? How absolutely bourgeois.
ANNA: I see. Why do you come here?
RADICAL STUDENT ACTIVIST: I don't come here for the overpriced drinks. I come here because of the bored western women who come here, who leave their tired businessmen husbands in the hotel rooms behind.
ANNA: You're cute. In a hostile way.
RADICAL STUDENT ACTIVIST: Fucking is a revolutionary act.
ANNA: Your hovel or my hotel?

Scene XXIV

In the hotel room. Anna, awake, lies in the middle of the bed.
To her left, Carl sleeps, curled up. To her right, the
Radical Student Activist, curled on her breast, slumbers.
Anna is awake with an insomniacal desperation.

ANNA: *(Singing softly.)* Two and two are four; four and four are eight; eight and eight are sixteen; sixteen and sixteen are thirty-two–
RADICAL STUDENT ACTIVIST: *(Groggy.)* Wo ist die Toilette?
(The Radical Student Activist rises and stumbles stage left.)

ANNA: In love-making, he's all fury and heat. His North Sea pounding against your Dreamer. And when you look up and see his face, red and huffing, it's hard to imagine him ever having been tiny, wrinkled, and seven pounds. That is, until afterwards. When he rises from sleep and he walks into the bathroom. And there he exposes his soft little derriere, and you can still see the soft baby flesh. *(As the Radical Student Activist comes back into the room.)* I've got to put a name to that behind. What's your name? Wie heissen Sie? *(The Radical Student Activist starts dressing in a hurry.)*

RADICAL STUDENT ACTIVIST: Auf Wiedersehn. Next thing you'll ask for my telephone number.

ANNA: No, I won't. I was just curious –

RADICAL STUDENT ACTIVIST: Ja, ja...und then my sign of the zodiac. I'll get cards from Hallmark und little scribblings like "I'll never forget the night we shared."

ANNA: Forget it.

RADICAL STUDENT ACTIVIST: There is something radical in two complete strangers committing biological necessity without having to give into bourgeois conventions of love, without breeding to produce workers for a capitalist system, without the benediction of the church, the family, the bosses –

ANNA: I have something to confess to you. I lied to you.

RADICAL STUDENT ACTIVIST: About what?

ANNA: I'm not here on business. I don't specialize in corporate takeovers. I don't work on Wall Street. I only told you that because I thought that was what you wanted to hear.

RADICAL STUDENT ACTIVIST: Okay. So you do estate planning? Income tax?

ANNA: No. You just committed a revolutionary act with a first-grade schoolteacher who lives in low-income housing. And I'm tired. I think you should go.

RADICAL STUDENT ACTIVIST: And your husband?

ANNA: Not too loud. And he's not my husband. He's my brother. A maiden librarian for the San Francisco Public. *(As the Radical Student Activist starts to leave.)* And by the way – the missionary position does not a revolution make. *(The Radical Student Activist leaves. Anna, depressed, lies down. Carl rises from the bed.)*

Scene XXV

CARL: And as she lay in the bed, sleepless, it swept over her – the way her classroom smelled early in the morning, before the children came. It smelled of chalk dust –

THE THIRD MAN: It smelled of crayola wax, crushed purple and green –

CARL: The cedar of hamster cage shavings –

THE THIRD MAN: The sweet wintergreen of LePage's paste –

CARL: The wooden smell of the thick construction paper –

THE THIRD MAN: The spillings of sticky orange drink and sour milk –
THE THIRD MAN and CARL: *(Simultaneously.)* And the insidious smell of first-grader pee.
CARL: It smelled like heaven.
ANNA: And the first thing I did each morning was put up the weather map for today on the board under the flag. A bright, smiling sun, or Miss Cloud or Mr. Umbrella. On special days I put up Suzy Snowflake. And when I opened my desk drawer, scattered like diamonds on the bottom were red, silver and gold stars. *(Beat.)* I want to go home. Carl, I want to go home.
CARL: Soon, sweetie. Very soon.
ANNA: I've had enough. I've seen all of the world I want to see. I want to wake up in my own bed. I want to sit with you at home and we'll watch the weather. And we'll wait.
CARL: We've come so far. We have to at least go to Vienna. Do you think you can hold out long enough to meet Dr. Todelsrocheln?
(Anna, miserable and homesick, nods.) That a girl. I promise you don't have to undertake his…hydrotherapy unless you decide to. I have a friend in Vienna, a college chum, who might be able to get us some of the blackmarket stuff. It's worth a shot.
ANNA: Then you'll take me home?
CARL: Then I'll take you home.

Scene XXVI

> *Music: the zither theme from "The Third Man." Carl and*
> *Anna stand, with their luggage, in front of a door buzzer.*

CARL: First we'll just look up Harry and leave our bags here. Then we'll cab over to Dr. Todesrocheln. *(Carl rings the buzzer. They wait. Carl rings the buzzer again. They wait. An aging Concierge comes out.)*
Entschuldigung. Wir suchen Harry Lime? Do you speak English?
CONCIERGE: Nein. Ich spreche kein Englisch. *(Carl and the Concierge start to shout as if the other one was deaf.)*
CARL: Herr Lime? Do you know him? Herr Harry Lime?
CONCIERGE: Ach. Ach. Ja, Herr Harry Lime. You come…too spat.
CARL: He's gone? Too spat?
CONCIERGE: Funf minuten too spat. Er ist tot –
CARL: What?
CONCIERGE: Ja. Ein auto mit Harry splatz-machen auf der Strasse. Splatz!
ANNA: Splatz!?
CARL: Splatz?! *(It dawns on Carl and Anna what the Concierge is saying.)*
CONCIERGE: Ja, ja. Er geht uber die strasse, und cin auto… spppllaattz!
ANNA: Oh, my god!
CONCIERGE: *(Gesturing with hands.)* Ja. Er hat auch eine rabbit. Herr rabbit auch – sppllaattz! They are…diggen ein grab in den Boden. Jetz.

CARL: Now? You saw this happen?
CONCIERGE: Ja. I...saw it mit meinen own Augen. Splatz. *(As he exits.)*
"Splatzen, splatzen, uber alles..."
CARL: Listen, darling. I want you to take a cab to the doctor's office.
ANNA: Where are you going?
CARL: Ich verlasse. I'll find out what happened to Harry.
ANNA: I wish you wouldn't leave...
CARL: I'll come back. Okay?

Scene XXVII

> *Anna climbs onto a table and gathers a white paper sheet around her. She huddles.*

ANNA: Some things are the same in every country. You're scared when you see the doctor, here in Vienna just like in Baltimore. And they hand you the same paper cup to fill, just like in America. Then you climb up onto the same cold metal table, and they throw a sheet around you and you feel very small. And just like at home, they tell you to wait. And you wait. *(As Anna waits, dwarfed on the table, the scene with Harry Lime and Carl unfolds. "The Third Man" theme music up.)*

Scene XXVIII *On the Ferris Wheel in the Prater.*

> *Carl holds the stuffed rabbit closely.*

CARL: I just came from your funeral.
HARRY LIME: I'm touched, old man. Was it a nice funeral?
CARL: What are you doing? Why are we meeting here?
HARRY LIME: It's best not to ask too many questions. The police were beginning to do that. It's extremely convenient, now and then in a man's career, to die. I've gone underground. So if you want to meet me, you have to come here. No one asks questions here.
CARL: Can you help us? *(Harry Lime at first does not answer. He looks at the view.)*
HARRY LIME: Where is your sister? She left you alone?
CARL: She's – she needs her rest.
HARRY LIME: Have you looked at the view from up here? It's quite inspiring. No matter how old I get, I always love the ferris wheel.
CARL: You were my closest friend in college.
HARRY LIME: I'll be straight with you. I can give you the drugs – but it won't help. It won't help at all. Your sister's better off with that quack Todesrocheln – we call him the Yellow Queen of Vienna – she might end up drinking her own piss, but it won't kill her.

CARL: But I thought you had the drugs –

HARRY LIME: Oh, I do. And they cost a pretty penny. For a price, I can give them to you. At a discount for old times. But you have to know, we make them up in my kitchen.

CARL: Jesus.

HARRY LIME: Why not? People will pay for these things. When they're desperate, people will eat peach pits, or aloe, or egg protein – they'll even drink their own piss. It gives them hope.

CARL: How can you do this?

HARRY LIME: Listen, old man, if you want to be a millionaire, you go into real estate. If you want to be a billionaire, you sell hope. Nowadays the only place a fellow can make a decent career of it is in Mexico and Europe.

CARL: That's…disgusting.

HARRY LIME: Look. I thought you weren't going to be… sentimental about this. It's a business. You have to have the right perspective. Like from up here…the people down on the street are just tiny little dots. And if you could charge 1,000 dollars, wouldn't you push the drugs? I could use a friend I can trust to help me.

CARL: When we were at Hopkins together, I thought you were God. You could hypnotize us into doing anything, and it would seem …charming. Carl, old man, you'd say, "Just do it." Cutting classes, cribbing exams, shop-lifting, stupid undergraduate things – and I would do it. Without knowing the consequences. I would do it.

THE THIRD MAN: Oh, you knew the consequences, old man. You knew. You chose not to think about them.

CARL: I've grown old before my time from the consequences. I'm turning you in.

HARRY LIME: I wouldn't do that, old man. *(Harry Lime pats a bulge on the inside of his trench coat.)* By the time you hit the ground, you'll be just a tiny little dot. *(Carl and Harry Lime look at each other, waiting.)*
And I think you have something I want. The rabbit, bitte.

CARL: No. You're not getting it. I'm taking it with me. *(Harry Lime puts his arms in position for a waltz and begins to sway, seductively.)*

HARRY LIME: Come on, give it up. Come to my arms, my only one. Dance with me, my beloved, my sweet – *(Carl takes the stuffed rabbit and threatens to throw it out the window of the ferris wheel. A Strauss waltz plays very loudly, and Harry Lime and Carl waltz-struggle for the rabbit. Carl is pushed and Harry Lime waltzes off with the rabbit.)*

Scene XXIX

Meanwhile, back at Doctor Todesrocheln.

ANNA: You begin to hope that the wait is proportionate to the medical expertise. My God. My feet are turning blue. Where am I? An HMO?
The problem with being an adult is that you never forget why you're waiting.

When I was a child, I could wait blissfully unaware for hours. I used to read signs and transpose letters, or count tiles in the floor. And in the days before I could read, I would make up stories about my hands – Mr. Left and Mr. Right. *(Beat.)* Mr. Left would provoke Mr. Right. Mr. Right would ignore it. The trouble would escalate, until my hands were battling each other to the death. *(Beat. Anna demonstrates.)* Then one of them would weep. Finally, they became friends again, and they'd dance – *(Anna's two hands dance together; she is unaware that Dr. Todesrocheln has entered and is watching her. He clears his throat. He wears a very dirty lab coat with pockets filled with paper and a stale doughnut. He wears a white fright wig and glasses. He also wears one sinister black glove. With relish, he carries a flask of a golden liquid.)* Oh, thank goodness.

DR. TODESROCHELN: Ja. So happy to meet you. Such an interesting specimen. I congratulate you. Very, very interesting.

ANNA: Thank you.

DR. TODESROCHELN: We must have many more such specimens from you – for the urinocryoscopy, the urinometer, the urinoglucosometer, the uroacidimeter, uroazotometer, and mein new acquirement in der laboratorium – ein urophosphometer.

ANNA: My goodness. *(Dr. Todesrocheln has put the flask down on a table. Quietly, his left hand reaches for it; the right hand stops the left.)*

DR. TODESROCHELN: Ja. Nowadays, we have learned to discover the uncharted mysteries of the fluids discharged through the urethra. We have been so primitive in the past. Doctors once could only analyze by taste and smell – but thanks to the advancement of medical science, there are no limits to our thirst for knowledge.

ANNA: Uh-huh. *(Dr. Todesrocheln's left hand seizes the flask. Trembling, with authority, his right hand replaces the flask on the table, and soothes the left hand into quietude.)*

DR. TODESROCHELN: So much data has been needlessly, carelessly destroyed in the past – the medical collections of Ravensbruck senselessly annihilated – and that is why, as a scientist, I must be exacting in our measurements and recordings.

ANNA: What can I hope to find out from these…specimens?

DR. TODESROCHELN: Ah, yes – the layman must have his due! Too much pure research und no application makes Jack…macht Jack… *(Dr. Todesrocheln loses his train of thought.)*

Fraulein Anna – I may call you Fraulein Anna? – Let us look at the body as an alchemist, taking in straw and mud und schweinefleisch and processing it into liquid gold which purifies the body. You might say that the sickness of the body can only be cured by the health of the body. To your health! *(His left hand seizes the flask in a salute, and raises the flask to his lips. In time, the right hand brings the flask down. A brief struggle. It appears the flask might spill, but at last the right hand triumphs.)*

ANNA: You know, even though I really grew up in the suburbs of Baltimore, I like to think of myself as an open-minded person –

DR. TODESROCHELN: The ancient Greeks knew that the aromatic properties of the fluid could reveal the imbalances of the soul itself... *(The left hand sneaks towards the flask.)*

ANNA: I'm always very eager to try new foods, or see the latest John Waters film –

DR. TODESROCHELN: – its use in the purification rites of the Aztecs is, of course, so well known that it need not be mentioned – *(The hand has grasped the flask and begins to inch it off the table.)*

ANNA: And whenever I meet someone who cross-dresses, I always compliment him on his shoes or her earrings –

DR. TODESROCHELN: It is the first golden drop that marks the infant's identity separate from the womb – *(The hand has slipped the flask beneath the table; his right hand is puzzled.)*

ANNA: But still, it's important to know where your threshhold is...and I think we're coming dangerously close to mine...

DR. TODESROCHELN: Until the last precious amber releases the soul from the body – ashes to ashes, drop to drop – excuse me – *(His left hand, with the flask, swings in an arc behind his body; he swivels his body to the flask, his back turned to us; we can hear him drink in secrecy. With his back turned...)* Ahhh... *(He orders himself. Composed, he turns around to face Anna again, and demurely sets down the flask. Its level is noticeably lower. Anna is aghast.)*
I can sense your concern. I have been prattling on without regard to questions you must surely have –

ANNA: Is that your real hair?

DR. TODESROCHELN: Of course, I can not promise results, but first we must proceed by securing more samples –

ANNA: I don't believe that's your real hair.

DR. TODESROCHELN: I will need first of all twenty-four hours of your time for a urononcometry –

ANNA: *(Increasingly scared.)* You look familiar to me –

DR. TODESROCHELN: Although I can tell you from a first taste – er, test, that your uroammonica level is high – not unpleasantly so, but full-bodied –

ANNA: Oh, my god...I think I know who you are... you're... you're... *(Anna rises to snatch his toupee. Dr. Todesrocheln suddenly stands, menacing. And the light change.)*

DR. TODESROCHELN: WO IST DEIN BRUDER? *(He takes off his wig and glasses and appears as the Doctor in the first scene, peeling off the black gloves to reveal latex gloves underneath.)*
You fool! You left your brother in the room alone! WO IST DEIN BRUDER?

> *Music: "The Emperor Waltz" plays at a very loud volume. Anna, frightened, races from the doctor's office to the hotel room. We see Carl, lying stiff beneath a white sheet. To the tempo of the Strauss, Anna tries to wake him. He does not respond. Anna forces him into a sitting position, the stuffed rabbit clenched beneath his arm. Carl remains*

*sitting, stiff, eyes open, wooden. Then he slumps. Anna
raises him again. He remains upright for a beat, and begins
to fall. Anna stops him, presses his body against hers, pulls
his legs over the bed, tries to stand him up. Frozen, his body
tilts against hers. She tries to make him cross the floor, his
arms around her neck. She positions him in a chair, but his
legs are locked in a perpendicular angle and will not touch
the floor. He mechanically springs forward. Then, suddenly,
like the doll in E.T.A. Hoffman, the body of Carl becomes
animated, but with a strange, automatic life of its own, and
faltering, falls back to the bed. There is the sound of a loud
alarm clock; the Doctor enters, and covers Carl with a
sheet. Then he pulls a white curtain in front of the scene, as
the stage lights become, for the first time, harsh, stark and
white.)*

Scene XXX *In the hospital lounge.*

*The Doctor holds the stuffed rabbit and travel brochures in
his hands. He awkwardly peels off his latex gloves.*

DOCTOR: I'm sorry. There was nothing we could do.
ANNA: Yes. I know.
DOCTOR: I thought you might want to take this along with you. *(The Doctor
hands Anna the stuffed rabbit.)*
ANNA: *(To the stuffed rabbit.)* There you are! *(Anna hugs the stuffed rabbit and
sees the Doctor watching her.)*
It's Jo-Jo. My brother's childhood rabbit. I brought it to the hospital as a little
surprise. I thought it might make him feel better.
DOCTOR: Sometimes little things become important, when nothing else will
help –
ANNA: Yes. *(They pause and stand together awkwardly.)* At least Carl went in
his sleep. I guess that's a blessing.
DOCTOR: If one has to die from this particular disease, there are worse ways to
go than pneumonia.
ANNA: I never would have believed what sickness can do to the body. *(Pause.)*
Well, Doctor, I want to thank you for all you've done for my brother.
DOCTOR: I wish I could do more. By the way, housekeeping found these
brochures in your brother's bedside table. I didn't know if they were important.
(Anna takes the brochures.)
ANNA: Ah, yes. The brochures for Europe. I've never been abroad. We're going
to go when he gets – *(Anna stops herself. With control.)* I must learn to use the
past tense. We would have gone had he gotten better.
DOCTOR: Anna – may I call you Anna? – I, uh, if there's anything I can do –
ANNA: Thank you, but there's nothing you can do –

DOCTOR: I mean, I really would like it if you'd call me for coffee, or if you just want to talk about all this – *(The Doctor trails off. Anna looks at him. She smiles. He squirms.)*
ANNA: You're very sweet. But no, I don't think so. Not now. I feel it's simply not safe for me right now to see anyone. Thanks again and goodbye.
(Anna starts to exit. The Doctor, wistful, watches her go. The lighting begins to change back to the dreamy atmosphere of the first scene. Softly, a Strauss waltz begins. Carl, in uniform, perfectly well, waits for Anna. They waltz off as the lights dim.)

END OF PLAY

UNFINISHED STORIES
by Sybille Pearson

Playwright's Biography

Sybille Pearson is the librettist of the musical "Baby" for which she received a Tony nomination. She is the author of the plays:"Sally and Marsha", "Phantasie", "Unfinished Stories" and "Watching The Dog". She is a recipient of a Rockefeller Playwrights Fellowship and has been a participant at the O'Neill Playwrights Conference, the Sundance Playwrights Conference and is a founding member of The Playwrights Circle at The New York Theatre Workshop. She is a teacher of musical theater at the Tisch School of the Arts at New York University, a member of the Dramatists Guild and a Board Member of The League of Professional Theatre Women / New York.

Playwright's Note

In Germany during the years of the Weimar Republic when Berlin vied with Paris as the cultural capital of Europe, German-Jewish intellectuals contributed brilliantly to a renaissance of literature, music, art and ideas. What many who lived through those years remembered as a lost paradise of arts, letters and humane life styles was destroyed by the Nazi counter-revolution when books were burned in bonfires, and artists and intellectuals were driven into exile or murdered. Among the most brilliant of the proscribed, exiled and executed were:

Erich Mühsam: the epitome of the cabaret poet, Mühsam's natural habitat was the literary cafe...socialist, Bohemian, satirist, anti-communist, anti-authoritarian, frequently homeless, contributor to the sardonic magazine "Simplicissimus". In March 1933, Mühsam was arrested by the Gestapo in a roundup of left-wing intellectuals and for 17 months endured beatings and torture in a succession of concentration camps until on July 9, 1935, he was murdered by the prison guards.

Kurt Tucholsky: critic, cabaret poet, novelist, celebrated for his social satire, political commentary, cultural criticism and chanson poetry, and for his satire, "one of the most feared of the intellectuals hated by the nazis". Despairing of Germany's future, ill and tired, he swallowed poison in Goteberg and died on December 21, 1935.

Ernst Toller: playwright and poet, an idealist, pacifist, political Utopian and passionate believer in human dignity, he joined the Independent Socialists led by Kurt Eisner and Gustav Landauer, and was elected deputy to the president after the bloodless Munich revolution of November 1918. With the failure of the revolution, Toller was imprisoned for five years during which he wrote plays which were concurrently produced in German's leading theatres. In exile after the nazis took over, Toller eventually, in 1938, hung himself in his room at the Mayflower Hotel in New York.

Two thoughts for the actors and director:

1. If there is a family trait that connects all the characters in Unfinished Stories, it is their lack of sentimentality. Walter abhors the sentimental. He sets the tone for the play as well as influencing the behavior of the family.

His patricianism is a question of quiet assurance, a certainty that he is being attended to. He takes for granted that being the center of attention is his privilege. He is a man of extraordinary human dignity with a sense of humor and the ability to show love to his daughter-in-law and grandson, but a man who can also be Prussian-like in accomplishing his determined objective.

2. Each character is always aware of Walter's presence in the room, especially Daniel and Yves. How near do I sit to him? Do I sit? Do I show him what I am feeling? Did he see what I just did? What did he think of what I just said? These are a few of the questions that are asked between the lines. Each character has a well-learned response and "cover". Where do these "covers" break? What is each character's behavior when they are alone?

This is a family that is too used to talking to each other indirectly, either through the walls of rooms or through this person to reach the other person. Each direct communication in the play is an unprepared moment for the character.

The life of the play depends on the above behavior and the inter-related life of the actors on the stage. They can never be aware of the audience but are deeply involved with each other. The credibility of the play depends on this moment-to-moment authenticity, on the creation of a family by the actors and director.

Sybille Pearson
November 13, 1992

CHARACTERS

WALTER, 80
DANIEL, 25
GABY, 54, Daniel's mother
YVES, 54

ORIGINAL CAST

"Unfinished Stories" was presented at the Center Theatre Group-Mark Taper Forum. The director was Gordon Davidson.

WALTER.............................Joseph Wiseman
DANIEL.............................Christopher Collet
GABY.............................Fionnula Flanagan
YVES.............................Hal Linden

SETTING

The set is a five-room Upper West Side apartment, delineated into playing areas by the use of trompe l'oeil.

In the front center is the LIVING ROOM, the most fully realized playing area. Its entrance is an archway. It contains a small desk, couch, two armchairs, a lamp, a phonograph, small tables, etc. The fourth wall is an imaginary picture window, looking out onto the Hudson River.

The other rooms are:

DANIEL'S OLD ROOM. The playing area is a sixties bean bag chair and a trunk covered with a shawl.

WALTER'S ROOM. The playing area is a single bed, a night table, a chair and a large bookcase which is the focal point of the entire set.

GABY'S ROOM. The playing area is an old carved wooden armchair, a desk and computer, and a Victorian coat rack for clothes.

THE KITCHEN. The playing area is a refrigerator and a table and four chairs.

THE BATHROOM. The playing area is the sink and the mirrored medicine chest above it.

There are corridors of trompe l'oeil HALLWAY that connect the rooms. To the right of the apartment is the FRONT DOOR, besides which is a coat rack.

Stretching into the wings is the playing area of the OUTER HALLWAY of the apartment building which leads to the unseen elevator.

(In a less elaborate set, each room can be defined simply by its own "practical" lamp.)

NOTE

When any of the characters enter onto the stage, they are *always* visible. Alone in their rooms, away from the others, they are as much in the action as when they speak to each other: their private reactions, at times, are in contrast to their public responses. The drama takes place in the entire apartment.

Unfinished Stories

Scene 1

Lights rise on Walter, an eighty-year-old man, asleep in his living room armchair. He is a frail man who speaks with a German accent. His cane lies on the floor beside him. A standing halogen lamp, bright, is lit behind him.

Enter Daniel, age 25, walks with a slight limp, dressed in well-used black jeans and jacket, carrying a car radio. He crosses the Outer Hallway, removes keys from his pocket, opens front door and enters through archway into the living room. He sees Walter and whispers into rest of the apartment.

DANIEL: Mom. *(He enters Gaby's room and turns on light.)* Mom? *(He returns to living room, looks at airmail letter on side table, then whispers to Walter.)* Don't wake up. It's Daniel. Sleep. *(Walter nods in his sleep.)* *(Daniel checks his watch, puts his hand on Walter's wrist and takes Walter's pulse. Walter wakes.)*
DANIEL: Hey Opa. *("Opa" is German for grandfather.)* *(Walter holds onto Daniel's hand. He speaks from the excitement of his dream.)*
WALTER: To feel a page in a dream! It was a book from Wegner's. I bought it...? 1924. December. Wintertime. Berlin. I bought it before I saw Mühsam. I ran to the train to meet Mühsam. I ran with the book under my arm and barked like a dog to keep warm. *(He barks and laughs.)* And the book was? *(He angrily turns off light.)* It goes in the light. It goes.
DANIEL: *(Calming.)* You'll remember it. *(The room is lit by the ceiling fixture in the archway and by the morning light that filters through the closed living room curtains of the fourth wall.)*
WALTER: *(Angry.)* I have lived too long.
DANIEL: It was a dream.
WALTER: *(With force.)* How do you speak? Erich Mühsam was no dream!
DANIEL: I don't know.
WALTER: I never told you.
DANIEL: You didn't.
WALTER: Na nu. *(He makes a decision.)* Na nu. *(*Na nu is a German sigh, an exclamation, changing with the speaker's mood.)*
DANIEL: I brought you the book review.
WALTER: Yes. *(Daniel gives it to Walter.)*
DANIEL: It's a month late, I know. But it's not last month's.
WALTER: Thank you. *(He points to desk chair.)* Bring that here.
DANIEL: Every time I'd try to get here. I'd put my off-duty on and...
WALTER: No more...
DANIEL: I'd say to them I'm not taking fares. I'm going to my grandfather's...
WALTER: No more. Bring the chair. *(Daniel brings his chair to "his place" by

Walter, but he doesn't stay in one place for long. Walter, having less energy after shouting, speaks quietly, but with his usual autocratic tone.) Tell me. You took my pulse?
DANIEL: Yeah. Did you like yesterday? The yellow bushes, in the park, turning into flowers...
WALTER: Forsythia.
DANIEL: Like they all got a signal, at the same time, and the seasons changed in an hour. Did you get to your bench? See Luther? The guy you sit with. The guy with the baseball bat for a cane.
WALTER: You were taking my pulse?
DANIEL: What can I say? I learned CPR.
WALTER: Where did you learn it? A school?
DANIEL: I didn't become a doctor. I still drive a cab.
WALTER: You think I'd like you to be a doctor?
DANIEL: You're a doctor.
WALTER: Not without a practice. Not for fifty years.
DANIEL: I still think of you as a doctor.
WALTER: "Des Menschen Himmel ist allein sein Hoffen." *(Daniel gestures he doesn't understand.)* Man's only heaven is his capacity for hope. A doctor should not be a doctor without this capacity.
DANIEL: You didn't have it?
WALTER: *You* find it.
DANIEL: *(Dismissive.)* Yeah.
WALTER: But don't be a doctor for me. I've seen enough to ever see another.
DANIEL: You go to one?
WALTER: *(Dismissive.)* Of course. *(Interrogating.)* Why did you learn this now?
DANIEL: You drive a cab at night in New York, if you get shot, you can tell someone what to do for you. *(Pause.)* I'm coming back. I'm joining the creatures of the day.
WALTER: What does this mean?
DANIEL: Starting today. I'm driving days. Taking the day shift.
WALTER: Good.
DANIEL: It's nothing to do with my not handling the night. Nothing to do with safety. I've got the reflexes. I can handle it. It's four years. It's...it's making a change.
WALTER: Na nu.
DANIEL: I'm thinking about...what do you think about my leaving the city?
WALTER: To do what?
DANIEL: You see, if I'd learned farming...
WALTER: Farming?
DANIEL: *(Continuing.)* If I hadn't screwed around with acting...
WALTER: You did what your father wanted.
DANIEL: I never studied acting cause he wanted me to.
WALTER: You haven't left your father's table, my boy.
DANIEL: I haven't lived here for four years!

WALTER: You will.

DANIEL: I've been driving for four years. Been in my own place for four years.

WALTER: *(Waves his hand.)* No more. Tell me about leaving the city.

DANIEL: I mean, sure, he's an actor but that was never why I went. I mean, that's so weak, man!

WALTER: No more! What will you do?–

DANIEL: Where did you always say I did my growing up?

WALTER: In the summer.

DANIEL: In the country, when Dad was doing stock.

WALTER: The first summer I moved in with you, when my wife died, you were five, and I came and lived here, and you... you would go nowhere without your bicycle. Remember? But then *we* walked. Five miles. Seven miles.

DANIEL: I figure it out in the country. I lose it when I come back to the city. What I'd like is a Christmas tree farm. *(Walter is dismayed but covers this reaction.)*

WALTER: Christmas trees?

DANIEL: It offends you.

WALTER: Offends me?

DANIEL: I don't have any religion.

WALTER: My boy. *(He gestures Daniel closer to him.)* My father would say, if a policeman asks your religion, you say Jew. This was before Hitler. Do not say to the policeman we are agnostics. He will spit and say, "You dirty Jew, you try to ingratiate yourself with us." We do not give him that satisfaction. But to a Jew also say Jew. If you say we are agnostics, he will spit and say, "You dirty Jew hater. Selbsthasser." I thought my father was a coward. I said to all what I was. Agnostic. There hadn't been a God in the house for four generations. My father stayed in Berlin. He was murdered as a Jew. So I say I am a Jew. Without a God and now with a Christmas tree. And I like it. I like to think of you in the country. Yes. *(Daniel, pleased, whistles a phrase from the Brahms' Violin Concerto.)* Brahms.

DANIEL: Your record, Opa.

WALTER: Yes. *(Walter gestures for Daniel to walk.)* Walk. *(Daniel walks as though he were in a doctor's office.)*

DANIEL: It's been okay. It was 3 years ago. I'm okay.

WALTER: Walk back. You may sit.

DANIEL: You're *my* doctor. Where's Mom?

WALTER: *(With a smile.)* On a street corner. Making trouble with her petitions.

DANIEL: Dad back?

WALTER: *(Curtly.)* I do not know my son's plans.

DANIEL: No problem.

WALTER: *(Gestures to desk.)* He sent something. A letter. He's to be back for some play somewhere, some time. I don't know. Why does he still act?

DANIEL: He's an actor.

WALTER: He has some talent, yes, but not the talent for the great roles. Why would you stay in a profession in which you did not have the talent for the great roles?

DANIEL: I don't know.

WALTER: This new wife of his? This "Karen." You've seen her? *(Daniel, uncomfortable with conversation, looks at himself in mirror.)*

DANIEL: I don't know. I met her.

WALTER: She is much younger than him. How much younger is she? *(Daniel shows Walter the beginnings of a pot belly.)*

DANIEL: *(Yiddish accent.)* "I see it but I don't believe it!" ...You think he's still alive?

WALTER: Who?

DANIEL: *(Imitates man with accent.)* "So who are you anyway?"

WALTER: I know this man?

DANIEL: Sure, you know him.

WALTER: Where?

DANIEL: The guy who rented us his house at the lake. In Peekskill.

WALTER: Peekskill? *(Sure of himself.)* I was never in Peekskill.

DANIEL: By the lake. A small lake. Like a pond.

WALTER: I know our summers!

DANIEL: We were all in the house. Dad was doing "La Mancha" in...

WALTER: There was Falmouth. Kennebunk. The Green Mountains. The summer theatre in Rhode Island. The one he played? In Maine! And you and Gaby and I found blueberries and walked and walked. I know all the summers with you!

DANIEL: You're right. It was the summer before you moved in.

WALTER: Na nu.

DANIEL: I'm not used to mornings. I need some juice. I'll get you some. *(Referring to light.)* You want that on?

(Gaby, a 54-year-old woman, in glasses, wearing a red coat, holding a fistfull of leaflets and a bag from the bakery, enters outer hallway and crosses to front door.)

WALTER: No. And no juice.

DANIEL: Raspberry syrup with seltzer. Himbeer Saft.

WALTER: Gaby made me one. *(Daniel enters kitchen.)*

DANIEL: I'll make you coffee.

WALTER: Gaby makes my coffee.

DANIEL: What do you want?

WALTER: *(Dismissive.)* Nothing. *(Walter and Daniel, in different rooms, allow their "public" faces to fall. Walter holds the Book Review, an old man, his energy gone. Daniel leans his head on the refrigerator. He does not get himself juice.)*

(Gaby enters apartment with energy. She walks into living room, takes off her glasses, opens the curtains that cover imaginary window of fourth wall. The stage is flooded with morning light.)

GABY: *(Tosses leaflets on Walter's lap.)* This is seditious?

WALTER: Gabriella.

GABY: *(Continuing.)* If you were a cop and you had a drug dealer passing out nickel bags over here and a woman passing out leaflets telling people their libraries are in trouble over there, who would you ask to move on? Put your

fingers in your ears, Walter!
(Gaby puts phonograph on. The record on the turntable is Otis Redding's "Satisfaction." The needle falls in the middle of the song. The volume is high! Gaby stands over the phonograph absorbing the music. Walter puts his fingers in his ears. Daniel crosses to archway and listens unnoticed by Gaby.)
(Yves, a 54-year-old man, wearing corduroy jacket, turtleneck and jeans, enters outside hallway, carrying a large leather shoulder bag. Yves puts finger to doorbell, then decides to take coffee out of a paper bag. He stands in hallway drinking coffee.)
(Gaby takes record off.)
GABY: *(Referring to petition.)* See what I start with.
WALTER: I have no... *(He gestures glasses.)*
GABY: "You can be a critic of your country without being an enemy of its promise." Your words.
WALTER: Tucholsky's words.
GABY: Did he tell them to me? You did. *(She gives Walter a warm kiss.)* Morning.
WALTER: You bring me the morning.
GABY: The only difference between European charm and Irish malarkey is the accent. *(Walter points to Daniel. Gaby turns and studies him.)* The bear's out. Daniel.
DANIEL: Came by to pick up some baseball cards.
GABY: You're out of hibernation.
WALTER: Baseball cards?
DANIEL: From when I kept them. I had Mantles that may be worth...
GABY: I have two books on...
DANIEL: I don't need books.
GABY: Joe Cool. *(Gaby exits.)*
DANIEL: I'm talking cash! Not the history of cards! *(Gaby is in hallway on way to her room.)*
GABY: That's why you should read the price guide.
DANIEL: *(Overlap.)* I can't believe this! I'm here two minutes and she's on about reading.
GABY: *(Shouts from her room.)* The price guide. Read the price guide! *(She crosses back into living room.)* It's at the library.
DANIEL: *(Not graciously.)* How does a library have a price guide for baseball cards?
GABY: Because I'm the librarian.
DANIEL: *(With a smile.)* I'll look at it.
GABY: You don't look bad for a morning.
DANIEL: I got some sleep.
GABY: Under the jacket, a new shirt?
DANIEL: It's not new. I just haven't worn it. *(He looks at a record and delivers next line as a throw away.)* I'm going to be driving days now.
GABY: *(Very pleased.)* No!
DANIEL: Mom, don't get happy.

GABY: I *am* happy.
DANIEL: You get *too* happy. *(Daniel exits into his old room. He looks at it for a beat, then removes shawl from trunk and looks for cards.)*
GABY: Who'd I meet? On the corner?
WALTER: Who?
GABY: The guys you sit with on the bench. Luther the Bad and Mike One Eye.
WALTER: Yes?
GABY: I couldn't believe it. Luther threatened me. With his bat. Blamed *me* for locking you in the house, called *me* over-protective! The only way I could get rid of the two was to tell them I'd walk you over to the bench myself. Get dressed. Give me twenty minutes.
WALTER: *(Hands her petitions.)* Mike One Eye and Luther never walk on the street together.
GABY: *(Directly.)* You lie. I lie. You're going out *today*, Walter. You hear me. *(Gaby takes petitions.)*
WALTER: Die Wärterin meines Lebens! *(The zoo keeper of my life.)*
GABY: Do I understand German?!
(She exits to Daniels's room. Walter turns light off and sits in chair. Yves drinks coffee in outside hallway. Gaby crosses into Daniel's room and places the petitions in front of Daniel.)
GABY: They cut the book budgets of the literacy programs again. By forty percent! *(She crosses into her room, puts her handbag on the chair, then crosses into Walter's room, takes the sweater off the back of his chair and tosses it onto his bed.)*
GABY: 50 thousand it costs them to put someone in jail, eight to put them on welfare and two thousand to teach them how to read. They can't make connections? What do they teach them at Harvard and Yale? *(The night table drawer is open. She looks in, closes it, and crosses to Daniel's room.)* The rally's Tuesday at noon.
DANIEL: You didn't throw *anything* out of here, did you?
GABY: What am I talking about!
DANIEL: Why ask me to go when you know what I'm going to say!
GABY: When are you kids going to start making noise?
DANIEL: This is your way, not mine.
GABY: Yours is shut down and hand it to them.
DANIEL: Twelve people walking in a circle is going to stop them? I haven't seen it working.
GABY: We had three hundred thousand at ...
DANIEL: How many did the papers say were there?
GABY: They never tell it straight.
DANIEL: "That's what I'm saying. Whatever you do, they've got the power.
GABY: I'm New York. I live here, which may mean I'm certifiable, but it doesn't mean I shut up or give up or stop fighting for this city, and a lit of it is lising. But when you lose, put something red on, something bright so you can keep on going, and if you think that's woman's thinking you can shove it!

DANIEL: Did I say …

GABY: *(Over-riding him.)* I am *no* Pollyanna. My grandfather went from a depression in Ireland to another in New York City. He kept a framed cartoon from the '30's in our living room. It was of a homeless man on a park bench and a squirrel in a tree above him. The squirrel says "Why didn't you save?" The man says, " I did."

DANIEL: *(Simply.)* We were born knowing that. It's not the sixties.

GABY: *(Direct and angry.)* The only thing you learned from the '60's is that we smoked grass.

DANIEL: I had one toke that night. One fucking toke!

GABY: I'm not bringing up the party.

DANIEL: It was one fucking toke!

GABY: One toke is enough to make you walk in front of a car. Enough to get your leg broken in nine pieces. Enough to get you out of acting school!

DANIEL: Oh man, is this weak!

GABY: Yeah!

(Gaby exits into hallway to cool down. After a beat, She crosses into Walter's room and opens night table drawer. She removes a leather case and looks in it. She finds a hypodermic syringe. She takes it out of case. After a beat, She puts it back in case, puts case in drawer and closes the drawer with energy, pushing aside any fears. She calls to Walter as she crosses to Daniel's room.)

GABY: Wear your sweater, Walter. *(She enters Daniel's room.)* Working days is going to give you a chance to look around.

DANIEL: Does.

GABY: Give you a chance to see what's out there.

DANIEL: Does.

GABY: Then what are we going at each other for? Enough. *(Gaby uses "enough" as a closure when she is finished with a thought. She picks up a newspaper clipping from trunk and holds it out to read.)*

DANIEL: You got the computer for your birthday?

GABY: I'm past birthdays.

DANIEL: It was last week.

GABY: Next week.

DANIEL: That's what I thought.

GABY: Baloney. *(She holds clipping to Daniel.)* What is this?

DANIEL: You should wear your glasses in the house.

GABY: I'd have to clean the house then.

DANIEL: Dad. In "La Mancha" when his beard was real. In Akron.

GABY: Got to get dressed. *(She points to petitions.)* Do me a favor. Put them on the backseat of your cab. *(She moves to exit.)*

DANIEL: I came in. He looked so fragile. His wrists. I was scared I'd break them.

GABY: The man's 80. When I'd visit my mother, and she was only in her 60's, if I hadn't seen her for two weeks, she'd look this grey small person. It scared me. After five minutes of being with her, she was tough, she was my mother. This is a spoiled European man. Spoiled by his mother, spoiled by his wife. He's not giving

that up. He's going to wait it out till he's 90, till I get his coffee right. Come more often to see him.
(Yves calls as he enters apartment.)
YVES: Hallo. Hallo. *(Gaby and Daniel are surprised and unsettled by Yves' entrance.)*
GABY: He's back. *(Gaby exits into Walter's room and makes his bed. Daniel returns to looking for cards. Walter, quickly, snaps light on. Yves enters living room.)*
YVES: "To have been Lutéce and to have become Paris – what could be a more magnificent symbol. To have been mud and to have become spirit!"
WALTER: Victor Hugo. Yes, but what book?
YVES: I haven't the slightest idea. For you. *(He takes newspapers out of leather bag and puts them on Walter's lap.)* Le Monde. Figaro, France-Soir, L'Equipe, Ein Berliner Zeitung. Avec les compliments du tabaconiste, cinquante trois bis rue des iles.
WALTER: *(Genuine.)* Thank you, Yves.
YVES: J'ai pensé à toi quand nos étions à Paris. *(Daniel exits to back hallway.)*
WALTER: Tu ne parles que francais?
YVES: Je suis retourné hier soir, Papa. Comment peut-on laver Paris de son âme?
WALTER: C'est peut-être pour cela que les Français ne se lavent pas aussi souvent.
YVES: Comment vas-tu?
WALTER: We will speak English?
YVES: I've been speaking French for two months. I only came back last night.
WALTER: I was afraid you'd gotten divorced from the English language, too. What is today?
YVES: Friday.
WALTER: You wrote Saturday.
YVES: A day early. I tell you, I will end my days an "insulaire" on lle St. Louis, eating nougat glace at Au Franc Pinot. And they still serve it as you had it. With that incredible pistachio sauce. It's there, father. Your Paris is still there ...
WALTER: *(Overlap.)* I have no Paris.
YVES: *(Continuing.)* There're still flowers in the butcher's window and parts of the city still smell of anise.
WALTER: *(Calls.)* Daniel. *(Daniel crosses to living room with record. Gaby crosses into kitchen with Walter's morning coffee pot and cup.)*
YVES: Daniel's here?
WALTER: *(Matter of fact.)* He comes almost everyday to see me.
YVES: How have you been feeling? *(Walter makes a dismissive gesture. Daniel enters.)* Daniel. Good to see you.
DANIEL: What can I say? I got up early. How's the Eiffel Tower?
YVES: Place for you, Paris. It can change your life.
WALTER: You begin to live in one of your operettas.
YVES: *(A phoney French accent.)* I was born there. I feel a part of it.
WALTER: You could barely walk when we left. You're a German of German immigrants. *(To Daniel.)* How many fools believed Paris would change their life?

You grow your trees. *(Yves takes record from Daniel and sings the "balladic opening" of The Who's "Goin' Mobile.")*
DANIEL: How do you know that? *(Yves sings another line.)*
YVES: I didn't like all your records. This one I liked.
DANIEL: The Who?
YVES: *(Yves sings the opening line of the chorus. He points at Daniel)* Next. *(Daniel sings the next line. They alternate till they join voices and sing together. Gaby crosses to her room. Yves is aware of her cross.)*
YVES: Windmills. Windmills. Windmills. *(He imitates Townshend's windmills.)*
WALTER: *(Interrupts.)* What do these say about Le Pen?
YVES: Pardon?
WALTER: What percentage does the National Front Party have in France now?
YVES: Karen and I walked. Ate. We went to the theatre.
WALTER: Le Pen is no surprise, yes? The French were Petainist fifty years before Petain. *(He includes Daniel.)* Le Pen. The leader of the National Front in France. A party of racism, xenophobia. What could be more congenial to the French? What do they say?
YVES: We didn't read the papers when we were there.
WALTER: Your new wife doesn't read newspapers?
YVES: We wanted time away from the news.
WALTER: You must have seen Le Pen on television.
YVES: We had the set taken out of the room.
WALTER: *(Exasperated.)* What did the concierge say about Le Pen?
YVES: We were on our honeymoon. We didn't talk politics.
WALTER: You were in France? How could you *not* talk politics?
YVES: We didn't.
WALTER: Why do I expect it? *(Daniel crosses to desk and looks for his cards. Yves crosses into kitchen.)*
YVES: I haven't had any coffee today. *(Walter closes his eyes. He is in pain. Yves, not looking for coffee, stands in kitchen. Gaby, impulsively, pulls her sweater off and puts on a new red sweater, then sits in chair and cuts the price tag off the sleeve. Walter speaks irritably to Daniel.)*
WALTER: Were you not getting me a himbeer saft?
DANIEL: I thought you didn't...
WALTER: Where did you think that! *(Daniel crosses into kitchen. Walter, now reveals his pain as he adjusts his body in the chair and lays newspapers on floor.)*
YVES: Trees?
DANIEL: *(Getting glass.)* I'm thinking of buying a Christmas tree farm.
YVES: *(Laughs.)* A Christmas tree farm.
DANIEL: Yes. *(Daniel mixes raspberry syrup with seltzer.)*
YVES: *(Can't stop laughing.)* I'm sorry... I'm sorry. I have this image of elves, Santa Clauses and you in red leder hosen, yodeling through your forest. *(He can't stop laughing.)* I'm sorry.
DANIEL: *(Slams icebox door.)* Never mind.
YVES: I'm sorry. I'm jet lagged. Don't be this sensitive. Please, tell me about these trees. What's the research you've done?

DANIEL: There was an article in the Times.
YVES: And?
DANIEL: *(Defensive.)* I know what I'm doing.
YVES: How can you know what you're doing if you haven't done any research?
DANIEL: *(Crosses into living room.)* I know what I'm doing... *(Gaby, in her room, makes a "general announcement.")*
GABY: I'm dressed, Walter. *(She stands and is ready now to meet Yves.)*
WALTER: *(To Daniel.)* In my room. I'll have it in my room. *(Daniel brings glass to Walter's room. Gaby enters kitchen.)*
YVES: "Come ye forth in triumph from the north with your hands and your feet and your raiment all red."
GABY: It's a sweater.
YVES: I saw you on the street.
GABY: When?
YVES: I was in a cab. Just now. You were talking to a policeman.
GABY: That was me.
YVES: Everything's been all right? Not too much trouble, I hope?
GABY: He gives me trouble? *(He points to bakery bag on table.)*
YVES: You have to go to 70th Street for his bread. Even mother didn't...
GABY: Your mother had no life but his. I do. *(He agrees to stop direction of conversation.)*
YVES: You have a point there. It's true. She didn't. I'm back now.
GABY: You're in the city now?
YVES: Last night...How about this week? You have any time this week?
GABY: Time?
YVES: We'll have lunch.
GABY: Lunch?
YVES: I can't today. I have an audition today at ten. *(Yves crosses into living room and gets his appointment book out of his shoulder bag. Gaby follows.)* Came back a day early. A new musical. An adaptation of Colette's "Indulgent Husband." Flew back for it. It's a great part. *(He finds wood to knock.)* Have a good chance on this one. I may break the curse of "La Mancha" yet. The producers are too young to remember my lifetime as a youthful Spanish Duke. *(Indirectly, towards Walter.)* It's New York. You play a part once here you're typecast forever. *(Daniel enters archway. Yves includes him in conversation.)* But the irony of ironies is...My agent got a call from a theatre in Florida. About? About my availability to play the old man, himself, Don Quixote. Can you believe it? There is now a possibility of my spending my last twenty years as an elderly Spanish gentleman. I can't knock it. *(To Daniel.)* "La Mancha" let me do it. Let me be an actor *and* have a family. Allowed me to send you to school. Allowed me to...
DANIEL: You're getting the money back for school. I'm paying you back.
YVES: Was I saying it for that? *(After a beat, he turns to Walter.)* We'll be moved in by Monday.
WALTER: I see.
YVES: *(To Daniel.)* The East Side. Karen's brother's building. It's a huge brownstone with a yard. We can do some barbecues. *(To Walter.)* The sliding

door's fixed. It'll be easier for you to get into the yard. I can have someone move your books in any time after Monday. *(The stage is silent.)*
GABY: *(Near tears.)* Danny and I will do it.
DANIEL: We'll use the cab. *(Daniel examines the arm of Walter's chair which is loose.)*
YVES: You knew Father was coming to live with us?
GABY: No.
YVES: For God's sake, why didn't you tell her?
WALTER: *(To Gaby.)* Forgive me. *(To Yves.)* I have moved many times in my life. It is impossible for me to move again.
YVES: I myself asked Karen's brother. I asked him for that apartment. You're the reason we asked for it.
WALTER: I am too old to move again.
YVES: Son arrested for taking aged father out of maid's room of Upper West Side apartment.
WALTER: It is impossible. *(To Gaby.)* Be kind enough to bring the autobiography, "The Journals of Erich Mühsam" from the library. Erich Mühsam. *(He spells.)* M-Ü-H-S-A-M. Thank you. Daniel, please carry the newspapers to my room. *(Walter exits to his room. After a beat, Daniel follows.)*
GABY: He's been living here for twenty years.
YVES: *(Covering all emotion.)* It's no skin off my nose... *(Yves opens book and looks in it. Walter sits on edge of his bed.)*
WALTER: You come tomorrow. Not another month. Tomorrow. I will tell you my life. You must come.
DANIEL: I will.
WALTER: *(Points to where he wants newspapers.)* There. I want to read them now. Thank you. *(Daniel puts papers on end of bed.)*
DANIEL: *(As he exits.)* Tomorrow. *(Walter sags onto his bed. His energy is gone. He remains in this position to end of Scene One. Daniel stands in hallway for a beat.)*
YVES: *(Looking in date book.)* Which day's good for you? Most any day this week's fine for me.
GABY: I don't know.
YVES: Thursday would be the best for me. But Wednesday, if it's after 1:00. Or Tuesday. We can have lunch. I can meet you at the Library. *(Daniel crosses to living room to look for cards in desk drawer.)*
GABY: I don't know how to do this yet. I don't know how to "lunch" with you, how to ask about your honeymoon. It's a year. You were gone this long when you were on the road. This is a divorce. You walk in like it's home. Ring the bell. I have to get to work. Enough. *(To Daniel.)* The cards aren't there. *(She exits to her room.)*
YVES: Take the day as it comes, lad. Take the day as it comes. You well, son?
DANIEL: Nothing much.
YVES: Is this early for you or are you driving...
DANIEL: *(Cuts him off.)* It's early.
YVES: *(Takes watch off wrist.)* I couldn't change it back last night. Two months

in Paris is hard to let go of.
DANIEL: It's 8:52. *(Yves resets watch.)*
YVES: I could have been born in Berlin. People weren't leaving Germany yet. I was born in Paris. That was *his* choice, not mine. Why? I don't know. I stopped wasting my time being upset about him telling me nothing a long time ago. You and I can talk. *(He over-dramatizes.)* But then, never say never. One day he'll take me on his knee and say: "Son. Let me tell you my life." And Brahms' Violin concerto will play and who knows? With music like that, I might even be forgiven for being born in Paris. Talk about romanticism! Imagine the mileage he'll get when he finds out my child was conceived in Paris. *(A pause. Yves looks at Daniel.)* Karen wanted it. She wouldn't have kept it a secret for long. I should get myself ready for the jokes. Older men, younger wives...
DANIEL: *(Yiddish accent.)*"I see it but I don't believe it."
YVES: *(Yiddish accent.)* "So who are you anyway?" *(Pause.)* You upset? Shocked?
DANIEL: It wasn't something I was thinking of.
YVES: Nor I. So who are we anyway? You think he's alive?
DANIEL: *(Shrugs.)* What was his real name?
YVES: His fate is ever to remain a family joke.
DANIEL: That was Peekskill?
YVES: That's right.
DANIEL: The summer Opa taught me chess.
YVES: I never could get myself pass the look on his face if I'd call a knight a horse...Can you let Walter know? I'll tell him myself. I mean, of course, I'll let him know. But he's always better when he's had a time to think about what he's being told. Of course, I'll understand perfectly if you can't.
DANIEL: Sure. *(Daniel exits to kitchen. Yves sits alone in living room. Gaby, with coat on, crosses into Walter's room.)*
GABY: Gaby.
WALTER: *(Sits up.)* Yes. *(She enters Walter's room.)*
YVES: *(To himself.)* I haven't sung in over eight weeks. *(Gaby opens night table drawer and takes out case.)*
GABY: What is this? *(She takes out syringe.)*
WALTER: *(Referring to drawer.)* You go into this?
GABY: This is a syringe. Why do you have it?
WALTER: I'm a doctor.
GABY: Why do you have it?
WALTER: For pain
GABY: You have that kind of pain?
WALTER: No. If I do.
GABY: *(An order.)* If you do, you tell me.
WALTER: Of course.
GABY: You're not going to the bench. *(She prepares Walter's bed. Yves sits alone in living room. He talks to Daniel in kitchen.)*
YVES:You know we have a yard. In the summer, whenever you want, use it. You

can use it for a barbecue.
DANIEL: Thanks. *(Yves speaks to an imaginary person on couch.)*
YVES: My lord. Its almost nine. *(He stands and calls to Daniel.)*
See you soon, son. *(Yves leaves the apartment and exits via outside hallway. Gaby turns Walter's light off and crosses to him.)*
GABY: *(Gently.)* Try to sleep now. *(Walter quotes from a German poem. Gaby does not understand the words but responds to the message which is emotional and reveals his love for her.)*
WALTER:
    "Denn mein Geheimnis ist mir Pflicht;
    Ich möchte dir mein ganzes Innre zeigen,
    Allein das Schicksal will es nicht."... Goethe.
(Translation.) "My secret is my writ;
    To show you all my heart would be my will,
    But fate does not permit." *(Gaby kisses his forehead.)*
GABY: Sleep now. *(Gaby exits Walter's room and stands by his door in the hallway. Daniel crosses into living room and puts The Who's "Goin' Mobile" on the phonograph. After a few beats, he grabs his car radio and exits the apartment. The lights dim to half light as the record plays.)*

Scene 2

    The lights rise on the next day. Saturday, 12 Noon. Walter is in his room, sitting on his bed, writing on a yellow pad. Daniel is in the living room. He fixes the arm of Walter's chair. He wears his jacket as he unscrews the knob on the arm of the chair. Yves is in the kitchen. He takes many small containers out of a large shopping bag and arranges them on a tray. Gaby is in her room, removing the wrapping from one of two hyacinth bulbs she has just bought. In the middle of removing the second wrapping, she crosses to Walter's room. She turns his overhead light on.

WALTER: Off.
GABY: *(With conviction.)* You should be with him. He's your son. He found a place. With a garden and air and sun light.
WALTER: You want that?
GABY: I don't want to find you've moved and forgot to tell me.
WALTER: I would never betray you that way.
GABY: I don't want it like yesterday. To find out Yves asked you to live with him from him. To find out you've pain because I find a syringe.
WALTER: Take it to your room. *(He takes syringe out of night table drawer)*
GABY: I don't want it.
WALTER: Take it. It upsets you.
GABY: It's not what upsets me.
WALTER: *(Points to door.)* You were there last night, watching me sleeping, like a ghost in the shadows.

GABY: Then you weren't sleeping.
WALTER: You have never done that before. I never wish to worry you. Please take this if you don't believe me. *(She puts syringe in drawer)*
GABY: I believe you, but it's new rules. I won't go on about having this room painted or your meeting your friends. That's your business. But you're not 60 anymore and I'm not married anymore. We're both in the next part of our lives. I don't know what that is. What I need is a promise. In English not German. That whatever it is, we're figuring it out between us.
WALTER: We will.
GABY: Our deal. *(As closure.)* Enough. *(Gaby rips paper off plant, stands on chair, removes dying plant from top of bookcase and replaces it with new plant)*
GABY: You know the big baloney from the union, the one who never comes to a meeting unless it's a "big" meeting...
WALTER: *(Interjects.)* Yes.
GABY: He said at the meeting. He said I'm not connected to the big issues. I said China could break into twenty pieces tomorrow and kids in welfare hotels still have to get to schools.He says that's woman's thinking and turns back as though I said nothing. What the hell's woman's thinking? You think what I say is woman's thinking?
WALTER: "A sense of decency is what we need." Tucholsky. "Power not filled with kindness will not last." Heinrich Mann. Tell him men say that.
GABY: I felt eleven. Like when I was handing out towels for the church, clean towels that were almost brand new, handing them to families living in rooms no bigger than this. I said to the priest, "If this is loving one another, we need a revolution of the heart." He smiled. As though I were going through a phase. I want to know how to say it!
WALTER: In your words. Gabriella's words. None will be better.
(Gaby is touched by Walter's words.)
GABY: *(Wiping tears.)* What a mess. That bastard got to me.
WALTER: *(Shrugs.)* He did.
GABY: *(Sits on bed.)* We're working the same causes we won in the '70s. I turn on the news and think I'm living in a "Saturday Night Live" skit. All I seem to do is yell at the old guys for not holding it together, wait for the new guys and they end up being the same as the old guys.
WALTER: Due to unfavorable weather, the German Revolution has taken place in music instead.
GABY: *(Grabs sheet of paper.)* I'm using that! Which one said it?
WALTER: Tucholsky.
GABY: Tucholsky. My words, yes, but I'm using this. *(She writes quote down. Yves crosses into living room and watches Daniel fix chair.)*
YVES: It's my first chair, for my first apartment, first piece of furniture I bought. A second hand store on Amsterdam. It's not there anymore.You'll need string to hold it after the glue's on.
DANIEL: This is new stuff. *(Yves brings corkscrew to kitchen and opens a bottle of wine)*
GABY: What are you writing?

WALTER: For Daniel. Times from my life.

GABY: Jesus, Mary and Joseph! The kid's going to wake up.

WALTER: Tell him he is to wait. Daniel must not leave.

GABY: *(Crossing to exit.)* He's not leaving.

WALTER: Why is Yves here?

GABY: I don't know. I just walked in. *(On exiting.)* I didn't mean a word about your living there. *(She crosses into her room and picks up second plant. They talk from room to room.)* Oh, there was nothing under Mühsam, no biography, no journals.

WALTER: Impossible. I was there when he wrote them.

GABY: Nothing in English. Nothing in German.

WALTER: American libraries.

GABY: *(Crossing into living room.)* He doesn't want you leaving. he's writing you his...

DANIEL: *(Cutting her off.)* Christ! *(He almost mouths his words.)* Did Opa call Dad?

GABY: What?

DANIEL: Jesus!

GABY: I didn't hear you. *(Gaby crosses to Daniel.)*

DANIEL: *(Softly.)* Did Opa ask Dad to come today?

GABY: No.

DANIEL: Why's he here?

GABY: I don't know.

DANIEL: He didn't ask him to come?

GABY: What's the matter with you?

DANIEL: You can't say anything around here without someone saying what's the matter with you! *(He stands.)* Tell Opa I'll call him.

GABY: Over my dead body. If you go, *you* tell him you're going.

DANIEL: *(Returns to fixing chair.)* Did I say I'm going? I'm driving a girl to the airport later. I'm fixing his chair now. I don't understand you!

GABY: *(Keeping her good mood.)* I'm not getting in to this. *(Gaby exits into kitchen. Yves quickly covers tray with kitchen towel.)*

YVES: What the hell's the matter with him?

GABY: *(Defending.)* Why does something have to be the matter with him? *(She speaks matter-of-factly.)* Why are you here?

YVES: I brought lunch for everybody.

GABY: Lunch?

YVES: I was so pressured yesterday. First audition in eight weeks. I was jet lagged. Everything was "left." Unresolved. I couldn't sleep last night. I should have called first.

GABY: I don't want you to feel you can't come here.

YVES: It feels...Everybody asking why I'm here.

GABY: *(Calls.)* Danny. Lunch.

DANIEL: I ate.

GABY: I'll get Walter. *(Gaby crosses to Walter's room.)* Yves brought lunch. *(Yves moves into hallway to hear better.)*

WALTER: *(Writing.)* I have no time for lunch.

GABY: Yves brought lunch. *(Yves returns to kitchen.)*

WALTER: I have no time! *(Gaby crosses back into kitchen.)*

GABY: He ate.

YVES: It was a last minute idea.

GABY: What's for lunch? *(Yves lifts dish cloth off tray.)*

GABY: My God.

YVES: I over did it. But free forks. *(He pulls a chair out for Gaby.)* Madame, we are ready to serve. *(Gaby sits.)* For appetizers, we start with two orders of fried dumplings from Ollie's for Daniel. He might want to take them with him. For father and all, we have a fois gras frais de canard. And new to you and for you. A tapenade. *(He gives her a baguette)* You use this for both. You dip it in. And the wine. The chardonnay you said you had at the what it was... library benefit.

GABY: *(Amazed.)* You found it.

YVES: Please start. *(She takes bites of food and drinks wine.)* The plats du jour. For father... and the three of these are from a new take out that has bistro food. Amazing. For father, I found a Cassoulet de Casteinaudary. Harricots. Beans, Sausages. Everything cooks for a year in white wine. For Daniel, a Choucroute à l'alsacienne. *(He shrugs.)* A try. And today is...?

GABY: Saturday.

YVES: *(Puts container in front of her.)* The Saturday lasagna from the Three Brothers Restaurant for you.

GABY: You went there too!

YVES: And since the thirteenth's your birthday. The birthday cake.

GABY: My god. *(He takes out of the shopping bag two boxes of graham crackers, a bag of marshmallows and a bag of apricots, stacking them on top of one another in the order mentioned.)*

YVES: Graham crackers. Marshmallows. The right ones?

GABY: Yes.

YVES: Apricots from Murrays. And graham crackers.

GABY: Thank you.

YVES: *(Sings.)* "Who doth ambition shun
And loves to live i' th' sun" *(He gestures towards Walter's room.)*
He's never seen me as Jacques. *(Sings.)*
"Seeking the food she eats,
And is she pleased with what she gets?"

GABY: It's terrific but I can't eat it. I had the lasagna for lunch.

YVES: Why didn't you tell me?

GABY: I thought everyone else was going to eat.

YVES: *(With emotion building.)* Come on. Let's hear it. The decadence of it! We could have fed a third of Ethiopia. Looking at me as though I were a fool...

GABY: I wouldn't.

YVES: *(Continuing.)* Never ever understanding "gesture." That there's a need for gesture in life...

GABY: This is lunch.

YVES: *(Continuing.)* Letting me think I can give something to you. Finally do something for you.

GABY: It's lunch we're talking about. Lunch.

YVES: Ever direct and literal.

GABY: Too admirable for any man to live with.

YVES: When I said that...

GABY: When you said that you meant it. Otherwise you'd be here.

(Daniel ties scarf around arm. Walter writes. A silent beat on stage.)
That's not all true. I wanted this, too. But you're not gone and I can't yell at you for being here. He's living here.

YVES: Who should come in and help you with him?

GABY: *(Affronted.)* Help?

YVES: They could live in Daniel's room.

GABY: That's my office.

YVES: It never became your office.

GABY: *(Point of fact.)*It's going to be my office.

YVES: You're going to start needing...

GABY: I don't need help. You always walk in wearing a sign saying, "Give it to me." He gives it to you. It's not that way with us.

YVES: That's a point.

GABY: He's 80. He's getting pains. Things have to change and we're together on it.

YVES: What does his doctor say? *(Daniel moves closer to kitchen to hear better.)*

GABY: You know when he left Fleisher.

YVES: I didn't know that.

GABY: You were here when he said he wasn't going back to Fleisher. Before you left.

YVES: He tells me fuck all!

GABY: Oh, no. Nobody was talking to anybody then.

YVES: What I know about him I know from my mother! He's had a year to tell me he wouldn't move. You always protect him.

GABY: No You put me between the two of you. *(Daniel enters kitchen. No one speaks. Yves puts lids on containers. Daniel opens and closes refrigerator. He exits to his room.)*

YVES: *(After a beat.)* When I was sitting in the yard. Before the rain. I watched a woman clean her window. When she finished, she sat by the window and had a cup of coffee. It was a simple moment.
(He gestures to the many containers.) I don't do things easily, simply. Karen and I are having a baby in December. Did you know?

GABY: No.

DANIEL: *(Entering kitchen.)* Why do you stop talking when I walk in a room?

GABY: Is the world about you?!

DANIEL: If it's about Opa, I want to know.

GABY: With your jacket on? Ready for the take off! That's how you want to know?

DANIEL: I just said...

GABY: You're going to the airport. *(She calls.)* Walter! Daniel left!
(She exits to her room.)

DANIEL: What'd she do that for? *(Walter grabs papers and cane, quickly gets out of bed.)*
WALTER: Wo ist Daniel? Er muss hier sein!
DANIEL: *(Crosses into living room.)* What the fuck's the matter with her? *(Yves follows him into living room.)*
YVES: *(Trying to calm situation.)* Let your mother alone. *(Gaby and Walter speak as they pass. All speeches overlap.)*
WALTER: Where is Daniel?
GABY: You can hear him!
DANIEL: *(To Yves.)* It's a fucking time warp in here.
YVES: You have to leave, leave.
GABY: Your slippers. Your robe. *(She crosses into Walter's room.)*
DANIEL: Whatever you do. You turn four years old in here. *(Walter enters archway.)*
YVES: *(Shouts.)* For God's sake, if you have a job, leave!
WALTER: *(To Yves.)* Why do you make him leave when you know I want him?
YVES: No one's making him leave! *(Yves exits to kitchen.)*
WALTER: You must stay today. You understand me?
DANIEL: I'm staying. *(As he walks into room, Walter refers to the papers in his hand, explaining himself in German.)*
WALTER: Euere amerikanischen Biblioteken! Wie können sie nichts from Erich Mühsam haben? Das sind nicht die richtigen Wörter! *(He reaches his chair.)*
DANIEL: *(Rushing to chair.)* You can't sit there. It's not dry.
WALTER: Wo ist es nass?
DANIEL: It's got glue on it. The arm. I fixed it. *(Walter crosses to other chair.)*
WALTER: Sehr gut. Danke. Zieh deine Jacke aus.
DANIEL: You're talking German. I don't understand you.
YVES: He wants you to take your jacket off. *(Walter falls exhausted into chair.)*
WALTER: I have been writing since yesterday. Forgive me... Sit, my boy. Tell me. If it's your work, I pay you for today.
DANIEL: I wouldn't take money. I'd never take your money.
(Gaby enters with robe and slippers.)
WALTER: *(Sharply.)* Not now. Not now. *(Gaby drops clothes on desk and exits into her room. She sits at computer, not turning it on, not working, but filled with emotion.)*
WALTER: *(To Daniel.)* Closer. Don't make me shout. *(Daniel pulls hassock over to chair. Gaby is in her room, from which she cannot hear Daniel and Walter. Yves is in kitchen, from which he can hear their scene.)*
WALTER: My father could write. I write like a student. A homework essay. With even a title. *(He give the pages to Daniel.)*
DANIEL: It's in German. *(Walter throws the paper on the floor.)*
WALTER: And I write it for you! Go to your work. Go now. *(He holds himself, rubbing his arms.)*
DANIEL: *(After a beat.)* You can tell me what you wrote.
WALTER: *(After a beat.)* I can do that. *(Daniel picks up papers. Walter takes them from him. Yves tosses forks in sink. Walter turns his head in the direction of*

the kitchen. He is aware of Yves' presence, aware that he can be overheard. He reads.) An acknowledgement. *(He shrugs.)* My title. *(He reads.)* Erich Mühsam was born in Lubeck in eighteen hundred...? *(To Daniel.)* 1878. 1880. He was my father's age. But unlike my father. My father was an elegant man. First violinist at the Berlin Philharmonic. Mühsam could never find his comb. He had a shaggy head and a large red beard. Always with a cigarette. Always with a poem. Important poems but, also...and he would make these up in front of you. He was a master of schuttelreime. Nonsense verse. I remember... "Man wolte sie zu zwanzig Dingen In einem Haus zu Danzig zwingen." I cannot translate this. They are puns. All Berlin knew them and knew his cabaret songs. He was a Bohemian. Poet. Revolutionary. First imprisoned for conscientious objection in the First War. To be a pacifist in Prussia! There was no cowardice in that man. Do not dismiss him as a Kaffehaus poet who slept in barns. He...*(Yves crosses into living room. With hope that Yves will stay:)* Yes? *(Yves waits a beat in the hope of being asked to join them. Neither can hold this moment too long, each anticipating rejection. Yves breaks moment by crossing to desk and removing Manhattan phone book. He returns to kitchen looking through book for a phone number.)* What? What did I say?

DANIEL: Not to dismiss him.

WALTER: My father dismissed him. But my father was a dismissive man. A vain man. We children were not allowed to see him in the morning till he was washed and shaved. You finished dinner and say excuse me and go watch TV. We were not allowed to leave the table until my father and his friends had finished talking politics. Besides the violin, politics was my father's passion. Not only did we have to have our political opinions by 12 years, we had to defend them as though we were defending our dissertation. When I told my father that Erich Mühsam was the prophet of our time... He worked for the liberation of the Society from the State, he warned against any "father state" be it Wilhelm,Fascist or Communist. My father, not looking at me, of course, waved his hand like a woman whose nails were still wet. "Any man who warns society about father states naturally attracts adolescents." Why that gesture? Why that moment out of so many before? I don't know. I pushed my dessert from my place with such force it fell into my sister's lap. She was too shocked to make a noise. I had lost all fear. My voice was strong. I blamed the condition, the ultimate demise of Germany on dinners like ours, eaten by intellectuals who could only define the needs of the country but refused to do the Kleinarbeit. The Kleinarbeit, the small work. Like Gaby does. The passing of leaflets, the gluing of posters. The daily work of change. "I will not eat your rich desserts anymore," I said. "I leave your table to meet a man who lives what you can only talk. I will meet Erich Mühsam's train." My boy! Mühsam and three other Jews were a revolution. Eisner, Toller, Landauer and Mühsam. Without a shot being fired. These four Jews, in 1918, were the government of the "Free State of Bavaria." In Bavaria. In München with its beer halls. A government of pacifists and poets supported by German workers. A government of Jewish intellectuals. When have you seen that in Washington? Amazing they lasted a day! Na nu. In three months Eisner was assassinated and Mühsam never forgiven. Never by the Freikorp, never by the SS. But that day he

came out of prison. That night I left my father's table to meet the ...
YVES: What's Fleisher's first name? *(The interruption allows Walter to feel his body's pain. He is weakened from his story telling. Daniel, deeply moved by the story, wishes it to continue.)*
DANIEL: How old were you when you left?
WALTER: Seventeen.
DANIEL: Where did you go?
WALTER: I took my books to a commune.
DANIEL: A commune?
WALTER: The '60's were the '20's in Berlin. We did what they did. Played our songs in the parks...
YVES: *(Calls.)* Gaby.
DANIEL: Don't stop.
GABY: Yes.
WALTER: Marched for free love. Discovered drugs...
YVES: What's Doctor Fleisher's first name?
WALTER: Walked naked in the parks. We... *(He stops himself. Gaby crossed to archway.)*
DANIEL: In the kitchen. *(To Walter.)* What were the songs?
WALTER: *(To Daniel.)* My stick. *(Gaby crosses to kitchen.)*
DANIEL: We'll take it to your room. *(Daniel collects Walter's written papers.)*
WALTER: My stick.
YVES: What's Fleisher's first name?
GABY: Harold. Why? *(Yves reopens phone book. Walter has not the energy to get out of his chair or to shout to the kitchen.)*
WALTER: *(Overlap.)* He is retired. He has no more office. Tell him that.
GABY: Why are you calling him?
DANIEL: His doctor's retired. He doesn't have an office.
YVES: Who do you see?
GABY: What's happened? *(She crosses into living room.)* Do you want to see a doctor?
WALTER: I do not ask for one.
DANIEL: It's Dad. *(He refers to Walter.)* He was talking to me. *(Yves crosses into living room. The speeches overlap.)* It's Dad.
YVES: Who do you see?
GABY: *(To Yves.)* He was up all night writing this.
YVES: I asked if my father sees a doctor!
GABY: Why can't you let them have this together?
YVES: *(To Walter.)* I asked if you see a doctor.
WALTER: No more.
GABY: *(Point of fact.)* He is a doctor.
YVES: He sat behind a desk of a pharmaceutical company in America...
GABY: When he wants a doctor...
YVES: He calls you Gabriella, he gets everything he wants.
GABY: *(Finishing sentence.)* He'll see one.
WALTER: *(Sharply to Gaby.)* I am in this room. *(Gaby moves away from Yves.)*

YVES: You haven't seen one since Fleisher.

WALTER: We don't do this now.

YVES: You're seeing my doctor. *(He takes his address book out of his bag.)*

WALTER: *(As much strength as he can find.)* We do not do this now. *(Yves crosses to phone.)*

YVES: If he's in, we'll go today. Someone has to take some responsibility.

GABY: Someone has taken responsibility!

YVES: *(On phone.)* It's Yves Wertheim. Is Dr. Meyers in today? Yes, yes, it was…it was a wonderful vacation… *(Walter speaks with as much strength as he can find. He waves his hand in a dismissive gesture, like a woman with wet nails.)*

WALTER: This is your stand? Your test? You are a man?

YVES: *(On phone.)* Yes, Paris is always wonderful…

WALTER: Did you need me this feeble?

YVES: Does he have time today? It can be anytime…

WALTER: Did you need me this broken? *(Yves slams down the phone.)*

YVES: Then die here! *(Daniel rushes at Yves, knocking the plant onto floor, pushing Yves off-balance. The men scuffle. Gaby crosses to Walter, protecting him.)*

GABY: Jesus God Almighty. *(Yves pushes Daniel aside.)*

YVES: What the hell was that?

DANIEL: Fight me.

YVES: Pull yourself together. *(Daniel rushes at Yves again. Yves pins Daniel's arms with a bear hug.)*

DANIEL: Fight me.

YVES: Pull yourself together.

GABY: *(Shielding Walter.)* Out!

YVES: *(Pins Daniel's arms.)* That's enough now. *(Daniel flails, unable to break the hold.)*

GABY: Get it out of here!

DANIEL: Oh, we're the father now. Big part. Father. "How've you been, son? That's enough, son."

GABY: Jesus. Let go of him.

YVES: *(Adding pressure.)* That is enough! *(Yves releases Daniel, pushing him away.)*

GABY: This will never happen in here again! *(Daniel continues the fight, verbally, from his corner.)*

DANIEL: You can't fight me. You can't take him talking to me. *(Daniel's line continues through the action.)*

YVES: Don't shout. *(Gaby stops Walter from walking near the broken flower pot as he crosses to exit.)*

GABY: Don't walk on that. *(She runs and picks up a shard.)* Your slippers?

WALTER: Leave me alone.

DANIEL: *(Continuing.)* You walk in for a number 'cause you can't fucking take him talking to me. *(Gaby gets slippers from desk.)*

YVES: Help your mother. *(Gaby crosses to Walter with his slippers.)*

WALTER: Leave me alone! *(Walter exits to his room.)*

GABY: I will. *(To Daniel.)* Get that off the floor! *(She exits to kitchen. Walter sits in the chair in his room, his door open, listening to the "noise" in the living room, hearing the specific lines that are in high volume.)*
YVES: You hear?
DANIEL: Why come here? You got your house on the East Side.
YVES: How much mileage do you think you have left playing the kid who hasn't found himself? *(Gaby comes in with brush and dust pan. She and Daniel speak at the same time.)*
DANIEL: What do you need here?
GABY: Why keep on him?
YVES: The boy who can do no wrong.
GABY: He's working days. What do you want from him?
YVES: You're working days? Why didn't you tell me?
DANIEL: Do you care?
YVES: The Jack and Jill Society. Danny and Gaby's Secret Club.
GABY: He did it without your help. Without the support...
YVES: Without the discipline. He needed a mother...
DANIEL: Don't fight.
YVES: Not another best friend...
DANIEL: Over me.
YVES: Not someone who undermines me.
GABY: You do that.
DANIEL: I don't need protection.
GABY: You gave up all authority when Walter walked into this house.
YVES: When did you stand with me? Together with me about the boy?
GABY: Didn't you hear him? *(Referring to Daniel.)* He just said...
DANIEL: *(Topping Gaby.)* No one can breathe here without your help!
GABY: What do you do here? *(Daniel refers to brush and pan in her hands.)*
DANIEL: You tell me do it. *You're* doing it. *(Gaby drops pan and brush at his feet.)*
GABY: Do it.
YVES: *(Overlap.)* Listen to your mother.
DANIEL: No one can make him a cup of coffee but you. *(Yves and Gaby speak at the same time.)*
GABY: When the hell are you here? You're in and out when you feel like it.
YVES: Your mother takes damn good care of him. Damn good care of you.
DANIEL: I'd be dead if I didn't forget what she taught me.
GABY: What'd you learn from me?
DANIEL: The first night, the first night I ever drove. A New York City taxi cab. Two in the morning. I pick up three dealers and take them to an alley in the Bronx so nobody'd think I was prejudiced.
GABY: *(Interjection.)* That was stupid!
DANIEL: *(Continuing.)* Your expectations are fucking mismatched with reality.
GABY: What do you know about reality?
DANIEL: *(Continuing.)* You live in a "We Are The World" video. He lives in "La Mancha." I'm out there. I'm the one out there at four in the morning, who's

had a gun to his head and gotten through the night.

GABY: The world's more than streets at four in the morning. You kids don't understand...

DANIEL: *(Interrupting.)* I'm not you kids.

YVES: That's enough shouting.

GABY: *(With force.)* You don't have any cop-outs.

DANIEL: Einstein wouldn't be great enough for this house.

GABY: All you need to do is look in his eyes to learn history.

YVES: Can we stop this now?

DANIEL: *(To Yves.)* I fail before I start with you. *(To Gaby.)* I don't have a cause, I'm a shit. If you can't be great, why do anything!

GABY: You're his grandson! You don't have the luxury to toke your life away.

DANIEL: I didn't have a fucking toke.

GABY: Who went partying?

DANIEL: From school.

GABY: Who walked into a car?

DANIEL: I walked home from school, from a fucking audition, not a fucking party.

YVES: You said...

DANIEL: An audition. An audition where I got the fucking part!

GABY: You didn't go to...? *(Daniel overrides her and continues his story as though it were a monologue at a comedy club: casual in delivery but driven by anger.)*

DANIEL: I got the fucking part. I'm going "Oh yeah, you got it! Oh yeah, you're good. Oh yeah, I can do it!" And then "Excuse me. Excuse me, man. You're going to take that part? I mean you're talking Shakespeare. You're talking great part. You're talking showing up the man from 'La Mancha,' man. I mean in front of Opa. That right, man?" Yeah, I'm taking it. Yeah, I'm telling Opa... Oh yeah, man? Who the fuck you kidding! You think you're going to be great enough for Opa? There's the car. I didn't need a fucking toke.

GABY: *(With feeling.)* I wish you could've...

DANIEL: Don't give me sympathy. I don't want fucking sympathy.

YVES: You could have, you could have told...

DANIEL: So someone would finally tell you something? You don't give a shit for anything here.

YVES: You're talking out of your ass.

DANIEL: *(Pointing towards Opa's room.)* Did you take him with you?

YVES: Did he come with me?

DANIEL: Did you ask him twice? It was "no skin off your nose."

GABY: Walter wanted...

DANIEL: *(Sharply.)* This is between us. *(Gaby grabs broken flower pot and exits to kitchen.)*

GABY: Then take it out of my living room. *(She throws plant in garbage pail and remains in kitchen.)*

YVES: I have things to do.

DANIEL Or was it you didn't have the balls to take him from Mom? *(As Yves collects his appointment book, he tears a tiny corner of a page.)*

YVES: *(Holding out corner of paper.)* Write down all you know about "balls."
DANIEL: *(Loud enough to reach Walter.)* Did you tell him you're having a baby? Did you have the balls to tell him you're having a baby? Did you have the balls to fight me?
YVES: *(With force.)* I have fought rejections, fears, doubts you haven't begun to see yet. *(Yves crosses and picks up his bag.)*
DANIEL: Nothing for you to walk out. Nothing you need here. He and I can talk. He's more my father.
YVES: Call me when you can apologize. *(Yves shouts to Walter as he grabs his coat off rack.)* It's what you wanted. It's yours! *(Yves leaves apartment, and crosses outer hallway. The stage is quiet. Daniel stands in archway. After a beat, Walter gets up from his chair and walks to his bed. After another beat, Gaby puts lid back on garbage pail. After another beat, Daniel crosses into kitchen.)*
DANIEL: I'm moving back to take care of him.
GABY: No.
DANIEL: I'm moving back.
GABY: *(Angry.)* What is it you all have to prove? *(She crosses away from him. Daniel exits into Walter's room.)*
DANIEL: We can finish in here.
WALTER: Go home.
DANIEL: We can do it tonight. I'm going to be here tonight.
WALTER: Go to the country. Go now.
DANIEL: I'm staying here now. Opa. I'm going to be with you.
WALTER: *(With force.)* I don't want you. I don't want you here!
(Walter turns off the night table light. Daniel exits room and stands in hallway. Gaby crosses into living room and puts on Terje Rypdal's record, "Chaser." Side two, "Ornen." Lights turn off Gaby, sitting on floor in living room. Then on Daniel in hallway. The music plays. The lights dim on the apartment. In this transition light, Gaby crosses to her room. Daniel crosses into his room, takes chess set and board and crosses into living room where he sets up the game.)

Scene 3

Lights up on the apartment in the middle of that night. Three a.m. Walter sits in his bed. The night table lamp is lit. Daniel sits in the living room. He is in semi-darkness. The halogen lamp lights Walter's chair, a small table with a chess set and a kitchen chair beside it. Gaby sits in her room, in the rocker, a tray in her lap holding solitaire cards. She is asleep. A standing lamp is lit behind her. Except for the three lamps, the rest of the apartment is dark. The Tube Light in the outside hallway flickers and burns out. Daniel sits quietly before crossing into Walter's room.

DANIEL: I know you're not asleep. I'm not asleep. I've been here.
WALTER: *(Acknowledging.)* Yes. You have been here. *(There is a beat of silence. Then, Walter gestures to Daniel to leave room.)* In a minute, in a minute.

DANIEL: I'm staying, Opa.
WALTER: *(Waving him out.)* Yes, yes. But go for a minute! *(Daniel goes into dark hallway. Walter opens plastic container which holds his dentures and places them in his mouth. As he replaces container, he knocks his alarm clock and tissue box on floor.)*
WALTER: Teufel!
DANIEL: *(In hallway.)* What are you doing? *(Gaby wakes and stands, when she hears Daniel's voice, she sits down.)*
WALTER: *(Muttering as he gets up.)* Impossible. Impossible.
(Daniel reenters room and sees Walter stooped over trying to pick up objects.)
DANIEL: I'll get that.
WALTER: *(With force.)* I can do it. *(Walter kneels and picks up tissues and clock. He has not the strength to get himself up.)*
DANIEL: *(After a beat.)* Can I help you?
WALTER: *(Angry at himself.)* Please. *(A beat of silence as Daniel helps Walter sit on the edge of bed. Daniel takes the objects from Walter's hand and places them on table.)*
DANIEL: *(After a beat.)* I found the board.
WALTER: *(Mutters.)* You are here. That's how it will be. *(A beat of silence.)*
DANIEL: I found the board.
WALTER: Board?
DANIEL: I went over the Gruenfeld Defense.
WALTER: Oh, yes. *(A beat of silence.)* Did Yves call?
DANIEL: No.
WALTER: Gaby?
DANIEL: She played records all night.
WALTER: I heard her. She is sleeping now?
DANIEL: Yes.
WALTER: *(After a beat.)* We'll have a brandy. I'll come to you. *(Daniel exits into living room, opens hutch cabinet and removes a bottle of brandy and glasses. Gaby tries to read book. Walter decides on his best robe, enters living room and sits in his chair. Daniel places Walter's glass beside chess board.)*
WALTER: Thank you. *(He refers to chess set.)* I gave that to you.
DANIEL: My first set.
WALTER: When did I give it to you?
DANIEL: The summer you taught me. In Peekskill. By the lake.
WALTER: You are a gentle liar. Perhaps you will be too kind.
DANIEL: For what?
WALTER: I do not know if Gaby knows, but I will tell her. Not you. Yves? Perhaps knows. May I have that please. *(Daniel brings afghan.)* Thank you. Sit. Malignancies of the gastro-intestinal tract metastasize early, earlier than diagnosable symptoms. A doctor would advise several possible procedures, only because the man is expected to say something. If he was honest, he would recommend nothing. I will not go to a hospital. This *must* be understood. Should it happen, should I be in a hospital, I shall be given morphine sulfate only. No resuscitation, nasogastric feeding, no mechanical respiration. No CPR, my boy.

(He pats his pocket.) I've written it down.

DANIEL: *(With difficulty.)* How do you know?

WALTER: To be a doctor is not only here. *(He points to his head.)* It's here. *(He points to his nose.)* I smell like a dying man. I am one. I know how I want to die. What I need…I need a witness to my wishes. *(He takes out a folded paper from his pocket.)* A defender of my wishes.

DANIEL: I'll be that.

WALTER: You?

DANIEL: Yes.

WALTER: What means your "yes"?

DANIEL: What do you mean?

WALTER: Listen, when Muhsam interviewed me for the Fanal, his magazine, to do the kleinearbeit, I wrote a letter for this interview. A letter pledging myself to him…that I would forever be a defender of his ideals… When I came into the office, he said, "No interview. Do you play chess?" Naturally, he learned more about a man by how he played, and we played. And by this watch, after an hour, he nodded his head. The very first animation he'd shown. And he said: "Oh yes. I know what you're going to do." I immediately changed my defense and lost.

DANIEL: He psyched you out.

WALTER: And learned much about me. Let us choose our sides. *(Daniel puts a white and a black pawn behind his back. Walter chooses the white pawn, which gives him the first move when he decides to start.)* What does your "yes," your pledge mean?

DANIEL: That I'll do it.

WALTER: Does it not rely on what your father thinks?

DANIEL: I don't give a shit what he thinks.

WALTER: You do. *(He gestures that Daniel move closer.)* I do not see your face. What were you to tell me? There is to be a new child?

DANIEL: Yes.

WALTER: He wasn't going to tell me?

DANIEL: You have to ask him.

WALTER: If I made you my witness, what might he say?

DANIEL: I can't say.

WALTER: Imagine. What would he say?

DANIEL: He'd want to know why you didn't ask him.

WALTER: Would he be angry at you?

DANIEL: I don't know.

WALTER: I'm being insensitive? These questions are too difficult?

DANIEL: They're not difficult.

WALTER: Good. Did he tell you he was having a child?

DANIEL: I said that.

WALTER: Yes. How did he tell it to you? What did he say?

DANIEL: That it happened in Paris.

WALTER: And he wanted this child to happen?

DANIEL: *(Irritably.)* I don't know.

WALTER: What did he say to you?

DANIEL: He was on his way out to an audition. The whole thing was a minute!
WALTER: Did he ask you to tell me?
DANIEL: He did.
WALTER: So he wanted you to tell me. And you said? *(Daniel refills his glass.)* And you said yes to him.
DANIEL: *(Proud of himself.)* But I didn't do it.
WALTER: *(Wrapping up case.)* Na nu.
DANIEL: That's my father and me. Not you and me.
WALTER: *(Gesturing to game.)* We are not playing?
DANIEL: Jesus! *(Daniel crosses into kitchen, flicks the light on, then off, and reenters living room. He stands in the darkness of the archway.)*
WALTER: That was a test, my boy. As they say it on the radio, only a test. You are staying there? *(Daniel enters and sits in chair by chess board.)* You see, my boy, *in* hospitals, *on* the many benches, sit the estranged...fathers, sons, mothers, husbands...incapable of allowing each other to die. "Let him see me once more. Let him open his eyes once more." This they say to their doctor, to me. In that "once more," love will be shown, finally exchanged. I am to put a tube in him. One here. One here. Keep him for me. You understand. Na nu. Which agony? You are the doctor. Which agony do you treat? Your patient's? Who needs to die, to be released from this pain. Or the agony of the man or the woman who's waited for love too long? The patient didn't leave a statement with his wishes.
DANIEL: I don't know.
WALTER: You are responsible. You have to have an answer.
DANIEL: The family.
WALTER: Na nu. Now, we are a different story. I have no wish to live. I will not see the end of this disease. I know how it ends. I have seen it too often. I tell you this. I have a statement here that needs a witness. You say you will be it. You sign. I ask you not to ask me more questions. I ask you to play chess. You do. *(He turns board so the white pieces face him.)* We play a game of chess. We say goodnight. I go to my room. I've had brandy. I inject morphine. Perhaps in the *morning,* I still breathe. Gaby finds me. She cannot let me die as I wish. She cannot be without hope. Na nu. In the hospital, you show the doctor my note. "Yes, he'll say, but what happened that day?" You will tell him a family argument in the afternoon. That I asked if Yves called. That he didn't. He is a romantic, this doctor. Decides that was the reason I took morphine. There are people like this. He will tell you of a machine that will give me, what he calls the gift of time, enough time, he tells you, so I might see this new child. And will you think, "There will be a new grandchild, a good one, the better one. I will be the one to take that from Opa?" That test will be harder than what we do here. *(He holds paper to Daniel.)* I am dependent on you. Dependent on my evaluation of you. *(Daniel takes paper to desk to sign his name. Walter hears Gaby as she leaves her room. Walter sharply.)* Put it away. *(He moves a pawn.)* Sit down. *(Daniel sits in chair and moves his pawn. Gaby crosses into kitchen, carrying a box of graham crackers.)* Gabriella. *(Gaby waits a beat then enters living room. She turns on a table lamp to give them more light.)* I apologize for my behavior. I never wish to speak to you in that way.

GABY: I lost it, too. I'm sorry.
WALTER: Did we wake you?
GABY: No. I was finishing a flier. And you?
WALTER: I was telling the boy how we swam at the Strandbad.
(Gaby puts her hand on Walter's shoulder and looks at chess game.)
GABY: Whose move?
WALTER: White.
GABY: It won't be too long then. You'll go to bed soon?
WALTER: Soon.
GABY: Good night. *(Gaby kisses his cheek.)*
WALTER: Meine Seele. My soul.
GABY: *(To Daniel.)* Night. *(She exits to her room, puts card game away, and readies herself for bed.)*
WALTER: Please. *(Emotional. Daniel gives him the afghan which has fallen. Walter wraps it around him.)* Turn it out. The Brahms please. *(Daniel turns table lamp off. He goes to record cabinet, finds the Brahms' Violin Concerto, puts it on and returns to chair.)* My move. *(Walter moves his man. Daniel moves his man.)* *(The concerto plays. After a beat, Daniel exits to kitchen. He dials phone carefully, with his back to the audience, his head bent down, he speaks rapidly but softly into phone. He cannot be heard under the music. Daniel picks up a graham cracker, crosses into living room and returns to the game. As the music plays, the lights dim and come up.)*

Scene 4

> *Yves, hurriedly dressed, runs across dark hallway to door, keys in hand. He enters apartment.*

YVES: Daniel. *(Gaby, hearing Yves, grabs her robe.)*
GABY: Yves? *(Yves enters living room.)*
WALTER: Unforgivable.
DANIEL: I signed it. I'm not backing out. But you have to tell him.
WALTER: *(Turns face from Daniel.)* Good night.
YVES: *(To Daniel.)* What is it? *(To Walter.)* You wanted to see me.
(Gaby speaks as she crosses hallway into the living room.)
GABY: Why are you here?
YVES: Daniel called me.
GABY: *(To Daniel.)* Why?
WALTER: He overreacts.
YVES: *(To Walter.)* Did you want to see me?
GABY: Overreacts to what?
YVES: *(Turns off stereo.)* It's goddamn three thirty in the morning! What is going on?
GABY: *(To Daniel.)* What are you overreacting to?
WALTER: Give him the paper. *(Daniel gives Yves the statement.)* You can go.

DANIEL: Go? *(Yves reads it and gives it to Gaby.)*
YVES: *(To Daniel.)* You can go now. *(Yves waits a beat for Daniel to exit. Daniel remains in place, looking at Walter. Walter looks straight ahead.)* What are you standing there for? You want him to tell me something, let him tell me.
GABY: *(With force.)* You were told to go. *(Daniel exits to his room. A beat of silence. Gaby switches on two lamps. Yves rereads statement.)*
WALTER: It was in a newspaper... how to write it. Many do it these days. The boy overreacted.
YVES: Just signing this?
WALTER: At 80, malignancies are common.
YVES: Why didn't you tell me this afternoon?
WALTER: *(Dismissing question.)* I didn't. *(A silent beat.)*
YVES: You drinking brandy?
WALTER: It's not good.
GABY: I didn't remember which. I'll make coffee.
WALTER: No.
GABY: All right. *(She sits.)*
YVES: *(Goes to brandy.)* I'll have some. Gaby?
GABY: No. *(A silent beat.)*
WALTER: Ich möchte nicht reden, wenn sie im Zimmer ist. (I do not wish to speak with her in the room.)
YVES: Du meinst doch nicht, das ich es ihr sagen soll? (You don't mean I should tell her?)
WALTER: Ich würde dir dankbar dafur. (I would appreciate it.)
YVES: Sag es auf Deutsch. Sie wird es nicht verstehen. (Say it in German. She won't understand.)
WALTER: Tu es! (Do it!)
YVES: *(Sipping brandy.)* I don't think it's that bad. *(A silent beat.)* Why don't Walter and I finish our brandies...the gentlemen in the drawing room.
GABY: *(After a beat.)* The gentlemen?
WALTER: *(To Yves.)* Yes.
GABY: Goodnight. *(Gaby exits to kitchen and pours herself a glass of wine to take to her room. After a beat, Yves remembers to say "good night." He says it in the direction of her room.)*
YVES: Good night. *(Yves studies chess game.)*
WALTER: Show me a picture of her. Your wife. *(Yves is taken off guard. He removes his wallet from his back pocket. Gaby stands in kitchen. She hears conversation. Daniel, isolated in his room, lies face down on his bed.)*
YVES: Don't know if I have... The ones we took in Paris haven't been... *(He looks through his wallet.)* A french air mail stamp. Daniel in "Our Town" in high school. Mother. Enough credit cards to stay in debt...I'll have to bring you one.
WALTER: She is young. What else?
YVES: A tall woman. Wonderful skin.
WALTER: *(After a beat.)* You are like a mouse waiting for the cat.
YVES: She's a lawyer. Has a Master's in Public Health.
WALTER: *(Approving.)* Oh.

YVES: *(With irony.)* One for Karen.
WALTER: And?
YVES: *(With love.)* And she's a giggler.
WALTER: A what?
YVES: She giggles. She can get silly. Can be that way with me, she says. Feels comfortable with me, she says. I am with her.
WALTER: Comfortable?
YVES: Why do I bother?
WALTER: I questioned a word.
YVES: Not question. Judge.
WALTER: "Comfortable." I think of chairs.
YVES: I feel comfortable... I feel good, I feel happy, I feel sexy, I feel talented with her...
WALTER: You must shout?
YVES: I don't feel shallow with her. I don't feel what I like is shallow with her. I can argue with her. I could get angry at Gaby. I never could argue with her.
WALTER: Gaby is a superior woman. *(Gaby stands, wanting to exit, but she sits down again.)*
YVES: Yes ...I'll bring Karen to you.
WALTER: This is Gaby's house.
YVES: Is this why you haven't asked to...
WALTER: Was I asked to a restaurant to meet her?
YVES: When did you tell me?
WALTER: I'm to tell you everything you do? Sois honnête avec toi-même. You thought I wouldn't approve of her.
YVES: *(After a beat.)* If anything, I wouldn't want her to see how I am with you. How I change when I'm with you.
WALTER: You become a werewolf?
YVES: Never mind. Just goddamn never mind.
WALTER: You are too quickly sensitive.
YVES: *(A German accent.)* Herr Professor. What should we do with him? *(He imitates teacher.)* Dismiss him for showing emotions. You. The child in the back. The one with the feelings. Out! Out!
WALTER: One can't talk to you. One can only destroy you.
YVES: What did you say when I told you I was marrying her? You know what you said? You said "yes." That was it. End of response. Conversation over.
WALTER: *(Overly dramatic.)* I was to beg you to stay? To keep this family together for me? This home for your father's last days?
YVES: That's not you.
WALTER: *(Accusing.)* How do you know?
YVES: I don't.
WALTER: It's not. *(Gaby stands.)*
GABY: *(Shouts.)* I am in here!
WALTER: We speak in my room. *(He points to his statement.)* Keep that. *(Walter walks as quickly as he can. Yves follows carrying the Mühsam papers.*

168 *Unfinished Stories*

Gaby exits kitchen crossing into archway. Walter passes by Gaby without any acknowledgment. Yves stops in archway. They whisper.)
GABY: What was he saying in German?
YVES: Wait for me.
GABY: What was he saying in German? What was it?
YVES: That he wanted to speak to me.
GABY: What else?
YVES: Nothing. Wait for me. *(Yves follows Walter into his room.)*
GABY: I've been waiting!! *(Daniel, hearing them walk by, sits up, hoping to be called to join the men. Sound: The door to WALTER's room closes. Gaby sits in living room. Daniel turns his head back into pillow. Walter falls onto his bed.)*
WALTER: The books. They go to Gaby. Tell her to...
YVES: I'll get her.
WALTER: *(With emotion.)* I run like a child. Humiliate myself. You will not get her. *(Closing topic forcefully.)* No more. *(He points to the first leather bound book on the top shelf of the bookcase.)* Take down Heine's book. The green one. The first one. Heine's book. Open it to the first page where it is marked. Translate.
YVES: *(Translates from book.)* Wherever they burn books, sooner or later, they will burn humans also.
WALTER: Tell her he wrote it 80 years before Hitler. Tell her each book in this case was burnt in Goebbel's fire. Tell her if she sells them, she must not sell them separately.
YVES: Yes.
WALTER: Tell her their order. *(He points to the different shelves.)* The first shelf. The authors who died before Hitler. Second. Those murdered by Hitler. The third. The exiles who lived out their lives. The last shelf. The exiles who took their own lives. That starts with the grey one. Second on the last shelf. There. There. Tucholsky. See it?
YVES: Yes.
WALTER: Read the names. Read from Tucholsky. *(Yves reads names off books. Walter closes his eyes.)*
YVES: Kurt Tucholsky.
WALTER: Suicide. Sweden. 1935.
YVES: Ernst Toller...
WALTER: In New York. '39.
YVES: Stefan Zweig...
WALTER: In Brazil. *(Yves stops reading names.)* Don't stop.
YVES: Ernst Weiss.
WALTER: Paris.
YVES: Carl Einstein.
WALTER: Paris.
YVES: Why did Daniel call me? *(Walter finishes naming the suicides.)*
WALTER: Walter Benjamin, Spain. Alfred Wolfenstein. Paris. Klaus Mann...
YVES: This is what you will do.
WALTER: *(After a beat.)* The boy told you.
YVES: He didn't.

WALTER: Good.

YVES: Gaby? *(Walter shakes his head.)*

WALTER: *(A fact.)* She has my heart. She knows that.

YVES: *(Points to books.)* This is what you will do.

WALTER: These are important men. Do not compare me. I merely quote them. As for me…*(He removes syringe case from drawer and puts it on night table.)* This pain is a voice inside me. Louder each day. I do not want it to become the only thing I hear. I have morphine. It is not difficult. I am not afraid of it.

YVES: There are things you can take for this pain.

WALTER: Yes, for a short time. Then it will be small doses of morphine and then, if I am lucky, a nurse will pity me and administer one that will end my life.

YVES: You don't know this, it's fifty years since you…

WALTER: We have said this today.

YVES: Fifty years since you were a doctor.

WALTER: Do you ask me to bear this for you?

YVES: No.

WALTER: Then allow me some dignity. *(A silent beat.)*

YVES: I will.

WALTER: Please do not tell my Gabriella.

YVES: No.

WALTER: You said a picture of your mother. *(After a beat, Yves removes small snapshot from wallet and hands it to Walter.)*

WALTER: In Berlin. Why have you this picture?

YVES: It's before the war.

WALTER: Yes?

YVES: I like to remember her then.

WALTER: You weren't born then.

YVES: I remember her stories.

WALTER: What does she wear?

YVES: As Rosalind.

WALTER: Oh yes.

YVES: In her school play. At her high school.

WALTER: *(Looking at picture.)* She was very attractive. At the Romanische Cafe. She sat with the poets at the poets' table. Then she painted and sat with the painters. Then with the actresses. Then with the dancers. Each table coming closer to mine. We were called the younger doctors' table. The five of us met at a worker's clinic where we gave our time. But at night we were…how do you explain? Where do you find writers, painters, critics, architects, dancers drinking coffee, drunk on wine, playing chess, reading papers, looking for women, looking for men. There was nothing here like this. No cafe like this. There was too much smoke, yes, but in the smoke was the Geist. I watched her at each table changing her life, changing her life, coming closer and closer to my table. For her "Alles war Schicksal." Everything was fate.

YVES: For you?

WALTER: Nothing was fate. *(He looks at picture.)* Beautiful. I can understand why you chose her.

YVES: Chose her?
WALTER: What child doesn't choose between his parents... Don't be naive. *(He returns picture to Yves.)* You expect too much of me.
YVES: I don't expect anything. *(Walter sits up and speaks with emotion.)*
WALTER: Come closer. Mühsam had a ticket. He could have left for Prague. A student, also wanted by the Gestapo, came, "Would you go if you could," Mühsam asked, "would you leave?" He gave him the ticket. "Have faith. Humanity will win," he said to the boy. The SS came the next morning. Beat Mühsam deaf, blind, broke his thumbs. They put a wild ape in his cell. The other prisoners were told to watch it bite the Jew. Mühsam put his arm around the ape and the creature kissed him. The animal was tortured in front of him, then killed. He said to the others, "Do not believe them, if they tell you I took my life." The next morning it was announced in the prison, then in the newspapers, that Mühsam had hung himself in his cell. Hung from a noose tied...said by those who saw...tied with intricate knots, by a blind man with broken thumbs.
YVES: Were you the student? *(Exhausted, Walter falls back onto the bed.)*
WALTER: *(With difficulty.)* It was '33. By then I had left without saying goodbye. I left in the middle of an argument about the amount of postage to put on an envelope. When I had already bought my ticket to Paris. When I knew I didn't have the courage to stay.
YVES: Many left. Many...
WALTER: I am not many. I do not excuse it.
YVES: It was the times. No one was who they were before.
WALTER: Do you romanticize this, too?
YVES: I'm trying to understand.
WALTER: We are this. *(He twines his fingers together.)* We are in here. We are one. You are fifty-four of my years. I am fifty-four of yours. How can we understand?
YVES: Things change.
WALTER: What magic do you think I have? What magic will make me this person you want?
YVES: It's not magic. It's working at it. It's making an effort.
WALTER: When may I be a man who has failed? When may I stop disappointing you? *(A beat of silence. Walter holds out his hand.)* If I had met you as a stranger at the bench. Old men in the sun with no last names, only the present. If I could have sat with you this way, with a coffee...but you are my son.
YVES: *(Without anger.)* What can I give you? What do you want?
WALTER: Give me your hand. Accept what we are. *(Yves puts his hand in Walter's hand.)* Na nu. I was responsible for the confusion in this family today. I apologize.
YVES: *(Accepting the moment.)* This is what you want.
WALTER: Yes... Go now. Go to your boy. *(After a beat, Yves exits into hallway. Yves stands in hallway for a few beats. Daniel, on hearing door, sits up. Gaby shifts her position. Walter opens the syringe case. Yves crosses to living room.)*
YVES: You're here. *(He pulls Gaby to him, his body trembles. Walter injects himself.)* You're here. You're here. *(Yves mumbles. until his body stops*

trembling. When it stops, Gaby speaks.)
GABY: What is it? *(Yves does not respond.)* What is it? What did he say? *(When Yves doesn't respond, Gaby: exits to Walter's room. On seeing Walter, Gaby begins wailing softly.)* Nonononononononono...
(Gaby's wail mixes with the sound of a siren. Black out.)

Scene 5

> *The siren stops as the lights come up. Eight a.m. the next morning. Daniel and Yves enter outer hallway. Yves unlocks door and they enter the apartment. All the lights are on. The apartment is as they left it when they took Walter to the hospital. Daniel crosses into kitchen, opens icebox, takes out a container from yesterday's lunch, grabs a fork and eats, leaving the icebox door open.*

YVES: Gaby. Gaby. *(Yves crosses into the living room, crosses into Gaby's room and returns to living room.)* She's walking. I know her. She's walking. *(He dials the phone. Daniel opens more containers. Yves on phone.)* We're back at Gaby's. He died at five... I'm with Daniel... No. She left the hospital after he died. She walked out while I was with Daniel. He was having an "encounter" with a policeman and she left. He thought father's watch was stolen in the hospital...
DANIEL: The cop should have taken after the guy!
YVES: *(To Karen.)* If he were wearing a watch...
DANIEL: Strung him up by the balls!
YVES: I'm on the phone. *(To Karen.)* Yes. *(Softly.)* I wish you were here with me. *(He hangs up, takes coat off and crosses into kitchen.)* You didn't have it for dinner. *(Yves gets a fork and eats.)*
DANIEL: Didn't have dinner.
YVES: *(Referring to Daniel's container.)* The cassoulet wasn't bad. *(He removes last container from icebox, leaving door open.)* You have the bread?
DANIEL: What is this?
YVES: Cassoulet. The French come closer to making the ankles of sheep edible than any other people.
DANIEL: What is this!
YVES: *(Pointing with bread.)* Beans, baked beans. Sausages instead of hot dogs. We were looking for the Au Franc Pinot and a man gave the directions pointing with his baguette.
DANIEL: *(Eating.)* I had a ninety-two-year old woman in my cab...
YVES: Excuse me, you don't want the pate?
DANIEL: No.
YVES: She was ninety-two?
DANIEL: She got in and told me her age, then didn't talk, then five minutes later told me she likes macaroni and cheese and got out.
YVES: *(Scraping the bits from container.)* Karen's father was with Mobil Oil and as a kid she lived in Lagos. She likes cold curry for breakfast.
DANIEL: What are the potatoes called?

YVES: What potatoes?

DANIEL: The ones he said the cooks had to inflate by blowing into each one with a straw.

YVES: Pommes de terre souffles.

DANIEL: I believed him.

YVES: He never stepped into a kitchen in his life.

DANIEL: He ate the cookie dough.

YVES: Cookie dough like...

DANIEL: What you make cookie's from.

YVES: Gaby baked cookies?

DANIEL: Mrs. Who lived next door gave me a bowl of it and told me how to bake them, and I was standing there, he didn't know I was there, and he ate it. Not all of it but he ate half of it. I was going to tell him he ate it?

YVES: When we ate Chinese, he ordered Moo Goo Gai Pan. That's like ordering Spaghetti O's. But he knew his French food. I once asked mother what restaurants they went to when they lived in Paris. She gave me his list. On the back of the list he had written: "Here I am a man. Not just a civilian." It was a list of bistros you could never find by accident. He knew his Paris. *(Daniel abruptly leaves kitchen. He crosses into living room.)*

DANIEL: *(To the world.)* Goddamn rude not being here. Fucking rude not being here. *(Yves closes icebox door.)*

YVES: She doesn't know we're here.

DANIEL: You don't walk out without telling someone you're walking out.

YVES: *(Crossing into living room.)* She'll be here. She's walking. *(Yves is exhausted. He sits on couch.)* I'll call the funeral home when they open.

DANIEL: What will they do?

YVES: Arrange for the cremation.

DANIEL: Where?

YVES: I don't know.

DANIEL: When?

YVES: They'll tell us.

DANIEL: We're not there? They just do it?

YVES: I don't know how these things work.

DANIEL: Nobody is there? You just let them do it?

YVES: I don't know how they...

DANIEL: I'll call them. *(He crosses to desk.)*

YVES: You signed it. He wants to be cremated...

DANIEL: Where's the fucking yellow pages?*(He crosses to kitchen and finds book where Yves left it earlier.)*

YVES: It's Sunday morning. They're not open.

DANIEL: *(With force.)* I'm being there.

YVES: *(Enters kitchen.)* You don't listen. I'm saying *he* didn't want a funeral, not that we can't...

DANIEL: He didn't want to be in a hospital. He didn't want his watch stolen.

YVES: We don't know if...

DANIEL: He had his watch on. He shouldn't have been in a hospital.
YVES: I'm not going through this again.
DANIEL: Why didn't you back me up? Why'd you let her call EMS?
YVES: That's what she wanted.
DANIEL: What *he* wanted. Why didn't you back me up with the cop? Why say you didn't know he had his watch on? *(Yves exits.) (Daniel speaks from kitchen.)* I was the one in the hallway. I saw where they left him. He was dead. Anyone could have gone up to him. *(Yves enters Walter's room. He spots watch immediately on night table.)*
YVES: *(With force.)* Come in here. Come in here. *(Daniel crosses into Walter's room.)* Take it! *(He tosses watch on bed. A silent beat. Being in Walter's room changes the tension, affecting both men.)*
DANIEL: He was pushed...pushed in a bag like he was garbage. And they're arguing, arguing over his body, arguing over who used the pay phone longer. *(Yves crosses to Daniel.)*
YVES: You were fantastic with the doctor. You were fantastic at the hospital. Do you hear what I'm saying?
DANIEL: *(Dismissive.)* Yeah. *(Daniel moves away.)*
YVES: He was in coma. *We* knew he was there. He didn't. You took on everybody. They listened to you. You lost it over his watch. It's nothing to what you did. *(A silent beat.)*
DANIEL: Did he say anything to you about me?
YVES: Like what?
DANIEL: About my calling you.
YVES: He wanted you to call me.
DANIEL: He said that?
YVES: He'd never tell me that.
DANIEL: Then he didn't say it?
YVES: Not directly.
DANIEL: Then he didn't say it.
YVES: No one did anything tonight he didn't want done.
DANIEL: He said to me it was unforgivable.
YVES: Everything to him was impossible, unforgivable.
DANIEL: That was the last thing he said to me.
YVES: You have to forget that.
DANIEL: I can't forget that.
YVES: You were in the middle. I couldn't call him. He couldn't call.
DANIEL: *(Breaking down.)* He said "We play a game of chess. We say goodnight." You don't understand. He didn't say goodnight... You don't understand. He didn't see me with the doctors. You don't understand. The last thing he was left... I was left... I failed him.
YVES: *(Grabs Daniel.)* You don't let him into your head. You keep him out of it.
DANIEL: I loved him.
YVES: And you showed it and that's no failure.
DANIEL: You don't know.
YVES: And stood up for him. That's no failure.

DANIEL: You don't know...
YVES: I know this. This is ours. Yours. His. Mine. You learned it here. In here.
This was your room. Your crib was there. You were this big. Passed from hand to
hand. My mother was here. Everyone was here. Everyone held you and said
something about you and passed you on. It felt like the game in which you start a
story and the next one adds something till it gets an ending. When Walter passed
you to me...O nouveau-né, this amazing new life...my hands shook. Gaby
thought it was that I was afraid I would drop you. It was as though he were
handing me the story he and I hadn't finished, which he hadn't finished with his
father, which I swore would have an ending before I ever had a child. You
understand. The failure is ours. Not yours. The failure is mine. *(After a beat, Yves
takes the watch from the bed and crosses into the living room. After a beat, Daniel
crosses into living room. Yves, controlling his emotions.)* What part was it? The
part you got?
DANIEL: Henry Five.
YVES: Yes. What did you do for them?
DANIEL: "If we are mark'd to die, we are enow..." *(Yves joins in.)*
DANIEL AND YVES: "To do our country loss; and if to live..."
YVES: "The fewer the men, the greater share of honor.
God's will! I pray thee wish not one man more."
DANIEL: You stayed an actor. You have a lot of courage. *(Yves turns to Daniel.)*
YVES: I wanted to take a book and read to him, read to him till he fell asleep.
DANIEL: *(Understanding.)* You couldn't.
YVES: Before I walked out, he said "Accept us for what we are." He had my
hand. It was a moment of peace. The first I ever felt. *(He gives Daniel the watch.)*
This is yours. Take it. *(Daniel takes watch. Gaby enters outer hallway. She
hesitates for a long beat by the apartment door.)*
DANIEL: He had it on the day he met Mühsam.
YVES: Don't romanticize it. It's a watch.
DANIEL: *(Not putting watch on.)* I know that. *(Gaby enters apartment. She
doesn't take her coat off, nor enters the main playing areas. She remains in the
hallways, intent on going to her room.)*
GABY: You can go home. We'll do it tomorrow.
DANIEL: Where were you? I looked at the coffee machine. I looked in the annex.
GABY: I left.
YVES: We'll meet tomorrow. We'll meet for breakfast.
DANIEL: I went back to the coffee machine...
YVES: *(At the same time as Daniel.)* She knows.
DANIEL: You said you were getting coffee.
GABY: I walked out.
YVES: She went for a walk.
DANIEL: I know the streets at night. I know where you don't walk.
And you don't walk on...
YVES: For God's sake, you were worried.
DANIEL: You don't have to patronize.
GABY: I don't need this!

YVES: Why don't we meet tomorrow. Should it be here?

GABY: Yes. The both of you can go.

DANIEL: We've been...

GABY: *(Letting anger out.)* This is not a men's club where I come to take care of the boys. Not a place to dump yourselves and call home till you've figured out your lives! You're standing where I live. What happens here is my life. I should have been told.

DANIEL: He said...

GABY: I don't give a damn what he said. I was here. You called Yves.

DANIEL: He's his father.

GABY: It was Walter I came home to, not you, not Yves. It was Walter I came home to.

YVES: Walter should have.

GABY: We had a deal. A deal I would have honored. It was he that didn't. It was he that lied to me.

YVES: You have to understand...

GABY: I don't want to understand.*(She crosses away from the men..)* I want him here. I want him in his chair. I want to hit him, yell at him. I want him here. I want him in his room. I want to ask him for his words. I want him here. I want to shout at the news with him. I want him here. I want to walk in his room, throw the Times on his bed, see him open it. I want to show him. There's your sense of decency, there's power filled with kindness. We did it. We did it for you and a hundred billion yous and for me *(She includes Daniel.)* and for you. We didn't. I walked from the Circle to Times Square, up Columbus, down Central Park. Streets we marched, made promises on.We were his hope, the next generation. We're this generation. What's out there is ours. *(With anger.)* And I don't know how. I don't know how to do it anymore.

DANIEL: *(Compassionately.)* How could you expect? What did you expect?

GABY: *(With passion.)* We expected.

DANIEL: You couldn't win. Read DeLillo. It fucking kills me...

YVES: *(Interjects.)* Not now.

DANIEL: When they see you coming. Kills me when they beat you up...

YVES: *(Interjects.)* Not now!

DANIEL: When they fuck over Opa, fuck over Mühsam.

GABY: Do something about it!

DANIEL: When you don't know how?

GABY: Yes.

DANIEL: What can I say to you ?!

GABY: Nothing! *(Gaby leaves the men. She goes from room to room turning the lights out, the lights left on from the previous night. She cannot enter Walter's room. His light stays on. She reenters living room and "opens" curtains to let in the morning sun light.)*

GABY: *(After a beat.)* You bring me the morning. He said it for 20 years. It got me every time. *(A silent beat.)* I thought he was apologizing. I thought he was apologizing for some stupid thing and he was saying good-bye. I didn't want to know. He walked in with his coffee pot, his Persian rugs, his turkey carpets, his bookcase and his books. He was my home.

YVES: He was. *(A silence.)*

DANIEL: He was home whenever I walked in. No matter that he didn't know I was coming. I thought it would follow he'd always be here. Everything doesn't follow.

GABY: Except for Germans. *(She laughs.)*

YVES: *(To Daniel.)* That's father's story.

GABY: His worst story. *(To Daniel.)* And he told it every midnight, every New Year.

YVES: *(For Daniel.)* A German thief, a thief in Berlin, in the twenties. He gets a hold of a German captain's uniform and puts it on. *(He imitates Walter in action and voice.)* Father buttoned the jacket. The thief, now dressed like a captain, says to every soldier he sees on the street."Soldier. Follow me at once."

GABY: *(Enjoying story.)* It's a true story.

YVES: He marches the soldiers to the Town Hall, orders them to put the mayor under arrest and then to seize the municipal funds. Here father would take a pause and look into his champagne glass. *(Yves imitates Walter with an actor's precision. It is as though Walter is in the room.)* He dismisses the soldiers. They return to their units. And the thief disappears with the money. When the Germans find this out, they do not punish the soldiers because, at least, they believed they were following orders. Na nu. *(A silent beat. Gaby is in silent tears.)*

DANIEL: *(Crosses to Gaby.)* Want me to stay?

GABY: *(Gently.)* Not tonight. I'm going to fall asleep next to the speaker.

DANIEL: I'll do it. *(He crosses to record cabinet and looks for a record for Gaby.)*

GABY: When did you read DeLillo?

DANIEL: I read.

GABY: What's so macho about telling me you don't read?

DANIEL: I never tell you I don't read. You kept assuming that.

GABY: Why didn't you unassume me?

DANIEL: I don't know.

GABY: Can you argue with me?

DANIEL: *(Not understanding.)* That's what we do.

YVES: Will you be all right?

GABY: Yes.

YVES: I'll call you tonight. *(Gaby wraps herself in the afghan and lies on the floor by the speaker)*

DANIEL: I'm driving to the country.

YVES: *(Getting his jacket.)* We can go down in the elevator together. We'll meet tomorrow. We'll see you tomorrow. *(Daniel cues needle onto record. The introduction to Otis Reading's "A Change Is Going To Come" is heard.)*

GABY: *(Looks at Daniel.)* Oh my.

DANIEL: The right one?

GABY: *(Surprised and moved.)* You know *my* music.

DANIEL: See you tomorrow. *(Gaby nods yes and closes her eyes. Daniel listens to the song for a few beats, then crosses to Yves. They exit apartment and cross*

outer hallway.)
DANIEL: Wait.
(Daniel reenters apartment. He crosses to the desk and picks up the Mühsam papers. As he crosses back to Yves, Daniel stops to carefully fold the papers and place them in his pocket. Daniel and Yves cross outer hallway together and exit stage. Gaby lies by the speaker. The music plays. The lights dim.)

THE END

WHAT IS THIS EVERYTHING?

an existential fairy tale
by Patricia Scanlon

Dedicated to Marc Raider

Playwright's Biography

Patricia Scanlon is a playwright and an actress living in New York City. Her plays and solo works include, *"What Is This Everything?"*, Westbank Cafe, Synchronicity Space Theatre, Ensemble Studio Theatre's One Act Marathon and L.A. *"Prophet In Limbo"*, the Public Theatre, *"The Age Of Doom"*, Home for Contemporary Theatre and Art, *"The Life And Hard Times Of Hildy Hildy"*, Soho Rep, *"Moons And Junes And Ferris Wheels"*, La Mama, *"By The Time I Got To Yesterday"* and *"The Shaken Baby Syndrome"*. Scanlon has performed her solo pieces at The Public, The Kitchen, La Mama, P.S. 122, The WestBank Cafe, Snug Harbor Cultural Center, and others. She has also performed her piece, *"Another Cup Of Coffee"* at The Lucille Ball Festival in Jamestown, New York as well as Theatre/Theater, Cafe Largo and The Pik-Me-Up in Los Angeles. Scanlon also writes and performs weekly in a staged soap opera, *"Nobody's Daughter"* as part of Cucaracha Theatre Company's *"Underground Soap"*. She also is a grant recipient of Poets and Writers.

Patricia would like to thank her sister, Barbara Wieland.

Playwright's Note

At the time in my life when I wrote this play, I had two choices. I could jump out the window. Or I could write the play. I wrote the play.

CHARACTERS

TRASH: A child-woman "just 30" on the edge of becoming something other than this pained, nervous, frightened sparrow she is now.

WAITER/FATHER: A large red-faced drinking man in between 50 and 60. He has the flavor of a twisted Jackie Gleason.

DIRTY DIGGIN MAN: He is between 30 and 40. He is very dirty and very "diggin." There is a fire in his head.

Although there are four "characters" in the play, FEAR hangs in the air like a fifth. At various points throughout the action of the play, each character looks as if he may commit an action of great violence.

ORIGINAL CAST

Originally developed at The WestBank Cafe with:

Trash...Patricia Scanlon
Dirty Diggin Man.......................Jeff Robins
Waiter / Father...........................James Gandolfini
Directed by Will Scheffer

Premiere Production at Synchronicity Space Theatre with:

Trash...Patricia Scanlon
Dirty Diggin Man.......................Jeff Robins
Waiter / Father...........................Robert Mooney
Directed by David Briggs

Subsequent Production at Ensemble Studio Theatre's One-Act Marathon.

Trash...Patricia Scanlon
Dirty Diggin Man.......................Brian Tarantina
Waiter / Father...........................Ed Setrakian
Directed by Billy Carden

SETTING

A landscape found inside a dream. The set is sparse. An old Naugahyde recliner sits atop a crooked staircase upstage right, a coffee shop counter and stools center stage, and a raked bed downstage left. Ideally, this bed may be the kind with a headboard and footboard of white bars to give it the appearance of a cage. Each area, when being played in and sometimes simultaneously while other scenes are being played, is accented with the use of boldly colored lighting, like one might imagine in the extremities of the mind's eye. The shadow of the Waiter/Father's chair is cast over other playing areas at certain points in the play.

TIME

We have the feeling that it is late, late, late at night, but actually it could be "anytime," a piece of time taken out of time.

What Is This Everything?

Scene 1

Sound: "Daydream Believer" by the Monkees. Lights up. Trash is sitting over an empty coffee cup at the counter of a coffee shop. The waiter is leaning against the other side of the counter doing a crossword puzzle. The Waiter spots a cockroach on the floor, smacks it with his newspaper, takes a napkin from the counter, wipes the floor, then turns off the radio.Sound out.

Trash wears an old dress. There are odd ribbons and things wrapped around her ankles and wrists. She also wears a dirty wedding veil which she has decorated with dead flowers and shiny trinkets. The veil is covering her face when the curtain rises.

TRASH: Excuse me. Excuse me. *(Pause. Lifting veil.)* Excuse me. I don't mean to bother you, but may I have some more coffee please.
WAITER: Sure. *(Pours, then cleans counter.)* You want something to eat with that? A donut? A grill cheese? Too much coffee on an empty stomach turns your insides to acid. Give ya the shakes. Always makes me jumpy. You sure you don't want something to eat?
TRASH: No. No thank you. *(Looks at the Waiter's face.)*
WAITER: OK. Suit yourself. I'll be in the kitchen. If you need me just holler.
(Trash watches him go, then looks out.)
TRASH: *(To herself.)* Despite certain observances...I guess part of me always thought you grew up, you did things and somehow you got happy. It was this feeling I had. This subtle expectation in my stomach. Like any moment something terribly exciting and wonderful might happen. Like when I went shopping at the mall with my friends and got a bottle of new perfume, "Love's Baby Soft" or something nice like that. I couldn't wait to get home. Take a shower, brush my hair out real nice and then, only then, put on some of my new perfume.
(Sound: Nat King Cole singing "Stay As Sweet As You Are.")
Then I'd sneak through the living room past my Dad.*(Lights up on Father sitting in the chair surrounded by empty beer bottles and Cheez-It boxes. Trash climbs up on the counter.)* who was always sitting in his chair drinking beer and listening to cornball music on the record player. I was told to tiptoe by, not look, 'cause you never knew whether he'd be swinging his fists or crying. And either way it was something nobody wanted to deal with.
(Trash jumps down into the Father's area.)

Scene 2

Father seems to have fallen asleep. He detects Trash sneaking by and

184   *What Is This Everything?*

watches for a moment before he says anything.
FATHER: Hey, hey. *(Trash jumps.)* Scared ya. Scared ya, didn't I? I don't miss a trick. Can't fool your ol' man. No siree. You got to get up pretty early to pull the wool over your ol' man's eyes. *(Stares hard at her. She nibbles on a candy necklace.)* You're a creepy kid. You know that. Always sneaking around spying on people. What are you looking for? Huh?
TRASH: Nothing.
FATHER: Look-atch-ya, with a big puss hanging down to your ass. Never see you smile. Wouldn't hurt you to smile at your ol' man once in a while – show a little appreciation. Smile for Christ's sake. Smile! *(Trash smiles.)* That's more like it. That didn't hurt, did it? Did it?
TRASH: No.
FATHER: You get more with honey than you do with vinegar, remember that.
TRASH: I will. *(Starts to move away.)*
FATHER: Hey, hey. How 'bout dancin' a step or two for your ol' man like you used to. Remember how you used to dance for me when you were a little girl?
TRASH: I don't remember.
FATHER: Sure you do. Just let the music in. Just let it move through you. Let it take you away. *(Sways his hands back and forth in the air, one of them still holding a beer.)*
TRASH: I don't remember. *(Trash crosses back to the coffee shop counter and sits on it. Sound out. Lights out on Father.)* I suppose I could have gone through the kitchen and out the back door and not had to walk by him at all. But somehow I think I enjoyed the thrill of it, the thrill of this downtrodden game of suburban espionage. Once I got to the front stoop I was home free. 'Cause just about anything might happen in those twilight hours between just-after-dinner and night. Davy Jones might drive by and ask me to marry him. Then he'd buy me a fancy outfit and I'd be a lead singer with the Monkees. That was just one of the wild possibilities. They were endless. *(Returns to her seat at the counter.)* I guess I always had this excited feeling back then. This vague idea that each life contained some uniquely marvelous eventuality. Even though all of the adults around me acted sort of...funny. Like something had come along and given them a bum turn. Like they'd had a secret they'd somehow... forgotten.

Scene 3

> *Lights up on the coffee shop. Trash is sitting at the counter. She is still drinking coffee.*
>
> *Dirty Diggin Man enters. He carries a dirty notebook and a stack of worn philosophy books. He sits at the counter.*

DIRTY DIGGIN MAN: What do you got to do to get a cup of coffee around here?
TRASH: Excuse me?

DIRTY DIGGIN MAN: What do you got to do to get a cup of coffee around here?

TRASH: *(Not looking at him.)* Just "holler." He's in the kitchen.

DIRTY DIGGIN MAN: Coffee. Yoo-hoo cup of java, please. *(The Waiter comes out of the kitchen and pours Dirty Diggin Man a cup of coffee, then exits. Dirty Diggin Man can't find a spoon, reaches over and grabs Trash's spoon.)*

TRASH: It's dirty.

DIRTY DIGGIN MAN: What?

TRASH: The spoon.

DIRTY DIGGIN MAN: Oh. *(Stirring coffee.)*

TRASH: You're welcome. *(The Waiter returns and resumes crossword puzzle. Dirty Diggin Man takes out a pencil. He holds it "white-knuckled" above his notebook and stares ahead into the deep distances of himself. Trash and Dirty Diggin Man gulp coffee. The Waiter silently refills their cups. Trash and Dirty Diggin Man sip and think, sip and think. They both look out. SOUND: music in. LIGHTS: black.*

Scene 4

> *Lights up on an even brighter coffee shop. Music continues. The coffee cups have become surrealistically large.*

DIRTY DIGGIN MAN: I got a glitch in my brain and I'm going nowhere. Same places over and over again. Saying bad things. Making me remember things I want to forget.

TRASH: It's making me hot inside. It's making me wish I could jump out of myself. This thing that I am. Who am I?

DIRTY DIGGIN MAN: Have I merely fallen like so much protoplasm into the one place I could fit?

TRASH: I don't like wondering where dead people go. Knowing just enough to know I know nothing.

DIRTY DIGGIN MAN: I know nothing and I know it well.

TRASH: All I know is that this not knowing hurts. I don't get where do you put the pain. Answer me that. Were do you put the pain? Cream, please.

DIRTY DIGGIN MAN: Twisted and dirty I sit inside myself waiting for an answer.

TRASH: My life is just not happening. It's just not taking shape. The way I thought it would. The way I expected it to.

DIRTY DIGGIN MAN: I have lost the taste of myself. I am losing the flavor of myself.

TRASH: I must break the back of this existence before it breaks me.

DIRTY DIGGIN MAN: The day is the salt. I am the wound.

TRASH: I wonder if the birds ever feel remorseful because their wings don't take them high enough?

DIRTY DIGGIN MAN: I don't think I'm living right. Something tells me I ain't living right. An inkling that I am off track somehow. Taken a corner but I don't remember taking the turn.

TRASH: There's this feeling like I've fallen down. Down inside myself. There is no buoyancy. Nothing to hold me up. My eyes don't look right when I look in the mirror. Like maybe there is something broken inside. People look at me funny.

DIRTY DIGGIN MAN: Sometimes I see these people and I get this feeling that they're doing all of their thinking outside of their heads. All this doing for doing and knowing not for what. All these busy, busy people scattered about obstructing one's view of the horizon. *(The Waiter throws the newspaper down and picks up another one from the small stack on the counter.)*

TRASH: No matter how much I bathe, I always feel dirty somehow. Like a dirty pillow in a clean pillowcase. Sometimes I think I'm giving off a funny smell. Like an old potato. *(Pulls a potato dripping with coffee out of the cup.)*

DIRTY DIGGIN MAN: *(Grabs the potato.)* I'll take that. *(Trash drinks coffee.)*

DIRTY DIGGIN MAN: I'll take that. Nobody cuts to the chase anymore. Everybody, everybody's afraid of the bottom line. Afraid of making the essential point. Like a dirty bum, I sit scratching the fat ass of my existence looking for the bottom line. The essential point.

TRASH: My vision is clouded. With visions of visions of visions of... revisions.

DIRTY DIGGIN MAN: *(Cued by "clouded.")* My vision is spattered with excrement from the past. *(To Trash.)* Sugar, please.

TRASH: When people talk to me, I am afraid that I will spill. That my insides will spill all over them. That they will say, "Hi, how are you?" And I will say, "Bluh-h-h-h-h-h-h-h-h-h-h-h."

DIRTY DIGGIN MAN: How do people contain themselves? How do they contain their questions? What? What? What is this hatred? This biting aching madness? This invisible hand that threatens to pull me out of myself?

TRASH: I find myself walking in small dizzy circles looking down at my wrists that hang limply by my sides like a tired answer. They whisper, "Slit me." Nothing I do. Nothing I say is ever quickly enough . Ever correctly enough. and I wonder what, what, what is this everything that has pushed and pulled me to this point?

DIRTY DIGGIN MAN: This, this, this way of living is just not acceptable.

TRASH: Nothing, nothing, nothing seems real anymore unless I am destroying it. *(Slams the counter hard with the flat of her hand.)*
(Lights black then in an instant come back up. Everyone is in his same position and the cups are back to normal size. Trash looks at her hand she has just slammed down on the counter.)

TRASH: *(Explains.)* Cockroach.

WAITER: Alright, this is enough. Sitting here all night gawking into your coffee cups. You know what's wrong with you kids? Huh, do you? Do you? You need an *objective*. That's what you need. An objective. You hear me? You get what I'm saying? An objective. Something to take your minds off yourself. Be good for ya.

DIRTY DIGGIN MAN: I got plenty objectives ... I *object* to everything.

WAITER: You know what time it is, wise-ass?

DIRTY DIGGIN MAN:
      The clock hangs like the devil

> Ticking on the wall
> Tick tock, tick tock
> Hear its ugly call.

TRASH:

> The clock hangs like the devil
> Ticking on the wall
> Tick tock, tick tock
> Death will come to all.

WAITER: Funny, mine must be a little fast. (*Exits with plunger.*) (*Trash and Dirty Diggin Man have been sneaking glances at each other. The sound of a toilet being plunged is heard. The Waiter reenters with dripping plunger.*)

TRASH: (*To Dirty Diggin Man, hesitantly.*) You a poet?

DIRTY DIGGIN MAN: Sort of. I think about stuff and if it feels like maybe it's true I write it down. So actually I don't end up writing that much.

TRASH: Well, if it ain't the truth, no sense writing it down. Is there?

DIRTY DIGGIN MAN: No. No, there isn't... I kind of like to think of myself as one of life's private detectives. "Naming the unnameable." There's a certain power in naming things. Gives you a distance on them. Gives you a little bit control over the hands that are trying to choke you, (*Glances at the Waiter.*) you know what I mean?

TRASH: Yeah. Yeah, I do... It's like if, if you can pull the hurt out of you somehow. Get it down on paper somehow, in words, right there in black and white, then it isn't sitting there inside of your guts anymore making things... (*Hunts for the right word to express exactly what she means.*)

WAITER: Hey, hey, hey. (*Trash and Dirty Diggin Man look at him.*) Scared ya, didn't I. Scared ya. Sorry, didn't mean to startle you. Look, I ah need your help. I got a toughie here. (*Indicates crossword.*) You kids know a three-letter word for poet? (*Pause.*)

WAITER: *Bum. B-U-M. Bum.* That's right. Now pay up and get out of here. I've been waiting to close up all night. It's making me sick being here with nothing to look at but the both of you. Look at you. Look at the both of you. You look like something right out of a horror movie. No kidding. All pinch-faced and worried. "Woe is me, woe is me." Look at you, all twisted and *to-o-ormented.* About *what?* A big fat *nothing.* That's right. That's right. And that's probably what you have in your pockets. *"A big fat nothing."* (*Makes an "O" with his thumb and index finger and pushes it in their faces.*)

DIRTY DIGGIN MAN: Look, man, I ain't crawlin' up your ass, now don't go crawlin' up mine.

WAITER: Now that's some poetry you got there. That oughta sell. Inside a Hallmark greeting card that-a-be nice. Catchy. (*Pause.*) You got a job?

DIRTY DIGGIN MAN: No. No, I don't. I can't find one that doesn't insist on my changing my way of thinking.

WAITER: God forbid. (*Begins to exit but changes his mind.*) Let me tell you something. I got two. That's right, two jobs. One in the morning. One at night. And I never missed a day a work in my life. Sometimes I'm pushin' say sixty-seventy hours a week. Someone offers me overtime, I take it. And you, look at you. You're sitting around scratchin' your fat ass, looking for the "meaning of life." You get up, you do what you gotta do, then you go to bed knowin' you done it. That's it. And every once in a while you buy yourself a nice meal. A steak. Lobster. Something nice. And a bottle-a-beer or two. That's it, that's life. Burns me up. Burns my ass see a young man like you sittin' around wasting his life. Sitting around with a big fat hair across his ass "thinki-i-n'" about "things." Just looking for somethig not to agree with. While I'm out busting my arse and then paying taxes up the wazoo taboot to support people like you. Freeloaders who refuse to live in the real world like the rest of us. Well, I got news for you, your ka-ka stinks like everyone else's. *(To Trash)* No offense. And I got even bigger news for the both of you - it takes real money to live in either world. World full of people like you, the world would go to hell in a hand-barrel before you could blink an eye. A world full of "thinka-a-a-as". A world full of "poets". Now that's something to think about. *(Wipes counter.)*

TRASH: My dear sir, one's thoughts are one's most crucial adventures. Do you know, I believe, I truly believe that one thought could change the entire world. One *important* thought. So *true. So pure. So utterly, undeniably unfalse that I believe it could change the entire order of things.*

WAITER: What a crock. *(Knocks a saucer off the counter; it falls to the floor and breaks.)* Damn it. *(Goes for dustpan and broom.)* God damn it. Jesus Christ almighty. God damn it. *(Dirty Diggin Man leans down over counter to Waiter.)*

DIRTY DIGGIN MAN: You see, sir, one shouldn't submit themselves to the mendacity of the marketplace. *(Trash joins Dirty Diggin Man leaning over the counter talking to Waiter. The Waiter continues to mumble curses under his breath.)*

TRASH: Yes sirree, sir, the human soul is becoming an endangered species.

WAITER: Jesus Christ almighty goddamn son of a bitch…*(This is the first time that Trash and Dirty Diggin Man look at each other.)*

DIRTY DIGGIN MAN: *(To Trash.)* What's your name?

TRASH: Trash. *(The Waiter is still struggling, bent over on all fours.)*

WAITER: Bag!!?!

TRASH: No. Just Trash. *(To Dirty Diggin Man.)* What's yours?

DIRTY DIGGIN MAN: Dirty –

WAITER: *Laundry!!?!*

DIRTY DIGGIN MAN: Dirty Diggin Man. *(To Waiter.)* You got that? Dirty Diggin Man. *(The Waiter stands up quickly and waves his dirty dishrag in their faces.)*

WAITER: And mine is dishrag! Dishrag! Now pay up and get out of here. Trash Bag! Dirt Bag! Get out of here. Get out of here. Your heads are going to bust right open you got 'em stuffed with so much garbage. All your high-and-mighty important thoughts. What? What? What? What does a person have to do all that "think-i-in'" about anyway? Poets, my fat ass. God knows what goes on in your minds. Scare one half to death, half to death just thinking about it. Gives me the heebee-geebees. *(Wipes counter with dishrag, the same spot over and over again.)* Busy hands are happy hands, that's what I always say. Busy hands are happy

hands. *(Trash has begun to bite in the air savagely at the Waiter.)* What's wrong with her? What's she doing? She a, a what do you call it epi – epileptic. *Spoon. Spoon.* Put *(Grabs a spoon. Dirty Diggin Man catches him by the wrist.)*
DIRTY DIGGIN MAN: She is biting the demons that nobody else seems to think exist. *(Starts biting too.)*
WAITER: This really is too much. Too damn much. You look like a couple of guppies. That's what you look like. A couple of rabid guppies. You really don't belong in this world. You really don't. *Now get out of here. Get out of here! Trash Bag! Dirt Bag!* *(Trash and Dirty Diggin Man exit biting. The Waiter grabs a donut from the pastry stand and gets a beer.)*
WAITER: *(With mouth full.)* You just do what you got to do and get on with it. *(Trash reenters and grabs Dirty Diggin Man's books from the counter.)* You hear me. Get on with it. "Poets," my big fat ass. *(Trash "bites a demon" and exits.)* How's this for a *poem?*

> Roses are red
> Violets are blue
> Just do
> What you Goddamn gotta do.

Or how's this? I got a good one.

> You wake up one day and all of a sudden you're fat.
> You wake up one day and all of a sudden you're old.
> You wake up one day and all of a sudden you don't know who
>   you are.
> And then it hits you.
> Maybe you ate too much.
> Or maybe you let life live you instead of you living life.

(Washes down the last of the donut.)

Scene 5

Lights up on Father in chair. Sound: "If I Ruled the World" sung by Tony Bennett. The Father is sitting exhausted in the chair, drinking beer and nibbling Cheez-Its. Now and then he is swept away by the song. As his energy gets higher, he may sing along. He may use the beer bottle as a microphone. Lights: fade out with end of song.

Scene 6

Red lights up on bed downstage right. Sound: "Room 43" by Ray Anthony. Trash and Dirty Diggin Man are doing "The Angst Dance". After the dance, the lights and sound fade.

Scene 7

Sickly yellow light. Trash and Dirty Diggin Man are kneeling on bed. They touch hands. Sound: A heart beat.

DIRTY DIGGIN MAN: I am afraid that I have lost touch with a certain power inside myself. That I am becoming an abstraction of the person I was meant to be.

TRASH: I am afraid that the doors I have closed are keeping out more than they are keeping in.

DIRTY DIGGIN MAN: I am afraid that the more I strive not to be mediocre and afraid, the more mediocre and afraid I become.

TRASH: I am afraid that even before I get up in the morning that I have done something wrong. Hurt someone. Somehow.

DIRTY DIGGIN MAN: I am afraid that I have become misshapen.

TRASH: I am afraid that I have become misconstrued. That what I am saying is not what I mean. *(Pause.)* Exactly.

DIRTY DIGGIN MAN: I am afraid that I have forgotten... how.

TRASH: I am afraid that I am not scooping up the day the way it should be scooped.

DIRTY DIGGIN MAN: I am afraid that at this precise moment I should be doing precisely something else.

TRASH: I am afraid that when people are talking to me they are not telling the truth.

DIRTY DIGGIN MAN: I am afraid that I am damaged beyond repair.

TRASH: I am afraid that I may kill myself. *(Pause.)* I have lost touch with the still place in me. That it no longer exists.

DIRTY DIGGIN MAN: I am afraid that someone will find out how sick I really am.

TRASH: I am afraid that someone will find out how afraid I really am. *(Sound: The heart beat stops. Pause. Trash and Dirty Diggin Man begin to pass a bottle of red wine back and forth.)*

TRASH: Your turn. *(Dirty Diggin Man thinks.)*

DIRTY DIGGIN MAN: I afraid that they will take my credit cards away. Cancel my accounts. Declare me "A bad credit risk."

TRASH: I afraid that the people I know aren't the "the right ones."

DIRTY DIGGIN MAN: I'm afraid that I'll never be able to find a job that I believe in.

TRASH: I afraid that I can't afford to dress like the woman I really am.

DIRTY DIGGIN MAN: I'm afraid that my hair style does not best complement my bone structure.

TRASH: I afraid that my lips are too thin to be considered truly beautiful.

DIRTY DIGGIN MAN: I'm afraid that there is another man inside of me and that his eyes are a different color.

TRASH: I afraid that stress causes premature aging.

DIRTY DIGGIN MAN: I afraid of crow's feet and losing the high curve of my buttocks.

TRASH: I afraid that when I reach the peak age for plastic surgery I won't be able to afford it.

DIRTY DIGGIN MAN: I'm afraid that the price of glory is too high.

TRASH: *I am afraid* of all of the dull people who have created all of the dull premises that my living has been forced to accommodate.

DIRTY DIGGIN MAN: *I am afraid* that they are biting at the poetry in my head with their idea of things.

TRASH: *I am afraid* that fear has become a habit.

DIRTY DIGGIN MAN: *I am afraid* we're all taught to be afraid.

TRASH: And I am afraid that I have been a very good student. *(Dirty Diggin Man crawls to the downstage corner of the bed, then stands trembling on the edge of the bed.)*

DIRTY DIGGIN MAN: What?

TRASH: What?

DIRTY DIGGIN MAN: What?

TRASH: What?

DIRTY DIGGIN MAN: What – I ask you – is man, but a God who stands afraid, trembling on the tiny edge of now!!! *(Becomes dizzy with his revelation and falls off the bed. As he falls Lights black.)*

TRASH: (In black) Are you alright? Dirty Diggin Man? Are you alright?

Scene 8

Lights up. Dirty Diggin Man is lying down with his eyes shut. Trash holds his head. Dirty Diggin Man moans. Trash echoes him. Sound out.

DIRTY DIGGIN MAN: When I close my eyes like this and squeeze them tight, I still see the same picture I saw as a child.

TRASH: What? What do you see?

DIRTY DIGGIN MAN: I see my grandmother sitting cluttered and cramped in a small dark room in a pile of her own feces. A bottle of booze in one hand, waving a kleenex in the other. Screaming, *"Wipe me, wipe me!"* Day I saw that was the day I decided I wasn't going to spend the rest of my life wiping other people's assholes.

TRASH: No way, baby. No way.

DIRTY DIGGIN MAN: You know what life is like, Trash?

TRASH: Tell me.

DIRTY DIGGIN MAN: It's a lot like going to the bathroom in the dark. You ain't ever sure if you're doing it right or if you're going to come clean.

TRASH: Yeah.

DIRTY DIGGIN MAN: What do you see?

TRASH: What?

DIRTY DIGGIN MAN: When you close your eyes tight. *(When she places her hands over her eyes light comes up on the Father asleep in the chair with a beer in his hand.)*

TRASH: Same thing as you. *(Dirty Diggin Man, shocked, sits up quickly, then down again, for his head hurts.)*
DIRTY DIGGIN MAN: Same thing?
TRASH: Well, not exactly.
DIRTY DIGGIN MAN: What then?
TRASH: Let's be quiet, Dirty Diggin Man. Let's just be quiet. *(Pause.)* What are you looking at?
DIRTY DIGGIN MAN: You.
TRASH: Is your head alright?
DIRTY DIGGIN MAN: Ah, my suffering – dear one – has become a tool. Its pointed, spinning head drilling a hole through the wall that separates me from life. That separates me from you.
TRASH: You're a nice man. *(Pause.)*
DIRTY DIGGIN MAN: Trash. There once was a boy who didn't feed his hamster for a week. Just because he wanted to watch something die.
TRASH: Dirty Diggin Man. There once was a girl that liked to smash glass against the wall just to hear it shatter.
DIRTY DIGGIN MAN: There once was a boy who liked to steal women's panties from the five and dime just for fun.
TRASH: There once was a girl that thought if she touched someone they would die just because she was dirty.
DIRTY DIGGIN MAN: There once was a boy who for a prank called women up and told them their husbands were dead just to hear the silence before the scream.
TRASH: There once was a girl who washed her hands until they were red and bleeding just to be safe.
DIRTY DIGGIN MAN: There once was a boy that tore the wings off butterflies and left them on the pavement, just because he liked to watch their wingless bodies tremble.
TRASH: There once was a girl who wished her father was dead just because…You know, sometimes I look in the mirror, Dirty Diggin Man, and I hate myself. With all my heart I hate myself. And funny thing is, is that I think something inside of me has grown to love this hate. Depend on it. I guess it gives me something to love and everyone needs something to love. Don't they?
DIRTY DIGGIN MAN: Yes, yes they do, Trash.
TRASH: When I was a teenager I used to listen to all those cornball love songs. And I used to believe them all. Like they were law. It wasn't so much the words, but the feeling they gave me. You know like this feeling right here. *(Indicating her solar plexus.)* It was like they opened up something inside of me, made me feel bigger than I was.
Than I am. You ever feel that way? So, so alive it hurts like you're almost vibrating with it?
DIRTY DIGGIN MAN: *(Intent upon her.)* Yes, yes I have.
TRASH: I wonder why people can't feel that way all the time?
DIRTY DIGGIN MAN: I feel that way now.
TRASH: You do?
DIRTY DIGGIN MAN: Yes.

TRASH: Me too. *(Pause.)* I'm not afraid of you. Somehow I get the feeling that the person you are right now is the person that you are.

DIRTY DIGGIN MAN: You're a nut.

TRASH: So. So are you. *(Pause. He hugs her from behind.)* Sometimes I have this dream that I'm in a gigantic ballroom. And there's music playing – there's no orchestra or anything that I can see – the music is just sort of pouring out of the walls. And in the dream, I am leaping gracefully, daintily, from one end of the room to the other without my feet once touching the ground. And the strangest thingabout this dream, the amazing thing about this dream is that I'm not surprised by this. It's like I'd been doing it my whole life. Flying across rooms like that. *(Dirty Diggin Man holds Trash's arms out like wings.)*

DIRTY DIGGIN MAN: "Does she dance? In the first blue hours. Will she wither like the dying flowers?"

TRASH: Is that yours?

DIRTY DIGGIN MAN: No, Rimbaud – but this is mine. "There once was a little girl that wanted to be loved. To be told that she was good."

TRASH: That doesn't rhyme.

DIRTY DIGGIN MAN: It doesn't have to.

TRASH: I have one. "There once was a little boy that wanted to be loved, too? And to be told that he was good?"

DIRTY DIGGIN MAN: Yes. Yes, there was. And a boy before that. And a boy before that. *(Pause.)* You know what I want to do?

TRASH: What?

DIRTY DIGGIN MAN: I want to love you in every little place. In every little place you've never been loved before. So that maybe – when you're near me – you can always feel your soul – alive and big like a miracle that nobody can take away. *(Pause.)*

TRASH: Dirty Diggin Man?

DIRTY DIGGIN MAN: Mmmmmmmm.

TRASH: Do you think that there is something profoundly wrong with us?

DIRTY DIGGIN MAN: No, Trash. I prefer to think that we're teetering on the edge of a new world.

(Dirty Diggin Man and Trash fall asleep in each other's arms. More light on the Father asleep in the chair. Sound: "Stay As Sweet As You Are." Trash rises slowly from the bed. Dirty Diggin Man still sleeps. Trash begins to dance. The Father opens one eye at a time and watches her dance. He gets up slowly and comes down the staircase. Trash turns. Trash and the Father look at each other. The Father exits. Trash returns to bed. Lights: fade slowly.)

THE END

JOINED AT THE HEAD
by Catherine Butterfield

For Kathy and Peter

Playwright's Biography

Catherine Butterfield is an actress/writer whose full length plays include: *"Joined At The Head"*, *"Life In The Trees"*, *"Under My Skin"*, *"Snowing At Delphi"*, and *"Sight Unseen"*. "Joined At The Head" was recently given a highly successful run at the Manhattan Theatre Club in New York, with Ms. Butterfield starring in it. She also received the Roger L. Smith Award for outstanding promise as a playwright (Kennedy Center/American Express Fund for New American Plays). *"Life In The Trees"* was produced at the GeVa Theatre in Rochester, NY where it played to SRO houses and won the Davie Award for outstanding accomplishment by a playwright in regional theatre. Her one-act, *"No Problem"*, was the winner of the 1988 Samuel French / Double Image Short Playwriting Competition and was subsequently published in 1989. Another one-act, *"Chemistry"*, was the winner of the Love Creek One-Act Festival in New York City.

She has also written two screenplays, *"A New Wrinkle"* and *"The Good Cause"*, as well as a one-woman show entitled *"BoBo's Birthday"* which she has performed across the country.

Acknowledgments

My deep and heartfelt thanks to : Gilbert Parker and Lynne Meadow for making this possible, Larry Corsa for making my life beautiful, Chris Casady Borgers, Maggie Marshall and Melanie Webber for the support only a girlfriend can give, Ginny Butterfield for never giving up on her flaky daughter, and most especially to the real life Maggy and Jim Burroughs, for sharing their lives with me and letting me see into places an outsider is usually never privy to. Their bravery and astounding good humor inspired the writing of this play and the living of my life.

Playwright's Note

In this production, it is important that the action be kept as fluid as possible. For this reason, I recommend a minimalist set and simple set pieces. The Manhattan Theatre Club production used furniture on silent casters, which whisked in and out as the two Maggies spoke and set the scene in very little time. The water fountain in the hospital would be wonderful but for reasons just mentioned I consider it optional.

As a playwright / actress, I am aware that there are certain actors' traps inherent in this script that I might as well mention now, to give you a running start on character. Following are a few suggestions which you should feel free to ignore, but I hope you won't.

1)   *In order for Maggie Mulroney's journey to be satisfying, I would like to encourage the actress playing her to dare to be a little tough, even unlikable at times in Act One. This is a woman without friends who is learning how to become one. We should feel her initial resistance to the intimacy Jim and Maggy encourage, a resistance which can then break down in Act Two.*

2)   *Maggy Burroughs is a full blooded, no bullshit kind of a person. The temptations are to a) fall into the self-pity trap, and b) play her as a saint. Avoid both of them, please. Nothing is less attractive on stage than self-pity, and nobody believes a saint.*

3)   *Although Jim's monologue in Act Two is his only chance to say what is really going on inside him, it is important that the actor playing him not regard this as an opportunity to pull out all the emotional stops. the more matter-of-fact this speech is delivered, the more powerful it will be. Please, no tears.*

"Joined At The Head" was presented at the Manhattan Theater Club and was directed by Pamela Berlin. The cast was as follows:

ORIGINAL CAST

Maggie Mulroney.......................................Ellen Parker
Jim Burroughs...Kevin O'Rourke
Maggy Burroughs....................................Catherine Butterfield
With: Neal Huff, Becca Lish, Elizabeth Perry, John C. Vennema, Sharon Washington, and Michael Wella

CHARACTERS

MAGGIE MULRONEY
JIM BURROUGHS
MAGGY BURROUGHS

ENSEMBLE ROLES:

ACTRESS #1   1st Political Woman, 1st Nurse, 2nd Woman at book signing (Christine), Mommy with baby carriage, Doctor, Arguing Woman (Optional: Make-up woman - segue into TV studio)

ACTRESS #2   2nd Political Woman, Muttering Woman, Visitor at Hospital, 3rd Woman at book signing, Nora, Mrs. Mulroney, Older Woman

ACTRESS #3   Engaged Woman, Coat Check Girl (Sandy), Woman in Wheelchair, 1st Woman at Booksigning (Kathy), 2nd Nurse, Younger Woman (Optional: Terwilliger assistant - segue into TV studio)

ACTOR #1   1st College Boy, Waiter #2, Waiter in Restaurant (Bill), Orderly, Young Man at Booksigning, First Man (final scene) (Optional: Lighting guy - segue into TV studio)

ACTOR #2   2nd College Boy, Waiter #1, Crystal Salesman, Visitor at Hospital, Daddy with baby carriage, Second Man (final scene) (Optional: Stage Manager - segue into TV studio)

ACTOR #3   Engaged Man, Man in Pajamas, Raymond Terwilliger, Mr. Mulroney, Arguing Man

In the production at Manhattan Theatre Club, the Ensemble did all of the scene shifts as well, rolling pieces of furniture on and off as they were needed, handing over telephones, refilling wine glasses (transition from first to second Maggie/Jim dinner scene,) etc. They were occasionally acknowledged by the three main characters, but were never intrusive to the playing of a scene.

Joined At The Head

ACT I

Lights up on Maggie.

MAGGIE: I was walking down Newbury Street in Boston on a very brisk, very clear day, late afternoon. Low on the horizon, the white winter sun shone directly in my face. It dazzled me, this light. I could see shadow forms of people coming toward me, but I couldn't make out faces, and I couldn't make out buildings, and I felt like I was almost blind, although my eyes were wide open. How to describe it – I felt like a camera with its lens open too far. And you know, it's funny about the drivers in Boston, they don't honk very much. They drive like madmen, but they don't honk. Which is unexpected to a New Yorker, who expects not only honking but yelling, sirens, distant gunfire. So here I was, having this strange, silent walk down Newbury Street, strange not only because it seemed so civilized, but because, being blinded by this light, my sense of hearing was unusually keen. And without meaning to, I found myself eavesdropping on a number of conversations.
(Two College Boys appear. They speak without noticing Maggie.)
1ST COLLEGE BOY: And then you know my mom asked her, "So tell me about yourself?" And she said, "Well, I was born and raised in California but I moved here to go to school." I mean, it sounded like the Dating Game. "I like tennis, skiing, and hope to become a dental hygienist." That kind of thing.
2ND COLLEGE BOY: Uh-huh. God, yeah.
1ST COLLEGE BOY: So everybody's passing the peas, and my Aunt Janice starts to talk about the trip she took to California, and it looks like everything's gonna be okay, you know?
(Two Women walk by.)
1ST POLITICAL WOMAN: Oh, yeah, like we won this war. He got exactly what he wanted, he trashed the place, and he's still in power. That's an interesting definition of victory for our side.
2ND POLITICAL WOMAN: The feel-good war of the 'nineties.
1ST COLLEGE BOY: But then my dad turns to her and says, "So what do you kids do for excitement?" And she says, "Well, Jim and I are still in the early stages of our relationship, so basically we stay in bed and have sex all day."
2ND COLLEGE BOY: She said that?
1ST COLLEGE BOY: Yeah. She'll say anything. I think that's why I'm so crazy about her. Listen to this one...
(Maggie comes up to a couple in their thirties, holding hands.)
ENGAGED MAN: Let me see it again. *(She holds up the ring on her finger.)*
ENGAGED WOMAN: It's so beautiful. I can't believe how beautiful it is.
ENGAGED MAN: I think we got the right one. I'm very proud of us.
ENGAGED WOMAN: So am I.
(They kiss. A Woman walks by muttering to herself.)
MUTTERING WOMAN: Don't let it be what I think it is. For God's sake, don't

let it be what I think it is.
(Two Men walk by.)
WAITER #1: I'm tired of that scrod joke. It wasn't funny ten years ago, and it's not funny now. Why can't they just order without making that stupid scrod joke?
WAITER #2: What scrod joke?
WAITER #1: Oh, please. You're a waiter in a seafood restaurant, and you've never heard the scrod joke?
ENGAGED WOMAN: You were wonderful. When that guy started to pressure us, we just walked out.
ENGAGED MAN: Actually, he wasn't pressuring us. He was just doing his job. I liked him.
ENGAGED WOMAN: Well, if you thought he was so wonderful, why didn't you buy from him?
ENGAGED MAN: I'm not saying he was wonderful. I was just kind of enjoying him.
ENGAGED WOMAN: *(Pause)* That's funny. I thought we were having the same experience, and now I find out we were having two different experiences.
ENGAGED MAN: We're having the same experience now, though, aren't we?
ENGAGED WOMAN: I don't know. Are we? *(They exit.)*
MAGGIE: That was it, really. Conversations. Fragments of conversations. Who knows where they were meant to lead? But I became so aware of how much life is going on all the time, how many stories, how many people are out there with their absolute reality that has nothing to do with my absolute reality. To them, I'm the backdrop. To me, they're mine. How often do we think of ourselves as backdrops for other peoples' lives? Not too often, I guess. We prefer to think of ourselves as being terribly significant. I remember being in New York once when a piece of scaffolding fell and bisected the head of a person a half a block ahead of me. I arrived in time to see the carnage, the hysteria. And I started thinking about the guy who'd been killed. An actor in his thirties, I read a few days later. The center of his own particular universe, until his universe was suddenly snatched away from him. All the rest of us, on that New York afternoon on 57th street, were the backdrop for the particular drama that was his life. How strange it would have been for him to know ahead of time that the supporting cast was going to play the show out without him. A play with a vacuum where the leading man is supposed to be? Impossible! We all live with that illusion, don't we? And we all parade the streets daily, back and forth, oblivious to the fact that the next piece of scaffolding may be meant for us. And convinced that really, deep down in the truest part of life, we are nobody's backdrop.
(She moves to an area with a bed and a telephone.)
I was in my hotel room watching endless reruns of gratuitous slaughter in the Middle East when the phone rang. *(She picks up the phone.)* Hello?
(The lights come up on Jim Burroughs, a man of thirty-eight. He is slightly overweight, slightly graying, if he'd been taking care of himself he would be a good looking man, but he hasn't been.)
JIM: Maggie?
MAGGIE: Yes.

JIM: Maggie Mulroney?

MAGGIE: Yes. Who's this?

JIM: Brace yourself for a blast from the past. This is Jim Burroughs.

MAGGIE: Jim! Oh, my God! I can't believe it. Where are you?

JIM: I'm right here. In Boston.

MAGGIE: Are you still living here?

JIM: Sure am. Well, Norville, actually.

MAGGIE: Oh, my God. You sound just the same! How did you get my number? How did you find out I was in town?

JIM: I read it in the paper. "Maggie Mulroney will be signing copies of her new book at the Harvard Book Store Cafe" – You're famous, Maggie, girl.

MAGGIE: I am not.

JIM: Well, you're as close to famous as anybody I've ever known.

MAGGIE: Jim, I can't believe we're talking to each other. I feel like we're still in high school.

JIM: Well, give or take twenty years.

MAGGIE: No.

JIM: Twenty years.

MAGGIE: That's impossible. What are you – I mean, how are you doing?

JIM: I'm fine, just fine. Yourself?

MAGGIE: I'm fine, too. *(A pause. They laugh.)* I'm sorry. I'm overwhelmed. I don't know what to say.

JIM: Me, neither. Twenty years is a lot to catch up on. Would you like to get together and try this in person?

MAGGIE: I'd love to. *(To audience.)* This, psychologically, is the moment in a conversation where you establish the boundaries of what is going to happen between a man and a woman. Naturally, both of us knew this instinctively.

JIM: We can have dinner. Maybe you can come over to the house. I'd love you to meet my wife.

(Maggie looks knowingly at the audience.)

MAGGIE: That sounds wonderful. You have kids, too?

JIM: No. No kids. We wanted to, but...oh look, we can talk about everything over dinner. How about tomorrow night?

MAGGIE: Great!

JIM: I'll pick you up at five.

MAGGIE: See you then. *(She hangs up.)* It was as easy as that. Twenty years of total silence, of not knowing, and rarely thinking about someone who was once a big reason you got up in the morning. And now, all at once, all of that is behind you. Suddenly, you're going to have a civilized dinner with him and his wife. Ain't life strange? *(Jim is standing next to two chairs stage left. Maggie approaches.)*

He picked me up alone. *(Maggie walks toward the "car" and Jim then walks right past him.)*

JIM: Maggie!

MAGGIE: *(Turning.)* Jim? Jim! *(She goes to him and they hug.)*

JIM: You didn't recognize me.

MAGGIE: No, I did, I do. It was the sun, it was in my eyes. *(To the audience.)* I didn't recognize him. He looked entirely different. I searched his face, trying to find the boy I'd known, but I couldn't find him. It was a little scary. *(They get into the "car.")*
MAGGIE: On the drive to his house I felt uneasy. Maybe this was a mistake. What could we possibly still have in common?
JIM: You look great, Mag.
MAGGIE: Thanks. You do, too.
JIM: Success agrees with you.
MAGGIE: Well, it's been a long haul. You should have met me a couple of years ago, you'd have said, "Poor Maggie. What a shame her life's not working out for her."
JIM: Really? Sure looks like it's working out now. *(Pause.)* I'm taking us through Newbridge. Just for old time's sake.
MAGGIE: Oh, good. It's been so long. Have things changed a lot?
JIM: You'll be amazed.
MAGGIE: At the changes?
JIM: At how much is exactly the same. You recognize this road?
MAGGIE: ...No, not really. At least, I .... Oh!
JIM: Remember now?
MAGGIE: Yes.
JIM: Our little detour.
MAGGIE: It's still there?
JIM: It sure is.
MAGGIE: *(To audience.)* We used to pull over in his van and make love. We had a special spot. A tiny dirt road right … wait, it's coming up. *(Maggie and Jim are both involved in the search.)* Right…
BOTH TOGETHER: There! *(They laugh.)*
MAGGIE: God, it's still there.
JIM: It's still there. Remember how we used to lie in the van and watch the stars come out?
MAGGIE: And then you'd drive me home at about eighty miles an hour on Lamarr Street. It was crazy. We took our life in our hands every night, and never gave it a second thought. We thought we were impervious.
JIM: Completely invulnerable.
MAGGIE: We're lucky we weren't killed.
JIM: It never even crossed my mind at the time.
MAGGIE: Me, neither. We were pretty wild, then, huh?
JIM: Pretty wild. *(They smile at each other.)* I don't think I've ever felt as sure of myself since.
MAGGIE: What do you do? I mean, for a living. Are you still a musician?
JIM: No. I'm teaching. At the high school.
MAGGIE: Really? Music?
JIM: No. English. One of life's little ironies, wouldn't you say? Me, the one who couldn't wait to get out of town, teaching English to the next generation of fuck-ups at the high school. Somebody up there really has a twisted sense of humor.

MAGGIE: Hey, but teaching, that's a wonderful thing to do. Not everybody can teach. I'll bet you're great at it.

JIM: I am great at it. I even like it. That doesn't mean it's what I want to do for the rest of my life.

MAGGIE: What do you want to do?

JIM: Oh, hell. What don't I want to do? I want to swim the Ganges. I want to be a film director. I want to find a cure for cancer.

MAGGIE: Nobel aspirations.

JIM: I want to be seventeen, and start all over again.

MAGGIE: Really?

JIM: *(Pause.)* No. No, I'm kidding about that.

MAGGIE: *(To audience.)* But he had tears in his eyes. It was funny, this happened a number of times on the drive, but since the rest of him seemed so completely under control I started to think he had developed an eye condition. Men are an odd breed. Their emotions sneak out in the strangest ways.

JIM: What do you want?

MAGGIE: Me? At the moment, I want to write a very, very good book. I want it to come easily, and naturally, and I want the muse to be sitting on my shoulder the entire time.

JIM: The whole time?

MAGGIE: Not even a coffee break.

JIM: What about marriage, children, that whole thing. Don't you want any of that?

MAGGIE: How do you know I'm not married?

JIM: I read an interview in the *Patriot Ledger*.

MAGGIE: Oh. Well, it's not a big priority with me. I give it thought from time to time, but it's not all that high on my list.

JIM: Uh-huh.

MAGGIE: It's really not. I get so annoyed with these people who think that if you're not married your life is a total failure. Sometimes I think I could win the Nobel Prize, and some people would still think I was a failure because I wasn't married. I mean, big deal!

JIM: Absolutely.

MAGGIE: It's not necessarily the end of the world.

JIM: Hey, it was just a question.

MAGGIE: *(Pause.)* Right. Sorry. It's just, you know, a question I get asked a lot.

JIM: Sure.

MAGGIE: *(To Audience.)* Okay, so I got a little defensive. Twenty years, and he still knew how to punch my buttons.

JIM: I've been writing some myself. Music, I mean.

MAGGIE: Really? I'd love to hear it some time.

JIM: It's not for general consumption. I mean, I'd never expect to market it or anything.

MAGGIE: So what? I remember how talented you were, Jim.

JIM: *(Brightening.)* Yeah – you know I do think some of it's pretty good. I really do.

MAGGIE: *(To the Audience.)* There he was, the boy I knew! He was still there. I just hadn't noticed.

JIM: So far, the only person who's heard any of it is Maggy. And, of course, what's she going to say? She loves me.

MAGGIE: Maggie?

JIM: Yeah. Didn't I mention that to you? My wife's name is Maggy, too.

MAGGIE: Really?

JIM: Yeah. Only she spells her with a Y. Wild, huh? The two big loves of my life, with the same name.

MAGGIE: *(To Audience.)* I hadn't known that. I mean about being one of two big loves.

JIM: You're going to love her. In some ways you're very much alike.

MAGGIE: You know, I always get a little nervous when people tell me I'll love someone because they're so much like me. Generally, I can't stand people who remind me of me.

JIM: I'm talking sense of humor, that kind of thing. In other ways you're very different. Do you remember Maggy McClintock?

JIM: No.

JIM: You probably will when you see here. She was a cheerleader.

MAGGIE: Jim. How could someone who was a cheerleader in high school be anything like me?

JIM: Basically, she did it just to spite everyone.

MAGGIE: Oh. That sounds like me.

JIM: As kind of an extended joke. She was a year behind us, I didn't know her then. I met her years later at a Fourth of July parade. We started making rude comments together about the floats, and realized we had causticity in common. It's a wonderful bond, being caustic together. Don't you find?

MAGGIE: I guess. *(To audience.)* My imagination was running wild. I was ready for some kind of cross between Christie Brinkley and Dorothy Parker.

JIM: Well, here we are. *(They stand and walk toward the door of the house.)*

MAGGIE: Wow. What a wonderful old house. How long have you lived here?

JIM: Six years. Uh, by the way. There's one other thing you should know about Maggy. *(Maggy appears at the door. Her head is wrapped in a brightly colored scarf.)*

JIM: She has cancer.

MAGGY: Hi, Maggie! *(She hugs Maggie.)* Good to see you. Come on in.

(They enter the house. It is very New Englandy – old, wood floors, wood burning stove.)

MAGGY: How was the drive out?

JIM: I showed her Newbridge, since she hadn't seen it in so long.

MAGGY: Hasn't changed, has it?

MAGGIE: No. It's kind of amazing. So much else has. I mean, in the rest of the world.

MAGGY: Actually, we have, too. You just can't see it at first.

JIM: *(To Maggie.)* Do you recognize Mag now?

MAGGIE: Uh, well, I kind of hate to say this, but no. *(To Maggy.)* You seem to recognize me.

MAGGY: Oh, sure. You haven't changed much. Would you like a glass of wine?

MAGGIE: Sure. Great.

MAGGY: *(Displaying a bottle of red wine.)* Jim bought this specially for the occasion.

JIM: Let me get that, honey.

MAGGY: No, no. I can get it. *(She works the cork off and pours.)*

MAGGIE: You have a beautiful home. I love what you've done with it.

MAGGY: Thanks. We got off to a good start on it, but lately it's had to take a back seat to other things. We hope to get back to it soon.

MAGGIE: How old is this house?

JIM: Over a hundred years.

MAGGIE: Wow.

JIM: Yeah. Lot of history. Lots of ghosts prowling around.

MAGGIE: Seriously?

JIM: If you believe in that stuff. Which I personally don't, but Maggy does.

MAGGY: Sure, why not? I plan to prowl around when the time comes, scare the shit out of everybody. Don't you?

JIM: *(Slightly uncomfortable laugh.)* Well, here's to us.

MAGGIE and MAGGY: To us.

MAGGY: Jim says you're here to do some publicity on your new book.

MAGGIE: Yeah. Book signings, that kind of thing.

MAGGY: It sounds like it's already a big hit. I can see why. It's really funny.

MAGGIE: You read it?

MAGGY: Oh, sure. Jim did, too.

MAGGIE: Wow, I'm flattered. How did you like it, Jim?

JIM: Fine, fine. Very good. Was that supposed to be your dad?

MAGGIE: Well, you know, with a few embellishments.

JIM: Interesting.

MAGGIE: Why?

JIM: I remember him so differently.

MAGGIE: Well, you know. It's fiction. Sometimes you have to distort reality to make things interesting.

JIM: Sure.

MAGGIE: And it's been so long since he died.

MAGGY: He died? You didn't mention that in the book.

MAGGIE: No. Too much of a downer. I wanted to keep it light.

MAGGY: Oh. That's too bad, though. How did he die?

MAGGIE: Uh, well, cancer, actually. *(There is a pause.)* So you were a cheerleader, huh? I'm trying to figure out why I don't remember you.

JIM: I'll get the yearbook. Maybe that'll jog your memory. *(He exits up the stairs.)*

MAGGY: I think you probably made more of an impression on me than I made on you. You were a pretty memorable figure at Newbridge High.

MAGGIE: Really? I always thought of myself as kind of disenfranchised and out of it.

MAGGY: No way. You were our resident angry young woman. I was completely in awe of you.

MAGGIE: You were?

MAGGY: Oh, yeah. I think a lot of us were. Do you remember a little thing called Moratorium Day?

MAGGIE: Sure. The protest day. "Let's get our Dick out of Cambodia."

MAGGY: I remember the day you were running around trying to drum up support for it. You came storming into the gym where we were practicing cheers and said, "Cut school tomorrow and come into Boston for Moratorium Day. Everybody who objects to this obscene war is doing it, even people like you." I liked that. Even people like us. Even hopelessly shallow rally girls were trooping into Boston for Moratorium Day.

MAGGIE: Tact was never my strong suit.

MAGGY: And remember Beth Folger? She said to you, "Do you realize what tomorrow is? It's the day before the game with Dover. We've got to practice." And you gave us a look of total disgust and said, "Why don't you girls stick your pom-poms up your pudenda?" Then you marched off.

MAGGIE: *(Laughing.)* Really? I'm not even sure that's proper English.

MAGGY: We got the point.

MAGGIE: I was such a big mouth back then. I'm surprised somebody didn't pop me one.

MAGGY: Oh no, I thought you were wonderful. I have to admit some of the other girls thought you were a bit of a crackpot. I mean, there you were fomenting revolution while the rest of us were setting our hair on orange juice cans. You kind of caught us by surprise.

MAGGIE: I never fomented revolution. I remember having a cause or two, but I mean I never blew anything up.

MAGGY: Yeah. I think I was secretly a little disappointed about that.

MAGGIE: Did you go to the protest?

MAGGY: No. I had some family problems. Wish I could have, though. I'll bet it was inspiring.

MAGGIE: Yeah. It was okay.

MAGGY: Oh well, next life. *(Jim comes down the stairs.)*

JIM: Here it is. The chronicle of our innocence. Mag and I page through it now and then when we need a good laugh. Check out the inscriptions.

MAGGIE: *(Reading.)* Here's one from Pam Brogan – "To a beautiful person and talented human being. Don't ever forget to seek the light and live forever free." Ah, the 'sixties.

JIM: Gone, but not distorted beyond recognition.

MAGGIE: How could we have worn our hair this way? My mom always used to say, "Your hair looks like you're hanging curtains." I had no idea what she meant.

MAGGY: I personally slaved for hours for that curtain effect.

MAGGIE: Mine was a product of sheer neglect. "To Jim, thanks for putting up with me in Chem class. You are a wonderful human being and I'm so glad I got the chance to know you. Best wishes forever, Gina Lazlo." God! Gina Lazlo! She took Chemistry? I always thought of her as a certified idiot.

JIM: A beautiful certified idiot, and if there was one thing Gina was definitely an expert in, it was chemistry.
MAGGY: *(Laughing,)* Listen to him. My Don Juan.
MAGGIE: Jim had a major crush on Gina Lazlo.
JIM: I did not. I mean I thought she was sexy and everything, but so did everyone else. I didn't have the nerve to come on to Gina Lazlo.
MAGGIE: Jim Burroughs, what are you talking about? What about the night of our senior prom?
JIM: What about it?
MAGGIE: You dumped me for her!
JIM: What? I did not.
MAGGIE: You most certainly did, too.
MAGGY: Jim! You dumped her at the senior prom?
JIM: No, I didn't...did I?
MAGGIE: Yes: Why would I make a thing like that up?
JIM: God...I did, didn't I?
MAGGIE: I had to hitch a ride home, it was completely humiliating.
MAGGY: You hitchhiked? In your prom dress?
MAGGIE: It was a night to remember.
MAGGY: Jim!
JIM: Yeah, but wait a minute. Then you broke my window, remember that? You went over to my house and broke my bedroom window with a rock.
MAGGIE: I did not.
JIM: You did, too!
MAGGIE: Well, you deserved it.
MAGGY: *(Laughing.)* This sounds like a really stable relationship you two had going.
MAGGIE: Oh, we were hopeless.
MAGGY: Well, I think it's time to bury the hatchet, don't you? I mean, it's been twenty years.
JIM: Maggie, I humbly beg your pardon for dropping you at the senior prom.
MAGGIE: *(Grudgingly.)* Okay. I forgive you. Sorry I broke your window.
JIM: My dad made me pay for it.
MAGGY: Jim!
JIM: Okay, okay. I accept your apology.
MAGGIE: Thanks. *(To audience.)* It was funny, I walked into this house and felt totally accepted. I wasn't a threat, there were no weird vibes. She seemed completely unfazed.
MAGGY: Are you married, Maggie?
JIM: Uh-oh. Look out.
MAGGIE: No, no. Can't find a man who isn't threatened by me. *(Pause.)* That sounds kind of obnoxious. I just haven't found the right guy, I guess.
MAGGY: I have a lot of girlfriends with the same problem. There's something funny going on between the sexes these days. Everybody's jockeying for position like a gun's going to go off any minute.
MAGGIE: Yeah. Or, I don't know. Maybe it's me.

MAGGY: Why would it be you?

MAGGIE: Oh, I don't know...

MAGGY: It's not you, Maggie. Don't worry about that.

JIM: Hey, how come Maggy can ask that question and it's okay, but I ask it and I get my head bitten off? This isn't fair. *(The phone rings.)*

JIM: That'll be the phone. Hello?...Uh, yes, she's right here. *(To Maggie.)* It's for you.

MAGGIE: Oh, thanks. *(She grabs her bag and takes the phone.)* Hello?... Shoot. *(She takes a little notebook from her bag, scribbles in it.)* Uh-huh... Okay...Okay...What time?...Okay. Thanks. *(She hangs up.)* Sorry, it was my service. Looks like I've got another interview coming up.

MAGGY: How exciting!

MAGGIE: It's not exciting at all, believe me. It's grueling. But you've gotta do it, it goes with the territory. It seems like someone else controls every move I make.

MAGGY: How did they get this number?

MAGGIE: I...gave it to them. Ooops. *(They all laugh.)* Let's find a picture of Maggy, where are the cheerleader pictures?

MAGGY: Jim, there's you.

MAGGIE: I remember that picture. Jim Morrison lives.

JIM: And Maggie, there's you.

MAGGIE: Oh, yuck. I hate that shot. I look like Squeaky Fromme.

JIM: *(Laughing.)* Squeaky Fromme!

MAGGIE: Feel free to disagree with me.

JIM: No, it's true. It's really true!

MAGGY: Oh, it is not. She looks pretty.

JIM: Okay, here we are, here we are. Here's my Maggy. With all her fellow leaders of the cheer.

MAGGIE: Where?

JIM: Right there. *(He points.)*

MAGGIE: *(Light dawning.)* Oh! *(She looks up at Maggy.)* I remember you!

MAGGY: Hi.

MAGGIE: Hi. *(To Audience.)* I did remember her. I never knew her, but I remembered her distinctly. She must have lived near the school – I took the bus, and I'd frequently see her walking as we passed. She always looked so put together: shiny hair that swung back and forth as she walked, usually some nice skirt and sweater that looked freshly cleaned and pressed. And yet an air of tension around her, as though she were walking in a perfectly constructed bubble. But tonight, the woman before me was nothing like my high school recollections. I looked at her and the same thought kept ringing in my head – this woman has cancer?

MAGGY: Are you hungry, Maggie?

MAGGIE: Yeah, I am.

MAGGY: Jim, you?

JIM: Starved.

MAGGY: Then let's go.

MAGGIE: *(To Audience.)* We went to an Italian restaurant.
(They sit at a table. A Waiter brings them drinks.)
MAGGIE: It was a wonderful evening. We laughed more than I'd laughed in ages. Jim was in particulary fine form. He told story after story about people and places I thought I'd long forgotten. The food was sensational, and although Maggy ate very little she kept encouraging us to eat.
JIM: ...and I was so upset that Ken Diamond got the Harvard Book Award instead of me, that when they told me I got the Brown Book Award, I was like, "Yeah, so what?" And you know, then I ended up going to B. U. and everything. And it wasn't until 1981 when I was typing up a resume that I said to myself, "Idiot! Why didn't you apply to Brown?"
MAGGIE: Maybe you just thought they were giving you a brown book?
JIM: *(Laughing.)* Yeah, that was it. "Ladies and gentlemen, we'd like to present Ken Diamond with the Harvard Book Award, and for Jim Burroughs we have this lovely brown book."
MAGGY: *(Laughing.)* As a consolation prize.
MAGGIE: Nothing written in it, but it is this lovely shade of brown.
(They are laughing convulsively by now. The Waiter walks by and looks slightly concerned.)
JIM: Oh, God. Is this really funny, or is there something wrong with us?
MAGGIE: I think this is what is called making a scene.
MAGGY: Oh, good. I've always wanted to make a scene. I'm waiting for the Maitre d' to come over and say, "Excuse me, but we couldn't help noticing that you three are making a scene."
JIM: "Perhaps you didn't notice the sign as you came in – absolutely no tee shirts, dogs or scene making in the restaurant."
MAGGY: And I'll say, "Please sir, take pity on a poor girl. I'm going in for chemo at nine in the morning, and this may be my last chance to make a really good scene."
JIM: "Avaunt!" he'll say. "Down with the sign! Let the scene making begin."
MAGGY: Avaunt? Do you really think he'll say, "Avaunt!?"
JIM: He's a Shakespearean actor on the side.
MAGGY: Ah.
MAGGIE: Um, so you're going to the hospital tomorrow7
MAGGY: Yeah. Chemotherapy.
MAGGIE: Are you... how do you feel about that?
JIM: Well, she'd rather be on the beach at Maui, but that wasn't one of the options.
MAGGIE: I'm sorry, that was a kind of a tactless –
MAGGY: No, that's a fair question. What would you like to know?
MAGGIE: I've just never really understood... I mean, what's it like?
MAGGY: First you feel like shit, then you feel better, then you feel like total shit, and then hopefully after that you feel much better. Somewhere along the way your hair falls out. It's a process.
JIM: What they do is, they bring you as close to the edge as they can without actually killing you. Then they count on the natural strength of your body to kick

in and build things up again.

MAGGY: Fortunately, I have a pretty strong constitution. In fact, aside from the fact that I have cancer, I'm in incredibly good health. But that's kind of like, "Aside from that, Mrs. Lincoln..."

JIM: The last one made her feel much better for quite some time. In fact, we thought we had it on the run. But it's deceptive.

MAGGY: We're kind of on the retreat right now. We're trying to gain back a little ground, but then even when you get it, it's like Kuwait. The enemy has gone in and trashed it so bad, you're not even sure it's worth having.

JIM: It's worth having.

MAGGY: Yeah. Yeah, it's worth having. I'm kidding.

(There is a pause. Some music plays softly in the background.)

JIM: Hey, Mag, listen. They're playing our song.

MAGGY: Playing our song? That's elevator music.

JIM: Oh, yeah? Listen.

MAGGY: *(Pause.)* Oh, my God. "Whiter Shade of Pale?"

MAGGIE: Muzak Procol Harum. Now I've heard everything.

JIM: *(Getting up.)* Dance with me baby. We can't let this opportunity go by.

MAGGY: Dance with you? Here? Are you crazy?

JIM: Not at all. You said you always wanted to make a really good scene.

MAGGY: That's true, I did, didn't I?

JIM: Your wish is my command.

(He whisks her into his arms and they begin to dance, laughingly at first, then she puts her head on his shoulder and they move more slowly. Maggie watches them.)

MAGGIE: *(To Audience.)* They were so in love. It was almost painful to watch. Maggy seemed so calm and serene, she didn't look ill in any way. Only later did I find out about all the pills she popped just to be able to be with us that night. Jim looked like a man who had just met the most beautiful woman in the world and who couldn't believe his good fortune that she had agreed to dance with him. I watched them in awe. I'd never seen anything quite like it. It was as though they were the only two people in the whole restaurant. The only two people in the universe.

(The music stops.)

JIM: Maggy Burroughs, you have just made a scene.

MAGGY: Thank you, my love. Another life long wish come true. *(They kiss and go back to the table.)* Maggie, are you feeling totally abandoned?

MAGGIE: No, just jealous. I want to make a really good scene.

MAGGY: Shall we all three dance the next dance?

MAGGIE: Maybe we should organize the other diners and form a conga line.

MAGGY: Yes! A conga line. What's playing?

(They listen. The next song has no beat whatsoever.)

JIM: Good luck, girls.

MAGGIE: Oh, well.

MAGGY: Maybe we should have a seriously dangerous dessert instead.

JIM: Ah, an inspired idea. Garçon!

(The Waiter approaches.)

JIM: Do you hate being called Garçon?
WAITER: Not if you're planning to tip well.
JIM: An honest man! I appreciate his bluntness, don't you? Well *(He looks at his name tag.)* Bill, we'd like to look at the dessert menu, if you don't mind.
(The waiter brings them three menus.)
MAGGIE: We looked at our menus. I don't know why, but I was feeling very happy. It was as if we were the Three Musketeers, all for one and one for all. I lowered my menu to speak, when suddenly I saw a look pass between the two of them. A look that was so emotionally charged it almost knocked me off my chair. It spoke of a deep love, the kind that can only spring from pain. But there was more. In his eyes I could see everything from fear to desperation to a kind of plea – "Don't leave me!" Her look to him was much more simple. "Courage," it said. In that moment, I realized why Maggy was not threatened by me. These two had something between them that went beyond emotions like jealousy. When you're dealing with something as earth shaking as death, jealousy is an emotion that just ceases to have meaning.
(Maggy closes her menu and addresses the audience for the first time.)
MAGGY: Excuse me, I hate to interrupt, but I've got to say something here. This woman is romanticizing. Now, I can understand why she's doing it, I mean she's a writer, I've read her stuff and I can tell her heart's in the right place. But this is my life here, and she's turning it into some kind of Gothic novel. *(To Maggie.)* Please. I don't mean to ruin your little whatever-this-thing-is, but there's a certain amount of bullshit going on, and I'd like to take the opportunity to set the record straight. You don't mind, do you?
MAGGIE: *(Horrified.)* What are you doing?
MAGGY: I just thought I'd correct a few misconceptions.
MAGGIE: No. I'm sorry, but it is not okay with me. Please sit down. *(Maggy remains standing.)* Maggy, come on. Okay, I'll admit I've allowed myself a little artistic license. But all writers do that. Now, maybe I haven't gotten all the facts completely straight, but since this is fiction –
MAGGY: This is not fiction. This is my life you're serving up before everyone, and I think I have the right to put in my two cents worth.
MAGGIE: Well, could you maybe do it after I've told the whole story?
MAGGY: No. Sorry. I thought I could at first, but that last monologue of yours was so over the top I just had to say something. Listen, I don't mean to rain on your parade. But I should think in the interests of accuracy, you'd like to hear what I have to say.
MAGGIE: *(Wounded.)* Fine. Go ahead.
MAGGY: I've hurt your feelings, right?
MAGGIE: No, no. Say what you have to say.
MAGGY: Okay, well –
MAGGIE: But I'd just like to add that this story is meant to be a tribute to you. I am working very hard to present your story in a light that will be an inspiration for others, and perhaps even immortalize you.
MAGGY: Immortalize me? Boy, are you barking up the wrong tree. I'm just one other person who got cancer. No more or less mortal than anybody else.

MAGGIE: Okay, perhaps that's true. But don't you see that the very act of making your life into a story suddenly gives it dramatic proportions? It invests it with a meaning that it might not have otherwise had.

MAGGY: Excuse me. Are you trying to tell me that my life didn't have meaning?

MAGGIE: No! Not at all.

MAGGY: Okay, good. Then since we both agree that my life had meaning regardless of whether you chose to put it down on a piece of paper or not, I think I should be able to address a few points here. *(To Audience.)* Don't you?

MAGGIE: Okay, okay.

MAGGY: You give me leave to speak?

MAGGIE: Speak, speak.

MAGGY: Thank you. *(To audience.)* Okay, first of all, let me just say that Maggie was right about one thing. I did like her. I still do. I had the same feeling she did when we met, that we were maybe sisters in another life, or brothers. Dragged slabs of stone up the same pyramid, whatever. And having the same name and all, that kind of heightened the effect. We ran with different crowds in high school: hers was the angry politicos, the early freaks and dope smokers that we all looked down upon. Mine was the party crowd. The funny thing is, I realize now I was really hanging out with the wrong people. I would have been a lot happier with all the angry ones, and I would probably be a lot healthier today if I'd started blowing off steam at an early age. But that's another story.

MAGGIE: Please don't tell it now.

MAGGY: Don't worry, I won't. Now, about this Three Musketeers thing...

MAGGIE: It was just an allusion. I didn't mean to suggest that we –

MAGGY: Yeah, okay, but it's still over the top. I mean, for God's sake, I'd only just met you that night. Jim hadn't seen you in twenty years. How could you suddenly see us as an inseparable threesome?

MAGGIE: It was the way I was feeling! I didn't say it was the way you were feeling. I don't have that many close friends in my life, and that evening was very important to me –

MAGGY: Why don't you have any close friends?

MAGGIE: I didn't say I don't have any. It's just that with my lifestyle, and the lifestyle of my friends – wait a minute, this is not where I want to go with this. This is your life we're examining here.

MAGGY: Why can't we do a little looking at yours while we're at it?

MAGGIE: Because that is not the intention of this piece! Now please, Maggy. I don't mind you putting in a few words, but let's not take this in an entirely different direction.

MAGGY: Okay, okay. Sorry. *(Pause.)* But I think you might want to look into that "no friends" thing some time in the future.

MAGGIE: Thank you. I will. Now, did you have anything more you wanted to add before I go on?

MAGGY: Yes. That look. The meaning of that look.

MAGGIE: That look was a devastating thing.

MAGGY: Yeah, okay, to you, maybe. To us, it was one of a thousand looks we'd given each other since this whole thing began. And listen, it's not fair to paint Jim as the wimpy one and me as some kind of saint. You didn't get to see the days when I was a whiney baby, or a total bitch and Jim was still solid as a rock. It's important you get that in, Mag. I want Jim to get his due.

MAGGIE: Okay.

MAGGY: And one more thing –

MAGGIE: Oh, come on, this isn't fair –

MAGGY: One more thing. I *was* jealous of you.

MAGGIE: ...You were?

MAGGY: Yes. But not for the reason you think. I was jealous because you were healthy, because you had your whole life ahead of you. I started wishing Jim had married you, so he wouldn't have to go through this shit with me.

MAGGIE: No.

MAGGY: Yes! Of course, yes. Do you have any idea of the guilt that a sick person carries around, knowing that they're ruining the lives of everyone they love? The whole experience is one big fucking drag, but the guilt thing is definitely a stand-out. *(Pause.)* Okay. I'm done. Carry on.

(She re-opens her menu.)

MAGGIE: *(Pause.)* Carry on? Carry on? You've just ruined my whole story here. How do you expect me to just "carry on"? Su

MAGGY: Well, come on. I mean, what was the original impulse behind this story?

MAGGIE: ...I don't know.

MAGGY: Yes, you do. You're just sulking.

MAGGIE: Well I think I have the right to sulk! I don't even dare say anything more about you, I'm afraid you're going to stand up and say it's bullshit again.

MAGGY: No. I won't. I promise.

MAGGIE: You know, you've taken the heroic aspect right out of this thing.

MAGGY: How? By telling the truth?

MAGGIE: By emphasizing aspects of your character that we don't need to know.

MAGGY: Sorry. This is me. Take it or leave it. Look, I promise, I won't say another word. I just wanted to start you off on the right foot. Now that I've got you going, things should go much more smoothly. By the way, I loved the opening. All those people walking around talking. Neat stuff. I don't know what it meant, but it looked cool.

MAGGIE: Thanks. *(To Audience.)* Sorry about that. I know how irritating it is to have the flow interrupted. I didn't mean this to be a Brechtian evening, I was hoping you'd be able to indulge your emotions from time to time. So feel free, in the future, to – OH, THIS IS HORRIBLE!

MAGGY: No, no. You can do it. Come on, I'm on your side.

(Maggie takes a deep breath, shakes out her arms.)

MAGGY: Good, that's good. Get relaxed, shake it out, good idea. Okay, let's go.

MAGGIE: *(To Audience. Reluctantly at first.)* Well, like I said, I found that look that passed between them incredibly moving. Whatever it meant. *(She looks to Maggy, who remains immobile.)* And I also felt very much on the outside of their experience, very alone for a minute. But as has been already said, why wouldn't I feel alone? I hardly knew them. We finished dinner, and Jim went to get the car.

(They get up from the table. Maggie and Maggy walk over to a counter, behind which stands a Coat Check Girl.)

COAT CHECK GIRL: *(Handing them their coats.)* How was dinner, Mrs. Burroughs?

MAGGY: Wonderful, Sandy. Hey, I thought you'd be in Europe by now.

COAT CHECK GIRL: Three more days. I'm so excited. I've always wanted to see Europe.

MAGGY: Me, too. Especially Italy.

COAT CHECK GIRL: Oooh, Italy. You've never been to Europe?

MAGGY: Not yet. Some day. *(Tipping her.)* Thanks, Sandy. Have a great time.

COAT CHECK GIRL: I will! I might never come back. I might go out there and change my whole life! *(She exits)*

MAGGIE: Change her whole life. You think she will?

MAGGY: Who knows? Anything is possible. We could open up the papers some day and discover she's become...what?

MAGGIE: Princess Sandy of Lichtenstein?

MAGGY: Sure, why not? *(They laugh.)* This has been good for us, getting out like this.

MAGGIE: Me, too.

MAGGY: I haven't seen Jim this happy in ages. He was really excited when he heard you were in town. You should have seen the detective work he did to find out where you were staying.

MAGGIE: Really?

MAGGY: Yeah. He really wanted us to meet each other. Am I different from what you expected?

MAGGIE: To tell you the truth, I didn't know what to expect.

MAGGY: I've changed a lot since high school.

MAGGIE: I guess we all have.

MAGGY: No, but I made sure I changed. It was a very conscious decision. And you had a lot to do with it.

MAGGIE: Me? What do you mean?

MAGGY: It's kind of a funny story. Are you going to be in town a while longer?

MAGGIE: Just a couple of days.

MAGGY: Oh, well, listen, if you should find yourself anywhere near Mass General, I'd love to say good-bye before you leave.

MAGGIE: Mass General?

MAGGY: Yeah. You know where that is?

MAGGIE: Yeah. I do. Well, hey, I'll see how my appointments line up.

MAGGY: Great! 'Cause otherwise, who knows when we'll see you again? Twenty years is a long time to waite.

(Maggy exits.)

MAGGIE: *(To Audience.)* Jim dropped Maggy off and drove me back to the hotel.

(Jim appears. He and Maggie get back into the car.)

MAGGIE: She's fantastic, Jim.

JIM: I thought you might enjoy each other.

MAGGIE: You two are good together.
JIM: Yeah. We do okay. *(Pause.)* She's a nurse, you know.
MAGGIE: No, I didn't know.
JIM: She works with children. She's taking a few months off right now, which is hard for her because she loves her work. But it'll work out fine. She'll have this chemo, we'll buy ourselves a little more time, and get back to life as usual.
MAGGIE: Good. That'll be good-
JIM: Yeah. That'll be good.
(There is a silence. We can hear the engine of the car. The street lights play on their faces intermittently.)
MAGGIE: Lamarr Street.
JIM: Yeah.
(There is another pause. Then, as if by mutual consent, Jim speeds up the car. We hear the engine being pushed further and further. The street lights accelerate as they play over their faces. Neither says a word for about thirty terrifying seconds. Finally, Jim slows the car down, pulls over and parks. There is a pause. Then he puts his head on the steering wheel and begins to weep. He sobs audibly, and Maggie puts her arms around him. After a moment, he stops. They look at one another. It appears for a moment as though they might kiss, but they disengage. He starts up the car again. They drive in silence.)
JIM: What's that stuff you use on your hair?
MAGGIE: Creme rinse. I've used it for ages.
JIM: Yeah- I remember. *(Pause,)* Maggy uses this herbal stuff. It smells really fresh. *(He drives a bit more, then pulls over.)* Well, here we are.
MAGGIE: *(Getting out.)* Will you call me? I want to hear how Maggie's chemo goes.
JIM: Sure. Or why don't you call me? I get kind of forgetful sometimes with all this going on.
MAGGIE: Oh, sure. *(She reaches out, puts a hand on his.)* It's going to be okay, Jim.
JIM: *(He pulls his hand away a little self-consciously, smiles.)* Oh, sure, yeah, I know. This is just a trying time. You look great, Mag, you really do. *(The engine starts, he waves.)* 'Bye!
(The lights go down on Jim.)
MAGGIE: The next day I took a walk down Newbury Street.
(Maggie walks over to a counter behind which stands a Salesman.)
SALESMAN: Hi, can I help you?
MAGGIE: Well, I'm kind of interested in this crystal thing. I've heard a little bit about it, and I was thinking of maybe getting something for a friend. Although, *(She half turns.)* I don't know. Maybe this is silly.
SALESMAN: Not at all. What kind of stone were you thinking of getting?
MAGGIE: Well, I don't know. She's not very well, and –
SALESMAN: How about amethyst? It will put her spirit in balance and promote tranquility.
MAGGIE: What? How could it do that? It's a stone.
SALESMAN: For thousands of years, stones have been recognized for their

healing powers.

MAGGIE: By whom?

SALESMAN: By those who know.

MAGGIE: Scientists? Geologists?

SALESMAN: Not everything that happens in this world can be embraced by the parameters of science.

MAGGIE: Oh, I see. Voodoo men. Witch doctors.

SALESMAN: Are you sure you're interested in purchasing a crystal? You don't seem, frankly, like the optimum candidate.

MAGGIE: I'm not the candidate. I told you, it's for a friend.

SALESMAN: What makes you think your friend might be a candidate?

MAGGIE: ...I don't know.

SALESMAN: How about a Sugilite?

MAGGIE: A what?

SALESMAN: A Sugilite. They've only been mining it for the past forty years, but already it's renowned for its intense healing powers.

MAGGIE: What does it look like?

(The Salesman takes a Sugilite out of the case.)

MAGGIE: Not very pretty.

SALESMAN: Beauty has nothing to do with a mineral's intrinsic power.

MAGGIE: Oh. Sorry.

SALESMAN: Have her – your friend is a woman?

MAGGIE: Yes.

SALESMAN: Have her put this by her bed, or even under her pillow.

MAGGIE: Under her pillow! We're trying to cure her, not kill her.

SALESMAN: Next to her bed then. And if the effects seem too powerful, tell her to move it farther away.

MAGGIE: This is ridiculous. It's a rock!

SALESMAN: Yes. I think we've established that.

MAGGIE: I'm not going to give a woman dying of cancer a rock to put under her pillow.

SALESMAN: You know, you're the one who walked in here. I don't remember anyone dragging you through the door.

MAGGIE: Okay, okay, I'll take it. Give me a big one.

(The scene changes to Mass General Hospital. A Nurse sits at a reception desk. An Orderly wheels a Young Woman by in a wheelchair. She looks scarily terminal. Maggie enters. She is visibly uneasy. She approaches the Nurses' stand.)

MAGGIE: Hi.

NURSE: Hi.

MAGGIE: Um, is this where I can find Maggy Burroughs?

NURSE: Maggy Burroughs, yes, she checked in about an hour ago.

MAGGIE: Great.

(A Man in Pajamas walks down the hall pulling his I.V. along behind him. He approaches Maggie.)

MAN IN PAJAMAS: *(His face suddenly radiant with joy.)* Diane?

MAGGIE: Excuse me?

MAN IN PAJAMAS: Oh, I'm so very sorry. I'm not wearing my glasses, and for a moment you looked so much like my wife. My apologies.

MAGGIE: Not at all.

MAN IN PAJAMAS: I hope you won't think me forward. You have very lovely hair.

MAGGIE: Thank you.

(Maggie watches him walk away.)

NURSE: You were saying?

MAGGIE: Uh, yes. Maggy Burroughs. I wonder if you could give her this. *(She hands the Nurse a wrapped box.)*

NURSE: Sure. Don't you want to see her?

MAGGIE: Oh, I'm sure she can't have visitors.

NURSE: Yes, she can. She's down in x-ray, but she'll be back soon. Why don't you wait?

MAGGIE: Oh, I really don't want to bother her.

NURSE: You won't be bothering her. I'm sure she'd love to see you.

MAGGIE: Gosh, I'd love to, I really would. But I'm on such a tight schedule.

NURSE: Why don't I just call down there and see when she –

MAGGIE: No! *(Attempting calmness.)* No, thanks a lot but I really just wanted to drop this off. I'll be calling her from New York, though. Maybe you can tell her that. I'll call.

NURSE: *(She's seen this before.)* Right. You'll call.

MAGGIE: *(To Audience.)* Don't look at me like that.

(She walks to an area with a table upon which are piled a number of books.)

MAGGIE: *(To Audience.)* I went to my book signing that afternoon.

(Three Women and a Man line up to get their books signed.)

MAGGIE: Cathy with a C?

FIRST WOMAN: No, a K.

MAGGIE: There you go.

FIRST WOMAN: Thanks, Miss Mulroney. I just want you to know, I've read all of your books, and I think you're terrific.

MAGGIE: Thank you.

FIRST WOMAN: I love your characters. They're so lonely and sad, but they're all trying real hard to understand their lives. I love that.

MAGGIE: Thank you.

FIRST WOMAN: Plus they're funny, of course.

MAGGIE: Of course. *(The Second Woman approaches.)* Hi. How shall I make this out?

SECOND WOMAN: Just say, "To my best friend Christine."

MAGGIE: *(Speaks to Audience as she signs the next book.)* I started to wonder, as I often do, why women seem to respond so directly to my stuff. Is there something about sad people you can laugh at that appeals more directly to the female psyche? Not that men don't respond, they do.

YOUNG MAN: I like the way you interweave the development of the theme with the exterior schematic.

MAGGIE: Thank you. *(To Audience.)* But not in such a personal way. Still, it's nice to have an audience. I'm probably one of the few people who enjoys book signings. All these people who think they know you, and like what they think they know. *(She stands, moves away from the table.)* The whole time I kept coming back to thoughts of Maggy. What were they doing to her? Was chemo painful? What was she feeling right now7

(The phone rings. Maggie walks over to an area with a bed, and picks up the phone on the bedside table.)

MAGGIE: Hello?

JIM: *(On phone.)* How did you know?

MAGGIE: How did I know what?

JIM: How did you know to buy her a Sugilite? I gave her one a long time ago, and she lost it. I kept wanting to buy her a new one, but she said there was a reason crystals went away from you, and a reason they came back.

MAGGIE: You mean she believes in that stuff?

JIM: Yeah, she does. You must, too, huh? Or you wouldn't have bought her one.

MAGGIE: ...Yeah, yeah, well, you know they have great healing powers.

JIM: She's sorry she missed you. Evidently you had just left when she came back from x-ray.

MAGGIE: Oh, what a shame. *(Guilty look at Audience.)* How is she?

JIM: She's doing okay. They were giving her something for the nausea, but she hated it so much she finally told them to stop giving it to her. So now she's doing the whole thing cold turkey. Everyone's amazed.

MAGGIE: Wow. Are you at the hospital?

JIM: Yeah. But I'm going home in awhile. It't been a long day.

MAGGIE: Is there anything I can do? Make you dinner, maybe? I make a mean chicken cacciatore.

JIM: Thanks, but what I really need is a good night's sleep.

MAGGIE: Oh. Okay.

JIM: Take a raincheck? How much longer are you staying in town?

MAGGIE: Well, I'm not sure. I was going to leave tomorrow.

JIM: Oh. Too bad.

MAGGIE: But it's possible I might have to stay in town awhile and do some research.

JIM: Something new? A new book or something?

MAGGIE: Maybe, yeah.

JIM: Oh. Well, good luck.

MAGGIE: Thanks. *(She hangs up.)* Why did I say that? Research on a new book, that was something that just popped out of my mouth. I really was due to go home tomorrow. I looked around the room of my hotel, with its generic attempt at cheerful decor and realized I needed some air.

(A few people start walking along the street. Maggie joins them. A Daddy and Mommy are pushing a baby carriage.)

DADDY: You're going to suffocate her.

MOMMY: What, you want her to freeze to death?

DADDY: I want her to be able to breathe.

MOMMY: She's breathing. Look at her, she's breathing.

DADDY: How can you tell? I can't even see her in there.

(Maggie peels off, stops. A doorbell sounds and an Older Woman approaches.)

NORA: *(Slight Irish accent.)* Yes, may I help you?

MAGGIE: I saw your Bed and Breakfast sign and was wondering if you had a room available.

NORA: For how long?

MAGGIE: I don't know exactly.

NORA: I see. Well, why don't you come on in? *(Maggie does.)* No bags?

MAGGIE: They're still at the hotel.

NORA: Ah. Moving out, are you?

MAGGIE: Yes. I'm looking for something a little homier.

NORA: Well, you've come to the right place. This is an old building, some might even call it a shade run down, but I prefer to think of it as homey, just as you say. We serve a Continental breakfast from seven to nine, free of charge. And there's a TV room on the first floor. I'm afraid there's no TV in it at the moment.

MAGGIE: That's fine. I'll take a room.

NORA: *(Entering her name in the register.)* Your name?

MAGGIE: Maggie Mulroney.

NORA: Mulroney, is it? Your family wouldn't hail from County Kerry, would they?

MAGGIE: I don't really know. My father told me, but I forgot, and now I can't ask.

NORA: Ah. Passed away, is he, your father?

MAGGIE: Uh, yes. When I was eighteen.

NORA: Pity. My dear father died last year, and I'm still half destroyed. And you only a teenager, you poor thing. And your mother, is she still living?

MAGGIE: Yes. She lives in Seattle. We don't see each other very often.

NORA: Why not?

MAGGIE: Um, I'm not sure. It's just the way things worked out.

NORA: Oh, Maggie, what a shame. Isn't life the saddest thing?

MAGGIE: *(To Audience.)* For a brief moment, I had the overwhelming urge to climb onto her lap and sob until I got uncontrollable hiccups, and fell fast asleep. Fortunately, I suppressed it.

NORA: Well, Maggie, I'm giving you my daughter's old room, with the view of the park. The nicest room I have available. Anything you need, you just ask. Nora Delaney's my name. And you'll meet my husband, Howard, at breakfast.

MAGGIE: Thank you, Nora.

NORA: You know, I've a feeling, were you able to ask, that you hail from County Kerry. I knew some Mulroneys from there, and you definitely favor them.

(Nora exits.)

MAGGIE: *(To Audience.)* Paying someone to be your family, this could be a whole new untapped market. Instead of hiring a prostitute, businessmen could hire some motherly type to come in and tut-tut over how hard it was at the office. Or to yell, "Get those dirty socks off the floor, ya louse!" depending on your inclination.

(She picks up a suitcase, carries it to her new room. It is a teenaged girl's old bedroom, with flowery wallpaper and one of those white bumpy bedspreads on the

bed. Maybe a stuffed animal. Maybe a poster. Kind of sweet.)
MAGGIE: Hmm. Nice. Makes me want to throw a slumber party. *(Sitting on the bed.)* County Kerry. Well, who knows? There was something kind of comforting about this woman suggesting that I might actually belong to a tribe somewhere. *(She bounces on the bed a minute testing the mattress.)* I considered for a moment calling someone to let them know I was staying. Then I realized there was no one I needed to call, except maybe my publicist. I have to admit, I got a little depressed there for a minute. *(Thinking of Maggy's "no friends" comment.)* Not that I don't have any friends, don't get me wrong. I just couldn't think of who they were at the moment. *(She stretches out on the bed.)* So. Here I was in a Bed and Breakfast, for no apparent reason. And there was Maggy, Jim's Maggy, lying in a bed across town, with poison dripping into her veins. I lay on the bed for a very long time, trying to figure out the correlation.

BLACK OUT

END OF ACT ONE

ACT II

In the dark, a phone rings. On the third ring it is answered by a machine.

JIM: You've reached the Burroughs residence. Here is the Maggy update as of Thursday: She is responding well to chemo, her condition is stable and we hope to have her back in a few days. Leave your message after the beep, and someone will get back to you.
(There is a beep. The lights come up. Maggie is lying on the bed with her head at the foot of it. On the nightstand beside her is a glass of wine and an empty wine bottle. She is on the phone.)
MAGGIE: Hi, Jim. It's Maggie. Maggie Mulroney. Guess what? I'm still here. I know you're at the hospital, but I just wanted to say that I'm thinking of you both, and…and I hope you're really kicking some butt with that chemo. *(Cheerleader.)* Let's go, our team, let's go! 'Bye. *(She hangs up the phone. To herself.)* That was really stupid.
(Black out. The phone rings again. It is again picked up by a machine.)
JIM: Hi, this is the Maggy Burroughs hotline. Maggy went through kind of a slump yesterday, but she's feeling much better today and can actually have visitors. I'm boring her to tears, so feel free to drop in and provide a change of pace. Mass General Health and Racquet Club, Cambridge Street entrance. 'Bye.
(Lights up. Maggie is lolling around on an unmade bed. She holds a young girl's doll in one hand and the phone in the other. During the call she plays casually with the doll's clothing.)
MAGGIE: Hi, Jim, it's Maggie again. I've been meaning to drop in on Maggy,

but I'm so darn busy. I've got an interview today and things are just crazy around here, so please give her my best and tell her I'm thinking of her. Um, okay, that's about it. 'Bye.
(She hangs up. To Audience.)
MAGGIE: I know, I know. But everybody tells little white lies on the telephone, don't they? The truth is, I kind of needed some time alone. My first night at the B & B, I bought a bottle of wine, drank it in my room and cried for about three hours. The next day I woke up with a monstrous hangover, walked over to the Charles River and threw things into it to watch them sink. I guess you might say I was going through a melancholy phase. I was on my way to a Bergman film retrospective when suddenly, I remembered I had an interview that afternoon.
(Black out. Pretentious PBS type music, and lights up. Maggie is in a TV studio. A lugubrious looking man with shadows under his eyes, Raymond Terwilliger, sits opposite her. He speaks to the audience.)
RAYMOND: Hello, I'm Raymond Terwilliger, and our guest tonight is Margaret Mulroney, whose book "Joined at the Head" is currently topping the New York Times Best Seller list. Miss Mulroney is in town at the moment, and we were lucky enough to get her to drop in to chat with us on "The Best of Boston." Welcome to the show, Margaret.
MAGGIE: Thank you, Raymond. A pleasure to be here.
RAYMOND: You're actually a Boston native, aren't you?
MAGGIE: Well, not really. I spent my adolescence here, however, which were rather important years for me. The Wonder Years.
RAYMOND: The Wonder Years?
MAGGIE: Didn't you eat that bread? Soft, white, easy to roll up into balls and throw in the cafeteria? That's where the TV show gets its name.
RAYMOND: I'm afraid I don't watch commercial television.
MAGGIE: Oh. Sorry.
RAYMOND: "Joined at the Head" has been doing so well in terms of sales, you might say there's something of a Margaret Mulroney groundswell going on these days. To what do you attribute this?
MAGGIE: I'm not sure. I've seen so many of my contemporaries fall in and out of favor, I would hesitate to attribute a rational explanation to anybody's popularity, least of all my own.
RAYMOND: Do you think the nation has gone into a period of self-examination, and that perhaps you exemplify the recent mood of the nation?
MAGGIE: Okay. That sounds good. Honestly, I don't know. I really liked my last book, and I could have offered you a very convincing explanation for its being a hit. But it wasn't, and this is. Go figure.
RAYMOND: "Joined at the Head" is a searing indictment of the father/daughter relationship. Is your –
MAGGIE: Oh, no.
RAYMOND: I beg your pardon?
MAGGIE: It's not a searing indictment of anything. It's funny.
RAYMOND: Be that as it may. Is your relationship with your father as cancerous as the one between Aggie, the protagonist in your book, and her father?

MAGGIE: Cancerous?

RAYMOND: By that I mean destructive, A sense of something rotting from within.

MAGGIE: Are you sure we're talking about the same book?

RAYMOND: Yes, I know, I've read all the kudos – "Hilariously funny." "Delightfully witty," etcetera. But I'm sorry, this reviewer found himself quite literally gasping for air while reading your book, the mood you created was so claustrophobic.

MAGGIE: Oh, dear. I'm very sorry.

RAYMOND: You're sorry your book is so powerful?

MAGGIE: Well, it wasn't my intention to hamper your breathing process. I was only trying to poke fun at some of the foibles of the father/daughter thing.

RAYMOND: And most would say you did exactly that. I'm merely trying to get deeper here, Margaret. To discover the real Margaret Mulroney.

MAGGIE: Is that absolutely necessary?

RAYMOND: What is your relationship with your father?

MAGGIE: Fine. Quite normal. He's deceased, unfortunately, but we were very close when he was alive. I think he would approve of this particular book.

RAYMOND: Is that necessary? That he approve.

MAGGIE: *(Flustered.)* Well, no, of course not. *(Nervous laugh.)* I'm starting to feel like I'm in therapy here. I hope your rates are reasonable.

RAYMOND: It has been said that while your women are fully fleshed out characters, the men in your books tend to be caddish, shallow, selfish, even perverted individuals. Why do you think this is?

MAGGIE: I wasn't aware that such a thing had been said.

RAYMOND: Well, surely Maxwell Roundtree couldn't be called a sympathetic character.

MAGGIE: On the contrary. I'd go out with him.

RAYMOND: You'd got out with him? An egomaniacal skirt-chaser without a moral bone in his body?

MAGGIE: He's smart, funny and successful. What more do you need in a man?

RAYMOND: *(Pause.)* You're not married, are you?

MAGGIE: *(Slow burn.)* No, as a matter of fact, I'm not.

RAYMOND: Anyone special in your life?

MAGGIE: I find it interesting that this question is asked of me so frequently. Tell me, if Saul Bellow were on the show tonight, would you ask him about that "special someone" in his life? I'm just curious.

RAYMOND: Touche. *(To the Audience.)* We've been talking to Margaret Mulroney, feminist author of "Joined at the Head." Tomorrow we'll be talking to Jean Kirkpatrick.

MAGGIE: I hear she's dating someone really cute these days. Ask her to tell you about him.

RAYMOND: *(Dourly.)* Ha-ha-ha. *(To Audience.)* This has been "The Best of Boston."

(Black out. A phone rings in the dark. Lights up on Maggie in her room asleep. She turns on the light and picks up the phone.)

MAGGIE: Hello?
MRS. MULRONEY: Maggie?
MAGGIE: Who's this?
MRS. MULRONEY: Who do you think?
MAGGIE: Mother?
MRS. MULRONEY: Of course. How are you, darling?
MAGGIE: How am I? Oh, I'm... fine, I guess.
MRS. MULRONEY: I saw you on that TV show. That man really raked you over the coals, didn't he?
MAGGIE: He sure did.
MRS. MULRONEY: What a terrible person. Why did they let him talk to you like that?
MAGGIE: It's his job, mom. I guess he didn't like me.
MRS. MULRONEY: Well, I wanted to scratch his eyes out. You, however, were adorable.
MAGGIE: Adorable?
MRS. MULRONEY: Absolutely. I love your new haircut. It creates a youthful illusion.
MAGGIE: Mom, what time is it?
MRS. MULRONEY: Oh, who looks at the time when your daughter is – are you ready?
MAGGIE: Ready for what? (*Mrs. Mulroney sings a birthday song culminating in "Happy Birthday, Famous Writer Daughter Of Mine, etc." I leave it to her how the tune of the song should go. During it, Maggie says "Mom," but not to be deterred, Mrs. Mulroney completes the entire song.*)
MRS. MULRONEY: I remember that day vividly. It was the most incredible pain of my entire life.
MAGGIE: Sorry.
MRS. MULRONEY: Wait till you have one. You'll see.
MAGGIE: In case you haven't noticed, Mom, it doesn't look like I'll be giving birth any time soon.
MRS. MULRONEY: Never say never. There was an article about you in the Seattle Times. Somebody read your book and didn't like it.
MAGGIE: Uh-huh. Well, thanks for sharing.
MRS. MULRONEY: No, listen, I bring it up because the guy was a jack-ass. Wait 'til you see the article, I'm going to mail it to you, you'll see what I mean. A total jack-ass. What's your address?
MAGGIE: (*Pause.*) I'm staying at the Copley Plaza. Send it there.
MRS. MULRONEY: What?
MAGGIE: I said, "I'm staying –"
MRS. MULRONEY: No, not you. Your father's talking to me...What?... Oh, your father wants to wish you a happy birthday.
MAGGIE: (*Pause.*) What?
MRS. MULRONEY: Hold on a second. Here, Bud.
(*A slight pause. Then a Man's voice.*)
MR. MULRONEY: Hey, baby, that you?

MAGGIE: ...Dad?

MR. MULRONEY: How's the birthday girl?

MAGGIE: How did you –?

MR. MULRONEY: Look, I heard about this lousy review, and I hope you're not going to let some joker from Seattle ruin your birthday. In fact, I tell you what I did for you. I rented out a hall, and you're gonna come out here and read your book page by page to all these clowns. We'll make them pay to hear it, and they're gonna love it.

MAGGIE: Daddy?

MR. MULRONEY: Because that's the only way to deal with these schmoes. Let them know who's boss. You're a comer, kid. And a comer doesn't let anybody stand in her way.

MAGGIE: Daddy, you can't...

MR. MULRONEY: Don't whine, Magpie. You know how I hate it when you whine.

MAGGIE: I'm not. I just –

MR. MULRONEY: You wanna make your old man proud of you?

MAGGIE: Well yeah. But –

MR. MULRONEY: You're not gonna let them treat you like a loser, are you?

MAGGIE: Dad –

MR. MULRONEY: Are you?

MAGGIE: No, Dad.

MR. MULRONEY: That's my girl. You're a good one, Magpie. Your mother and I love you very much.

MAGGIE: I love you, too.

MR. MULRONEY: Now, I've rented this hall, and we're going to force this stuff down all the nay-sayers' throats, and before you know it, they'll be begging for more. My daughter is not a loser!

MAGGIE: Dad, you can't be doing this.

MR. MULRONEY: What do you mean? I've already sold the tickets, called the newspapers –

MAGGIE: I mean, you can't be talking to me on the phone right now.

MR. MULRONEY: Why not?

MAGGIE: Well, I mean...you're dead, Dad. *(Long pause.)* Dad? Daddy? *(There is a click.)*

MAGGIE: Daddy! Daddy, wait! I'm sorry, I didn't mean it! Come back! Daddy, please, talk to me!

(There's a knock at the door. Nora enters.)

NORA: Maggie? Are you all right?

MAGGIE: Uh, yes.

NORA: I hope you don't mind my barging in on you, but I couldn't help hearing–

MAGGIE: No, no. Sorry...I embarrassed my father.

NORA: How's that?

MAGGIE: In my dream. I think I really embarrassed him. By pointing out that he was dead.

NORA: Oh. Yes. He probably considered it bad form. Mine does, too. Would you like me to fix you a cup of tea? It might calm your nerves a bit.

MAGGIE: No, thank you, Nora. I'm sorry to have woken you.

NORA: Oh, you didn't wake me, it's still early yet. Howard and I were playing Scrabble. Terrible cheater, Howard. He's probably trading in his tiles as we speak.

MAGGIE: Oh, dear.

NORA: You know, this may not be the best time to mention it, but there certainly are a lot of phone messages piling up for you downstairs.

MAGGIE: I know.

NORA: Your publicist, your editor, a man from the Boston Globe. Sounds like a fascinating existence, being a writer.

MAGGIE: Did anyone call who said they were a friend?

NORA: Well, not specifically, dear, but I'm sure many of them were. *(Pause.)* I should be getting back to Howard. Will you be all right?

MAGGIE: Yes, I'm fine. Thanks for looking in.

NORA: Of course. Tell your father not to take things so seriously.

MAGGIE: I will. Good-night.

(Nora exits. Maggie looks at the audience.) This is getting kind of confusing. I didn't mean to get into all this stuff about my family, it just kind of slipped out. I hope you'll bear with me, sometimes you just veer off track a little, you know? So let's get back to the important stuff. I called Maggy and Jim's house frequently. *(She dials. Jim's voice.)*

JIM: This is the Maggy Burroughs hotline. If all goes well – *(Maggie hangs up.)*

MAGGIE: But all I got was the machine. It was frustrating. I was feeling kind of nervous and edgy and didn't know what to do about it. I asked myself – What could I do to calm myself down?

(A doctor enters. She is looking at a chart.)

DOCTOR: Well, you seem to check out okay. Blood levels normal, heart good, mammography negative. You're in good health.

MAGGIE: *(Getting off the bed and moving toward her)* I don't know. I'm not sleeping very well lately.

DOCTOR: You have a slight tendency towards anemia, but nothing to worry about. Pop a few folic acid tabs now and then.

MAGGIE: "Pop a few folic acid tabs?"

DOCTOR: Yeah, sure, what the hell.

MAGGIE: And what about the headaches?

DOCTOR: Ever heard of aspirin?

MAGGIE: Yes, I've heard of aspirin, but what if it's more than a headache? What if it's something serious?

DOCTOR: You want me to run a CAT scan? I'll be happy to run a CAT scan.

MAGGIE: Why? Do you think I need one?

DOCTOR: I just told you. I think you're perfectly normal. Physically, that is.

MAGGIE: Then why do you want to run a CAT scan?

DOCTOR: I don't. I'm humoring you.

MAGGIE: Look, I'm a little nervous, okay? I just don't feel up to par. Isn't it possible that you missed something?

DOCTOR: Well, of course, that's always possible. I gave someone a clean bill of health once and he dropped dead the next day.

MAGGIE: What?

DOCTOR: But it's very unusual. We can't know everything.

MAGGIE: This isn't comforting. Somehow I'm not feeling better for this experience.

DOCTOR: Have you thought about maybe taking a vacation?

MAGGIE: I'm on vacation. Sort of.

DOCTOR: I see. Well then, perhaps you should go back to work.

MAGGIE: Have I told you how helpful you've been? You've really been wonderfully helpful.

DOCTOR: My pleasure. Drop in any time.

MAGGIE: *(Long, confused pause. Then, to Audience.)* You know what? I'm lost. I'm sorry, I thought I knew what I was doing here, but I don't. I'm very embarrassed, I shouldn't have gotten you all out here on false pretenses. So I tell you what – let's just stop here. Maybe a little time away from this will clear my head.

(Maggy enters.)

MAGGY: What are you doing?

MAGGIE: I'm sending everybody home.

MAGGY: Why?

MAGGIE: Because I'm lost. I don't know where I'm going. I thought I did, I thought this was going to be a moving tribute to you, and now all this other stuff is coming out.

MAGGY: What other stuff?

MAGGIE: About me. Who needs it?

MAGGY: Evidently you do.

MAGGIE: No. I don't. It's immaterial. It's off the point. *(To Audience.)* 'Bye, everybody. Thanks for your patience and your –

MAGGY: Don't anybody move! *(To Maggie.)* This is ridiculous. Tell your story.

MAGGIE: I can't. What are you doing here, anyway? You said you'd never interrupt again.

MAGGY: Well, obviously I spoke prematurely. I had no idea you'd pull a stunt like this. This is highly irresponsible. You owe it to these people to continue. Now talk.

MAGGIE: No.

MAGGY: Okay then, I will.

MAGGIE: *You* will?

MAGGY: Somebody's got to.

MAGGIE: But not you. It's my story.

MAGGY: But you're not telling it. And you can't just leave a story dangling like this. It's extremely bad manners. *(To Audience.)* Okay, when last we left our heroine –

MAGGIE: I'm not the heroine. You are the heroine.

MAGGY: Oh. What are you?

MAGGIE: I'm the narrator. My life serves as a backdrop for your story.

MAGGY: Oh. Okay. When last we left our backdrop, she had just come back from a trip to the doctor, which is something I'll bet about 99% of all people do when they find out someone they know has cancer. She had decided to stay on in Boston in order to be near Jim and me. She then proceeded to avoid us for the next three days.

MAGGIE: What do you mean? I didn't avoid you. I called constantly.

MAGGY: But you never came to the hospital once.

MAGGIE: I was busy!

MAGGY: I see.

MAGGIE: I was! I had an interview, and meetings with –

MAGGY: Excuse me. I'm trying to tell a story here. Do you mind? Thank you. You also saw a dream about a rather strange phone call from her parents.

MAGGIE: *(To audience)* Which I ask you to disregard.

MAGGY: Although I myself found it rather interesting. Then, let's see, right after that I came home. It was nice to be back home after five days of staring at the same walls at Mass General, but I felt like total shit. I had mucositis, which is like fifty zillion cankar sores all along the lining of your mouth and down your throat. It was the worst.

(She lies on a sofa. Jim enters carrying a milk shake with a straw in it.)

JIM: Here you go. *(He hands her the drink.)* Do you think you can have a little of this? Try to take a sip.

(Painfully, Maggy takes a small sip. Just the act of swallowing is excruciating.)

JIM: Come on, honey, just a little more. You've got to keep up your strength.

(The phone rings. Jim picks it up.)

JIM: Speak.

MAGGIE: Oh, Jim! I thought I'd get your machine.

JIM: We just got home.

MAGGIE: How's Maggy feeling?

JIM: Pretty well under the circumstances.

MAGGIE: I'm so glad. Can I talk to her?

JIM: Not at the moment. She's kind of lying low.

MAGGIE: Sure, yeah, of course. Well, I just wanted to check in on you and see how things were. Let you know I'm thinking of you.

JIM: That's nice of you, Mag. Thanks.

MAGGIE: And, you know, if there's anything I can do...

JIM: Thanks. When she's feeling better, we'd like to have you out to dinner.

MAGGIE: That would be great. Well, love to Maggy.

(She hangs up. Lights out on her. Maggy is reaching for a pillow.)

JIM: Let me get that for you. *(He puts it behind her back.)* How're you feeling?

MAGGY: A little achy.

JIM: You could be run over by a steamroller, and as they peeled you off the pavement and asked you how you felt, you'd say, "Oh, a little achy." C'mon, drink this.

MAGGY: Jim, please, go away.

JIM: Sorry, I'm here for good. Get used to it. Now drink. *(She takes a sip.)* Thank you. It's good to have you home, sweetie.

MAGGY: It's good to be home.

JIM: Maggie sends her love. She left about twenty-five messages on the machine while you were in the hospital.

MAGGY: You didn't call her back?

JIM: No. Too busy.

MAGGY: I wish you had. I think she's lonely.

JIM: Lonely? No way. She's doing great. Flying here, flying there, book signings, interviews. This is the kind of life she always wanted. Honey, try to take another sip of this, okay? Then I promise I'll leave you alone for twenty minutes. I know it hurts, but if you don't take liquids, you'll get dehydrated.

MAGGY: *(Standing and approaching Audience.)* And that's exactly what did happen. I got dehydrated, and it was back to the hospital for me. Interestingly, Maggie still did not visit, although she sent many strange and exotic gifts. Jim did, however, finally return her calls, and the next night they had dinner at our house.

MAGGIE: We don't need to do that.

MAGGY: What?

MAGGIE: The dinner. It was just one of those old time's sake kind of dinners, and it had nothing to do with you.

MAGGY: Hey, who's telling this story?

MAGGIE: I don't see how you could possibly tell a story about a dinner you weren't at.

MAGGY: Maybe I'll surprise you.

MAGGIE: I'd rather you didn't.

MAGGY: Come on. You're stuck. I might as well take a stab at this, don't you think? *(Silence.)* Okay. *(To Audience.)* Maggie went over to dinner at our house the night I went back to the hospital. Here's what I think probably happened. *(Lights up on Jim and Maggie. Jim is playing a tune on the piano, a beautiful lyrical song with no words.)*

MAGGIE: Jim, that's beautiful.

JIM: You really like it?

MAGGIE: Oh God, yes.

JIM: I wrote it for Maggy.

MAGGIE: Really? She must have been so touched.

JIM: Yeah. She likes it. Do you remember this? *(He plays a song from an earlier time. A less mature attempt at a love song.)*

MAGGIE: I thought you might have forgotten that one.

JIM: How could I forget the first love song I ever wrote? You were such a lovely girl. You still are.

MAGGIE: Oh, no.

JIM: Yes, you are. You know, I feel I could only say this to you, and please try not to judge me – it's such a relief to be with someone who's healthy. God, I hate myself for saying that. But poor Maggy, I feel like I have to be so careful with her all the time. She's so fragile, it's like being with a wounded bird. I broke one of her ribs once making love, just snapped it in two. And we were both trying to be so careful, it was like making love to a teacup. But I broke her rib anyway. I heard it break.

MAGGIE: Oh Jim, how horrible.

JIM: Maggie, sometimes I wonder how much more of this I can take. And then I hate myself, because she's the one who's going through the pain. What the fuck right do I have to cave in?

MAGGIE: You're not caving in, Jim. It's hard. No one comes out a hero at a time like this. It's hard.

JIM: Come here. *(She moves toward him. He kisses her. She responds.)* Please forgive me. *(He kisses her again.)* Please, please forgive me.

(They are in each other's arms, obviously on their way to other things. Maggie breaks away.)

MAGGIE: No, no, no, no, no. You've got it all wrong. God! How could you even think such a thing?

MAGGY: How could I think such a thing? Isn't that where all this has been leading?

MAGGIE: No! Jesus, Maggy, give me a little credit. Or forget me, give Jim a little credit. He would no sooner have made a pass at me than he would have cut off his arm.

MAGGY: Really?

MAGGIE: Of course, really. Honestly! You really shock me sometimes.

MAGGY: Well then, what happened? If he didn't make a pass at you, what happened?

MAGGIE: I really don't want to get into it.

MAGGY: I think you'd better, don't you? To clear up this misconception.

MAGGIE: It has nothing to do with this story, Maggy, it's extraneous and completely off the track.

MAGGY: What track? I thought you were stuck.

MAGGIE: *(Pause.)* All right, all right, I'll try to encapsulate it.

MAGGY: Good. *(She exits.)*

MAGGIE: *(To Audience.)* I went to dinner at Jim's that night. I'll make this quick, then we'll move on to other things.

(Maggie moves into position next to Jim, who is again playing the love song to Maggy.*)

MAGGIE: Maybe the problem was that I'd had too much wine with dinner. I always tend to take life too seriously when I have wine in my system. Everything seems so goddamn meaningful.

(Jim's song comes to a close.)

— MAGGIE: Jim, that's beautiful.

JIM: You like it?

MAGGIE: Oh God, yes.

JIM: I wrote it for Maggy.

MAGGIE: I had a feeling. You're so talented. I always thought you were going to end up being a famous musician.

JIM: Instead of a loser high school teacher?

MAGGIE: Jim, that's not what I —

JIM: Hey, I'm kidding. Look, there was a time when I thought so, too. You and I always vowed we'd get out of this place and make good. You're the one who did it.

MAGGIE: Are you sorry you didn't?

JIM: I was at first. Then I met Maggy. I wouldn't change a thing now – except for this little cancer thing, which is kind of cramping our style.

MAGGIE: *(Pause.)* Would you like to talk about that? I mean, I just want you to know that I'm here for you if you want to –

JIM: Thanks. No. I'm fine.

MAGGIE: The other night in the car –

JIM: Little moment of insanity, Mag.

MAGGIE: That wasn't insanity, that was a perfectly natural response to a terrible situation.

JIM: It's nothing to worry about. Hope you'll forget it happened.

MAGGIE: It was good it happened. I'm just glad I was the one you chose to –

JIM: Maggie, I didn't choose anything. You just happened to be there, okay? No big deal. *(Pause.)* Hey, remember this one?

(Jim plays the second song.)*

MAGGIE: *(To Audience.)* I couldn't believe it. First he pulls the rug out from under me, then he tries to make up for it by playing me a love song. *(An edge in her voice.)* Yeah, that's pretty. Play that Van Morrison tune I used to like.

JIM: *(Stopping.)* What?

MAGGIE: What was it called? "Blue Money" or something?

JIM: You're kidding me, right?

MAGGIE: Why would I be kidding?

JIM: I'm playing a love song I wrote you almost twenty years ago and you tell me to play Van Morrison?

MAGGIE: I like that song, I really do. But you just said it, times change. I mean, look at us. We're hardly teen-agers anymore. It's kind of embarrassing.

JIM: This is vintage you, you know that? Christ! You haven't changed a bit.

MAGGIE: Why is it vintage me? What do you mean?

JIM: Oh, forget it.

MAGGIE: No, I want to know. Why is it vintage me?

JIM: You always used to do this, Maggie, always. How many times did I have to tell you, you do not stop someone in the middle of a song?

MAGGIE: Well I'm sorry, but I was just –

JIM: I don't care! It is so fucking rude. Not to mention controlling.

MAGGIE: Oh, I'm controlling? That's very funny from someone who always had to call the shots.

JIM: Oh, yeah. Turn it around. Now it's my fault.

MAGGIE: It is! It's been the pattern from the beginning. Who dumped who at the senior prom?

JIM: The senior prom again. Maggie, I wasn't going to mention this, but since you keep on bringing it up – I didn't dump you at the senior prom. You dumped me.

MAGGIE: I did not:

JIM: Yes, you did. You don't remember this? You told me your father had always said I was a loser, and you didn't want to be saddled with a loser for the rest of your life.

MAGGIE: I never said that!

JIM: Yes, you did. Believe me, Mag, it's not the kind of thing a guy forgets.

MAGGIE: *(To Audience.)* A loser. Oh, my God, I probably did say that.

JIM: Maybe that's why I ran off that night with Gina Lazlo.

MAGGIE: Jim, I'm so sorry. I don't know how I could have been so cruel.

JIM: Your dad had just died. You were having a hard time. I was a moody musician with pipe dreams of grandeur and very little compassion. Who wouldn't have dumped me?

MAGGIE: You're awfully understanding.

JIM: Only in retrospect. To tell you the truth, I was pretty pissed off there for a couple of years. After Maggy got sick, though, I looked back on that time and realized what was really going on with you. It's a bitch. There's no way around it.

MAGGIE: I know. I wish you'd allow yourself to be comforted a little, Jim. This New England stoicism is so unhealthy.

JIM: Hey, don't talk to me about what's unhealthy, okay? I don't remember you being so warm and wonderful while your dad was wasting away. *(Pause.)* Christ, that was a low blow. I don't know why, but being around you seems to strike a raw nerve in me. That's why I haven't been returning your calls.

MAGGIE: Oh. I hadn't realized you didn't want to talk to me. I thought you were just too busy.

JIM: I was. Oh, God, Mag. Don't take this as rejection.

MAGGIE: I'm trying not to. Give me a minute.

JIM: I just can't talk about this. Cancer, Mag! You must remember what that's like.

MAGGIE: *(Pause.)* Yes, I do. And I'm really sorry.

JIM: Oh, boy. Just like old times, huh? *(He puts his arm around her.)* I'm being an asshole.

MAGGIE: And I'm being hypersensitive. It's a magic combination, isn't it? I feel just like I'm sixteen again. I hated being sixteen.

JIM: *(Raymond Terwiliger.)* Ah, the Wonder Years.

MAGGIE: Oh, no. You didn't see that interview, did you?

JIM: 'Fraid so.

MAGGIE: Oh, *no.* I was desperately hoping no one ever watched that show.

JIM: It's big with hospital waiting rooms. Good soporific. Listen, the guy's a moron. You should have seen him with Larry Bird.

MAGGIE: Do you think he's right about my book?

JIM: Well, I think he's right that your father would approve.

MAGGIE: What's that supposed to mean? *(Jim shrugs.)* You don't like that book, do you?

JIM: Hey, who am I to judge? It's selling like hotcakes, everybody loves it –

MAGGIE: What's wrong with it? Come on, Jim, you're an English teacher. You're one of the most perceptive people I've ever known. Since I've endowed you with the power to make me listen to you, you might as well take advantage of it and tell me what's wrong.

JIM: *(Pause.)* Okay. In my opinion, it's dishonest.

MAGGIE: (*Devestated.*) Dishonest.

JIM: It's not your dad. It's some swell guy that you cooked up in order to make America laugh, but it's not your dad. Now if that was your intention, fine, then you succeeded. But if you were trying to capture your dad and the essence of your relationship with him, well, I didn't buy it.

MAGGIE: I see. Well, what did you want me to write? That I was a delinquent teenager who never lived up to his expectations? That he died before I could ever make him proud of me?

JIM: If that's the truth, yes.

MAGGIE: Oh, yeah, that sounds fascinating. The story of one woman's failure. That'll sell millions for sure.

JIM: Well, you're right. I suppose if selling millions is what you're after, you might have to dress it up a bit.

MAGGIE: It's so easy to be righteous from a distance, isn't it?

JIM: Maggie, I'm not judging you, I'm really not. I'm just surprised to see the old firebrand I knew turning out such innocuous stuff. Sorry. (*Maggie gets up.*) You're mad at me, right?

MAGGIE: This is just a little more honesty than I can take in one evening.

JIM: Mag, I'm your friend. What am I supposed to do, lie to you?

MAGGIE: I'm your friend, too. But once every twenty years seems like just about enough right now.

JIM: Are you going?

MAGGIE: Yeah. It's late, anyway. Thanks for dinner. I'd better get home.

JIM: Maggie. (*She turns.*) I was looking forward to showing you the great guy I've turned into. How happy ten years of marriage has made me, how I finally managed to acquire some compassion along the way. I'm sorry I screwed it up.

— MAGGIE: (*Pause.*) You didn't screw it up, Jim. You did just fine.

(*Maggie gets in the car and starts to drive. Soon she is sobbing. Maggy enters and gets into the seat next to her.*)

MAGGY: How come everybody in this story seems to cry in their cars?

MAGGIE: Leave me alone.

MAGGY: This is very reckless driving, Maggie. You're on Lamarr Street driving like an idiot.

MAGGIE: Who cares? We're all just gonna die anyway.

MAGGY: Oh, that's a fine attitude, I must say. Come on. I know you're upset, but this is your car and someone's got to drive it. Pull yourself together, Mag. Please.

(*Maggie stops crying. She begins to concentrate on driving the car.*)

MAGGY: Thanks. You were making me nervous.

MAGGIE: I told you we didn't need that scene! Your name was barely mentioned!

MAGGY: I was there, though. I was clearly there.

MAGGIE: What was I looking for from him? Why didn't I get it?

MAGGY: Maybe you did get it and just didn't realize it.

MAGGIE:What do you mean?

MAGGY: What do you think you were looking for?

MAGGIE: Approval. As usual. The never ending quest for approval.
MAGGY: Hm. And all you got was friendship. Tough break. *(She stands.)* Well, 'bye.
MAGGIE: Are you leaving?
MAGGY: Yeah. I think you're back on track now. Drive carefully, will you? You could kill yourself driving like that.
(Maggy exits.)
MAGGIE: *(To Audience.)* So anyway, where was I? Oh, yes. Maggy was doing about as well as could be expected, according to the hospital, and... and I was still scared to visit her, and... Listen, let's do this another way. Here are all the things that happened from this point on. This story is just going to have to tell itself.
(The phone rings. Maggie picks it up.)
MAGGIE: Hello?
JIM: Maggy's worse. An infection has set in, she's running a high fever. *(Pause.)* Hello?
MAGGIE: Yes, I'm here.
(Black out. Lights up on the hospital. Maggie enters carrying a plastic bonsai tree. She walks up to the front desk.)
MAGGIE: Excuse me.
NURSE: Yes?
MAGGIE: I wanted to check on the condition of one of your patients. Margaret Burroughs.
NURSE: *(Paging through files.)* Burroughs. I'm sorry, she's passed away.
MAGGIE: What?
NURSE: *(Pause.)* Oh, no, wait. That's Burris. Margaret Burroughs. Stable. Sorry about that. Haven't had my morning coffee.
MAGGIE: Please have it now.
JIM: *(Entering.)* Maggie! *(He takes her by the arm, leads her away from desk.)* It's good to see you.
MAGGIE: How is she?
JIM: She's being pumped full of antibiotics. She really gave us a scare, but the doctor says she'll be fine.
MAGGIE: Oh, what a relief.
JIM: It's amazing how quickly she bounces back from these things. She's got a lot of fight in her, that girl. But hey, I'm sorry to have dragged you out here in the middle of the night.
MAGGIE: No. I'm glad you called. I...I have very strong memories of this place.
JIM: You do?
MAGGIE: I used to visit my father here.
JIM: Oh. Well hey, Mag, you don't need to stick around. I'll tell Maggy you dropped by and –
MAGGIE: No. I'd like to see her. I mean, if she can handle visitors.
JIM: Yeah, she can. In fact, she asked for you. She thinks you're a kindred spirit.
MAGGIE: Are you okay? You look exhausted.
JIM: I'm fine, I'm fine. Why don't you go on in? It's Room 36. I'll be in in a minute.

MAGGIE: Okay. Listen, about last night –
JIM: Magpie, let's do ourselves a favor and forget about last night.
MAGGIE: *(Smiling.)* Magpie. You call Maggy that, too?
JIM: No, that one's yours. All yours. Now get on in there.
MAGGIE: Thanks.
(Maggie exits. Jim's face goes from hopeful and encouraging to a mask of grief.
He goes over to a water fountain. Washes his face as he drinks from it.
Straightens up and looks at the audience.)
JIM: Here's what you won't hear from them about me. You won't hear about the
nights I lie awake looking at Maggy, thinking about what a wonderful mother she
would have made. Or how beautiful our children would have been. You won't
hear about how I lust for her, even now, even with tubes running out of her body.
How I fantasize about making her well with my ejaculations, as though it were a
life-giving fluid that could wash through her entire body and render her clean
again. Or about the other side of that, the self-hatred that goes along with forcing
yourself upon a sick person. Even though she pretends it's voluntary, that she
wants it, too. You won't hear about the anger, an anger so strong and vicious it
feels like it could wipe out cities. Anger at the world, at fate, at this fucking roll of
the dice that is your life. And anger at Maggy, for letting herself get so sick. For
doing this to me and ruining my life. You particularly won't hear about this last
because I don't tell it to anyone, least of all myself. You won't hear about my
dreams, dreams of flight, of other women, of another life, the one with her we
didn't get to have. You won't know what comfort I take in these dreams, the true
happiness I find in them. And the strange sensation of waking up to discover that
it's your life that is the nightmare, not the dream. "Don't cry, Jim, it's only your
life. You're asleep now, everything's okay." You won't hear about the people I
work with, and how they've reacted to all this. How some are compassionate and
caring, and others treat me like I'm perhaps a carrier and they're going to get it
themselves. Still others act as though nothing has happened, and I'm probably
overreacting. And more than one woman is already shooting up flares – "I'm
available when all this is over!" Vulture women. If they knew my fantasies
regarding them, every sphincter would open in abject fear. You won't hear about
the effort it takes to stay positive, to keep hoping, to never let her know I've given
up. And you won't know, because she couldn't possibly realize herself, how
desperately and deeply I love her. My partner. My life partner. The one I'm joined
to forever. My love. My wife.
(He takes another drink from the water fountain, slicks back his hair.)
JIM: I just thought you should know.
(He exits. The lights come up on Maggy. She is lying in bed with her eyes closed,
listening to nature sounds from a tape recorder. Maggie enters.)
MAGGIE: Maggy?
MAGGY: Hey! Come on in. *(She turns off the pate recorder.)* Don't be shy. You
look like you think I'm going to drop dead before your eyes.
MAGGIE: Actually, I think you look pretty good. I mean, you don't look ready
for the Olympics, but you look better than I imagined.
MAGGY: Kind of makes me wonder what you imagined.

MAGGIE: How do you feel?
MAGGY: Fine. A little achy. *(Looking at the gift.)* What is that?
MAGGIE: I don't know. I found it in the gift shop.
MAGGY: I hope you weren't planning on giving it to me.
MAGGIE: No, no. I've been really needing something like this for my apartment. *(They laugh.)* I keep buying you the most ridiculous things. I don't know why.
MAGGY: They're not ridiculous! I've been listening to these tapes all day. They're great.
MAGGIE: What do they say?
MAGGY: Oh, there's nature sounds, and subliminal messages. "You're feeling better every minute," that kind of stuff.
MAGGIE: I never trusted those things. I'm always afraid they're really saying something like "Kill the landlord."
MAGGY: But you got it for me anyway.
MAGGIE: Well, yeah.
MAGGY: And what about my crystal?
MAGGIE: Oh, the crystal's different. Those things are potent.
MAGGY: *(Laughing.)* Oh, no, what have I reduce you to? Buying gifts that go against all your convictions and then pretending you believe in them.
MAGGIE: Well, you never know.
MAGGY: No, you never really do. *(Pause.)* You know what? I was a little scared, meeting you again after all these years.
MAGGIE: You were? So was I.
MAGGY: Why were you scared?
MAGGIE: I was afraid it would be awkward and horrible. That our faces would all hurt from fake smiling.
MAGGY: Oh, I hate that.
MAGGIE: Why were you scared?
MAGGY: Because I felt guilty.
MAGGIE: Guilty?
MAGGY: About being the one who got Jim. Sometimes I worry that I got him under false pretenses.
MAGGIE: What do you mean?
MAGGY: I almost told you about this the other night. Jim and I met at a Fourth of July parade, did he tell you that?
MAGGIE: Uh-huh.
MAGGY: He was standing there watching the floats, and I kind of sidled over and stood next to him. I remembered him from school. In fact, I remembered him as your boyfriend. It was surprising to see him standing there by himself all those years later, looking sort of lost and lonely. I just assumed he'd married you and gone off to become a big shot somewhere – you know, Brown Book Award and all.
MAGGIE: *(Smiling.)* Yeah.
MAGGY: Anyway, there I stood next to Jim looking at the parade, feeling kind of stupid, and here's what I thought: "If I were Maggie Mulroney right now, what would I say?"

MAGGIE: Uh-oh.

MAGGY: And at that moment a float went by with Gina Lazlo on it. She was looking a little the worse for wear – to tell you the truth she kind of peaked in 12th grade. She was all dolled up as some kind of overweight sex goddess on a float that said Bigelow Pontiac – she married Robbie Bigelow, did you know that?

MAGGIE: No!

MAGGY: Yes! So here she is on Robbie's float waving a wand, you really had to be there to appreciate the full impact, and I said, "Living proof. You drive 'em off the lot, and they lose their value instantly." *(Maggie laughs.)* Hey, it was a start.

MAGGIE: I like it.

MAGGY: Yeah, so did he. He looked at me like I'd just arrived on the Planet, one of those "what have we here?" looks, you know?

MAGGIE: Yeah.

MAGGY: And I felt like a million dollars. Suddenly, with my new personality, I felt so free and liberated. It was great. But after awhile I started to worry. I said to myself, "This isn't really you. Who is it?" Of course I knew the answer right away. It was you.

MAGGIE: But that's not me. I don't feel free and liberated at all.

MAGGY: Well, you seemed like you did to me. You seemed absolutely ferocious. I loved your optimism, your sense that anything was possible. And most of all, I loved your anger, because that was one thing I just couldn't express myself. My mother was an alcoholic. Even conscious, she was never what you would call presentable. I spent all my time trying to fool everybody, convince them we were a normal family. And for the most part, I managed to pull it off – But God! I was so angry underneath. At my mother, for taking away my childhood. But mostly at myself, for being such a "good girl," for letting everybody push me around. You don't know how much I wanted to go to that demonstration in Boston with all of you and scream at the top of my lungs, "This is wrong! This is wrong! This is –"

(Her face contorts.)

MAGGIE: Are you okay?

MAGGY: Where's that bowl?

(Maggie finds the bowl and hands it to her. Maggy dry heaves into it.)

MAGGY: Sorry. Thought I was going to lose it for a minute.

MAGGIE: Do you want the nurse?

MAGGY: No, no. This happens all the time. Don't worry about it, I'm fine.

MAGGIE: A glass of water, maybe?

MAGGY: Sure. Thanks. *(Pause.)* Anyway, where was I? Oh, yeah, pretending to be you. I kept telling myself it wasn't that big a deal. Then last week Jim called and said he was bringing you home to meet me. You know what it felt like? It felt like the real Maggie was coming back to town.

MAGGIE: No.

MAGGY: I just couldn't shake that feeling.

MAGGIE: But Maggy, that's just not true. There is no "real Maggie." There's just you and me. Listen, I was kind of worried before I met you, too. I was thinking to myself, "Here's the woman who lived the life I didn't have. Let's see what it's like." Then I met you, and realized how egotistical that was. You're not living the life I didn't have. You're leading your own life, which is unique and distinct from anybody else's. And as for being anything like me – I should only be so lucky. You just blow me away with your strength, and your courage, and your humor in the face of this thing you're going through. You don't remind me of me at all.

MAGGY: But Maggie, that's exactly what I see in you. Strength, courage, and humor. How can you say we're nothing alike?

MAGGIE: I don't know.

MAGGY: I don't think you see yourself very clearly, Mag. You ought to start taking a closer look.

MAGGIE: I'm trying, I really am. But it's hard, you know? I think it's a writer thing. You spend all your time looking at other people's lives, you get out of the habit of looking at your own.

MAGGY: No, that's not it.

MAGGIE: It's not?

MAGGY: I don't think so.

MAGGIE: *(Pause.)* No. I'm afraid if I look, I'll see someone I really don't like at all.

MAGGY: Yeah, that's it.

MAGGIE: You know that one?

MAGGY: Oh, yeah. It's a scary one. It hurts like hell for a while, but after that you feel much better.

MAGGIE: Funny. Isn't that the way you described chemo?

MAGGY: Yeah, it is. Surviving the cure is the toughest part.

MAGGIE: I want you to get better, Maggy. I want you to beat this thing.

MAGGY: I will. Don't you worry, I will.

(Maggie and Maggy embrace. They hold one another for a long moment. Then they release.)

MAGGIE: *(Pause.)* It's my birthday today.

MAGGY: Really? You didn't tell anyone!

MAGGIE: I don't usually celebrate it.

MAGGY: Well, I think it's high time you started. *(She hands her back the weird looking plant Maggie gave her.)* Happy Birthday, Maggie.

MAGGIE: *(As they laugh.)* Thank you, Maggy. I can't think of anyone I'd rather share it with. *(Pause.)* Jim's out there.

MAGGY: I know.

MAGGIE: He tells me we have a reunion coming up, did you know that?

MAGGY: Yeah. I'll go if you go.

MAGGIE: Deal. *(Suddenly she laughs.)*

MAGGY: What?

MAGGIE: I can't believe that Gina Lazlo actually brought you two together.

MAGGY: Hey, there's one good reason to make that reunion right there.

MAGGIE: Check out how much she's depreciated?

MAGGY: You bet.

MAGGIE: Well…I'll see you, my friend.

— MAGGY: My friend, you absolutely will. 'Bye.
(Maggie exits. Jim approaches.)
JIM: Everything okay?
MAGGIE: Yeah. Yeah, everything's fine. She looks so pale.
JIM: That's temporary. She'll be back on her feet soon.
MAGGIE: Absolutely. *(Silence.)* Well!
JIM: Listen, I'm going to stay with Maggy for awhile, but I thought tomorrow we could maybe take a spin around Newbridge. Check out some of the places you haven't seen yet.
MAGGIE: I'd love to, but you know what, Jim? I think I have to go back to New York.
JIM: Oh, I'm sorry. We'll miss you. Finished all your research, huh?
MAGGIE: Yeah, pretty much. It's time to go home and take stock. But listen, I'm planning on seeing you both at that reunion.
JIM: Oh, we wouldn't miss it.
MAGGIE: *(Pause.)* I can see it, you know.
JIM: What's that?
MAGGIE: What you were trying to show me last night. The person you've become. I think you're an amazing man, Jim.
JIM: I don't feel too amazing. I feel pretty goddamned ordinary, if you want to know the truth.
MAGGIE: Well, you're wrong. To me, you're a great man.
JIM: *(Hugging her.)* Best of luck to you, Mag.
MAGGIE: Thanks, Jim. You, too.
(Jim exits. Maggie stands thinking for a moment. Then she looks up at the audience.)
MAGGIE: I was just thinking. We are now coming to a part of the story that I wasn't going to get into when I first began, but I see now that it would be kind of dishonest not to. The only thing is, there are a number of ways to go about this. I'm not sure whether a clinical explanation is in order here, perhaps an itemization of the medical procedures –
MAGGY: *(Sitting up in bed.)* Oh, please, no. That would be really boring.
MAGGIE: You think?
MAGGY: Oh, definitely. So far you've managed to avoid technical jargon, it's probably the only reason people are still here.
MAGGIE: Oh, thanks a lot. Okay, you're so smart, you tell me. How do I do this?
MAGGY: I don't know. A couple of jokes first, to loosen everybody up?
MAGGIE: I think jokes would be in bad taste at the moment.
MAGGY: Maybe you're right. How about a little music? "Adagio for Strings?"
MAGGIE: "Adagio for Strings?" Now who's romanticizing? *(To Audience.)* What Maggy's trying to help me with can actually be said very simply, so I might as well say it. She died.
MAGGY: Well, that wasn't very imaginative.
MAGGIE: Sorry. Sometimes it's better to come right out and say it.
MAGGY: Yeah, but just bang, she died? That's kind of drab, don't you think?

MAGGIE: I'm just trying to be honest.

MAGGY: Okay, honest is good. But there are so many more colorful ways to say it. "Gave up the ghost." "Passed on to a better world." "Shook hands with Elvis."

MAGGIE: Maggy, I'd like to end this with a little decorum.

MAGGY: Sorry. You're absolutely right.

MAGGIE: *(To Audience.)* It was six months later. She had another round of chemo, and I guess this one took her just a little too close to the edge. I went to the funeral. Jim was a mess. It was as though everything just broke loose inside him, now that he didn't have to be strong for someone else. We both went to the reunion, but it wasn't much fun. Even though Maggy was in the class behind us, I felt like she belonged there more than either one of us. She would have gotten such a kick out of Gina Lazlo Bigelow, sexpot turned Born Again Christian.

MAGGY: No!

MAGGIE: Yes!

MAGGY: Oh, I wish I could have been there.

MAGGIE: You'd have loved it. And me…I took Maggy's death pretty hard, myself. I went back to New York, took one look at my apartment, and decided to move out of the city. I'd had a long standing offer to teach at this college in Iowa which I'd never really taken seriously, an inner voice had always said to me, "Nah, that's a loser thing to do." But for some reason that inner voice had stopped talking. I picked up the phone and told them I'd be out within the week.

MAGGY: Did it help?

MAGGIE: It didn't hurt. I wrote a furious novel about women in the nineties which left everyone bewildered. They kept looking for the jokes. But that's another story.

MAGGY: Please don't tell it now. *(She exits.)*

MAGGIE: Don't worry, I won't. *(She looks back. Maggy is gone. A pause.)* It's funny, though. I mean funny in retrospect. I keep thinking about the walk back from the cemetary the day of Maggy's funeral. It was another one of those eerily clear days when sound travels like lightening and the sun is like a klieglight. And I was wrapped up in my own story, I really didn't want to hear anybody else's. But I just couldn't help it, there they were, all around me.

(The same late-afternoon light appears from the first act. A number of people start to emerge from the wings.)

MAN: You've got to look at the whole picture. Your problem is that you fragmentize.

WOMAN: What does that mean, anyway?

MAN: You look at the fragments.

WOMAN: I most certainly do not, and I resent that.

(They exit. Two Women are talking.)

YOUNGER WOMAN: Oh, we were deeply in love.

OLDER WOMAN: You were? I didn't even know you knew him that well.

YOUNGER WOMAN: Well, I don't, but we had the most incredible weekend. We fell so in love, it was very intense.

OLDER WOMAN: A weekend? That qualifies as being deeply in love?

YOUNGER WOMAN: We totally grokked each other in a Heinlein kind of way.
OLDER WOMAN: I have absolutely no idea what you're talking about.
(They exit. Two Men walk by.)
FIRST MAN: Do you know what the chances are of that happening again?
SECOND MAN: Nine hundred and eighty-nine to one.
FIRST MAN: Oh, you are such a wise ass.
SECOND MAN: No, really. Nine hundred and eighty-nine to one.
FIRST MAN: How could you possibly calculate such a thing?
SECOND MAN: Okay, there's nine players on a team, right?
FIRST MAN: Yeah.
SECOND MAN: And nine planets. Also there are seven days in the week, right?
FIRST MAN: Yeah, yeah, yeah. This is bullshit.
SECOND MAN: No, listen. How many cards in a deck?
(They exit. For a moment, Maggie is alone.)
MAGGIE: *(To Audience.)* I couldn't help listening to their conversations.
Everyone with his own story. Each person deeply involved in her own activity.
And it was the events of the day, I guess. Suddenly it all seemed to be too much.
I'm afraid I started to feel very, very sorry for myself. Because I couldn't help
noticing that while everyone else seemed to be in the company of another person
or persons, I seemed to be the only person on the whole street who was walking
entirely alone.

*(During the previous, the People have re-emerged, walking in couples, threes. As
they move off stage, one of them peels away and joins Maggie, who is walking in
the opposite direction. She is Maggy, without the scarf, with a full head of shining
hair. Maggie sees her. They smile. Together, they walk directly into the light.)*

BLACK OUT

END OF PLAY